To Anthony

From an ex RAF "sprog"

Best wishes.

John Misseldine'

SURVIVAL AGAINST ALL ODDS

SURVIVAL AGAINST ALL ODDS

Sunday, 8th June 1942:
Shot down over France

JOHN MISSELDINE
with OLIVER CLUTTON-BROCK

GRUB STREET · LONDON

Published by
Grub Street
4 Rainham Close
London
SW11 6SS

Copyright © Grub Street 2010
Copyright text © John Misseldine and Oliver Clutton-Brock

British Library Cataloguing in Publication Data
  Misseldine, John, 1922-
  Survival against all odds : Sunday, 8 June 1942 - shot down
  over France.
  1. Misseldine, John, 1922- 2. Fighter pilots--Great
  Britain. 3. World War, 1939-1945--Personal narratives,
  British. 4. World War, 1939-1945--Aerial operations,
  British.
  I. Title II. Clutton-Brock, Oliver.
  940.5'44'941'092-dc22

  ISBN-13: 9781906502751

Cover design and formatting by Sarah Driver
Edited by Sophie Campbell

Printed and bound by MPG Ltd, Bodmin, Cornwall

Grub Street Publishing only uses
FSC (Forest Stewardship Council) paper for its books.

CONTENTS

DEDICATION

To my wife Mauricette
and to my family.

———

In memory of
my brother Geoffrey (1920-2007),
who took part in the Normandy landings,
and
those who helped me in my time of need,
some of whom lost their lives.

PREFACE

O ver the years, I have read many books on the exploits of
famous wartime airmen, and have written this book primarily for the benefit of my grandchildren, explaining how an
ordinary youngster attained his goal of becoming a pilot and, in
particular, flew Spitfires, firstly on 611 and then 65 Squadron,
without any success in combat! But also how I escaped Occupied
France, under the nose of the enemy, on the run, with the help of
men and women who put their lives on the line so that I could
return to England and defend our skies.

The story started out to recount highlights of my time in the RAF
that I remembered, supplemented by reference to letters that I
wrote to my parents during the war that passed into my hands after
their deaths. My flying log book acted as a diary, covering most of
my time in the RAF; photographs, my lecture notes during training
and pilots notes for the Spitfire, as well as other single-engine fighter planes that I flew, also helped. In addition, where it was necessary, over the years I made notes, visited places to confirm certain
facts and also made use of some reference books. Later on, when I
put pen to paper, it became evident that my early life had a bearing
on my years in the RAF and the aftermath.

Older people will remember, and younger people will be aware
of, the events that happened during the years of the Second World
War, 1939-1945. In particular, the Dunkirk evacuation at the end of
May 1940, and the furious combat that took place over England
during the summer of that year, especially the aerial battles over
London that reached their zenith on 15th September – the day

when the pilots of Fighter Command had their greatest success over the Luftwaffe.

Few people, however, would have attached any significance to an event that took place two days later, on 17th September 1940. And why should they? The fact that it was my birthday would have had little interest to anyone outside my family and circle of friends. To me, however, it was very important. Having attained the age of eighteen, it was now possible for me to enlist for military service and, hopefully, join the Royal Air Force Volunteer Reserve (RAFVR) to train as a pilot for the duration of the war. This desire was sparked off in 1938 when I paid five shillings (25 pence) for a five-minute flight in the front seat of a two-seater open cockpit airplane, and made me dream of becoming a pilot. Oddly enough it was another flight in a bi-plane in 1999 that stirred me to complete this story of the ups and downs, good times and difficult times, errors and, in particular, the part that Lady Luck played during this period of my life.

Although I was christened John, my Grandfather Brown always called me Jack. I liked it, and during my RAF career, and later in the Royal Air Force Escaping Society (RAFES), I was known by this Christian name, as well as, during my escapade through France, the French version, Jacques. But at all other times the family use John.

By a happy chance, Diana Morgan of the RAFES introduced me to Oliver Clutton-Brock and, thanks to his experience, guidance and research abilities, he has added considerable depth to this story.

John Misseldine
Grasse,
France.
August 2009.

PROLOGUE

Flying a Spitfire for 611 Squadron over northern France on 8th June 1942, I was covering the tail of my section leader when I saw a large number of German aircraft that were climbing towards us. My leader dived in to attack with me protecting him, looking behind, above and below our aircraft. I was so occupied with this that I was surprised, when looking forward, to find that my leader had abandoned the attack and had climbed away in a hurry, leaving me alone. I was faced with a dilemma: should I try to catch up with him and continue to guard his rear, or look after myself and attempt to attack the enemy? During those few seconds of indecision, the pilot of one of the enemy aircraft must have positioned himself in a blind spot under my tail. He was either a veteran pilot, or a very lucky one, as his burst of fire hit my Spitfire and flames appeared in the cockpit. In addition, my aircraft no longer responded to the controls. As the petrol tanks in a Spitfire are in a vulnerable position immediately in front of the pilot, the danger of the aircraft exploding was very real. There was only one thing to do. GET OUT...

They say that a drowning person sees the events of his lifetime pass through his mind and, as I lay in the wood, after parachuting out, I had a feeling like that. My thoughts turned to my family, my childhood, teenage years, the time I spent training to become a pilot in the RAF and, especially, the time I had spent on 611 Squadron leading up to my present life-threatening situation, shot down in Occupied France.

Chapter 1

SEEKING A CAREER

I was born on 17th September 1922 in a flat in Islington, North London. My first real memory of my life was in March 1926, when my father decided to move from a flat that he rented in Queens Park to a house in Harrow. This had become necessary as my mother was pregnant and expecting her third child in June. Barbara was in fact born on 11th June, a sister for me and for my elder brother, Geoff, who had been born on 26th September 1920.

The house at 40, Manor Road, was one of some sixty that were being built on a site that was an extension of the old Manor Road. The houses were practically identical, having a sitting room (lounge), dining room and a kitchen that had an Ideal boiler to supply hot water, and led to the scullery where there was a gas cooker, a sink and a larder facing down the garden. On the first floor there were two main bedrooms and a third, smaller one. As was normal in those days on construction sites, they built the houses first and then laid the gas mains, electric cables, as well as water and sewage pipes. It was only when this was completed that the road was surfaced and paving stones put down. In consequence during that period, when it rained, like other new residents, I was frequently walking in mud. A temporary narrow-gauge railway line had been built, that ran down the length of the road, on which side-tipping iron trucks loaded with building materials were pushed by the workmen to the houses under construction.

One of my first memories was of an incident that happened just before my fourth birthday. It was a weekend and, as there were no workmen about, my brother Geoff and his young friends living nearby thought they would give me a birthday treat. Loading me into one of the trucks they gave it a push. All went well for the first few yards but, as the truck gathered speed on the gradient it went out of control. Fortunately, at the end of the line, the workmen had placed a pile of sand that stopped the runaway truck, and I was thrown out, landing in the sand without injury. But my shorts and shirt were torn and dirtied so that, when I returned home with my brother, my mother scolded us and forbade us to go near the trucks again. Soon after, I sustained an injury to my forehead resulting from running up the stairs and into the bedroom that I shared with my brother, my intention being to help my mother make the beds. However, in my haste I tripped on the bedside rug and fell head first onto the corner of the wardrobe, suffering a gash above my right eye. Our local doctor, Doctor Morrow, who came round immediately, had some difficulty in stitching up the wound as apparently I wriggled around a lot and broke a needle before the wound was closed.

Approaching the age of five, I was becoming more aware of life. All the houses in our road had been completed; the tarmac road had been laid, as had the stone flags that made the pavement. With very few cars about in 1927, in fact there was only one family in the road who owned a car, a familiar sight was horse-drawn vehi-cles. Among them was a milk cart that came early in the morning, when my mother would take a large jug out to the milkman, who ladled milk out of a churn into it. During the day the greengrocer's cart came round, followed by a butcher's cart and, once a week, a fishmonger. About once a month we would hear the sound of a bell and watch a character approach, swinging a hand bell, probably obtained from a town crier of a bygone age, and pushing an elon-gated cart on two wheels shouting "Any old rags and bones". He seemed to do very well, as his cart was frequently piled high with discarded clothes, but I never found out what he did with the bones. He must have been a forerunner of the modern recycling efforts! Another character was the knife grinder, who came singing down the road pushing a contraption like an over-sized wheelbarrow with extended shafts, on which he had a plank to sit on so that he could put his feet on a peddle system that was linked to a large grinding wheel above. His main trade was sharpening knives, scissors and hedge cutters.

At the beginning of September 1927, mother took me to Greenhill School on St Anne's Road, in the centre of Harrow, where I was enrolled in the infant's class. My brother had been going to this school for two years, and had already moved up into the junior section, which I joined the following year. The school had been built at the end of the nineteenth century, with the classrooms illuminated by incandescent gas lights, and in winter it was heated by a solitary coal fire near the teacher's desk. Whilst normally my friends and I used to sit at the back of the classroom out of the teacher's direct gaze, during the winter we tried to find a place near the front where it was warmer – not without some arguments. We lived about a mile from the school and, as in those days there were no school meals or buses, at 12.15 pm the lunch break bell sounded, and we had to hurry home to eat, so as to be back at school by 1.45 pm. On rare occasions mother gave us tuppence ha'penny to go to a fried fish shop near the school to buy a piece of fish and a portion of chips wrapped up in newspaper. We enjoyed this, as it left us about an hour to play games in the playground before the afternoon session of lessons.

One snowy winter's day, when I was seven years old, Geoff and I were on our way back to school after lunch at home, and passed a boy called Dungey. As we did so I called him 'Dungey's mess', a parody of Dungeness that I had recently learnt about in a geography lesson. Not surprisingly he chased after me and, to avoid being caught, I ran across the road to safety but, in looking back to see if he was following, I failed to see an approaching car, and was sent flying through the air to land in a snow drift. Geoff came over and helped me to my feet and though I had a cut on my hand and felt groggy I was also soaking wet. Arriving at school, my brother took me to my form mistress, Mrs Inkpen, who told me to sit on a stool near the fire to dry out. A little later the headmistress came into the classroom and, having heard about the incident from the car driver, asked me for my version. After listening to my explanation she said: "I won't punish you this time for calling another boy a name and running into the road, as I think you have learnt your lesson." I didn't think that it was very sympathetic but she did, however, send for my brother and told him to take me home to tell my mother that it would be a good idea for me to see a doctor. With the ejection from the iron cart, the injury to my temple and now this, I began to wonder what other calamities awaited me.

My father, who was born on 14th October 1894 and christened Edward, and whom we affectionately called 'Pop', was employed as a depot manager for a coal firm in Highbury.

Dad was a member of the St Leonard's Church choir in Kenton and, at an early age, both my brother and I also became choristers. This meant that we attended Matins at 10.30 am, High Mass at 11 am, bible class at 3 pm and Evensong at 6.30 pm. Additionally, on the Wednesday of each week, we had choir practice at 6 pm, where we enjoyed singing under the watchful eye of the choirmaster. He had an easy-going manner, so much so that we took advantage of his nature and played pranks on him, which he usually took in good humour. However, disaster struck one evening when we decided to hide his bowler hat in the vestry, and one of the choir boys suggested that an ideal place would be to put it in the lavatory pan, placing it carefully so as not to damage it, and then close the lid. We were in the middle of singing a hymn in the church when we heard a shout from the vestry. Apparently the curate had arrived to listen to the practice and had needed to use the toilet. As the 'little room' had little illumination, he failed to notice that there was something in the pan until his effort rebounded off the hat and over his cassock. As a punishment we were all suspended from the choir for a week.

At the age of eight I had joined the Wolf Cub pack run by the church, and in my second year, with other members of the pack, we accompanied the senior Scouts on a camping trip to the home of scouting at Gilwell, where I saw Lord Baden-Powell, who had founded the Scout Movement in 1907 and which had taken root in many other countries.[1] It was an international affair that enabled me to meet other young people from different nations. It was quite an experience. The Duke of York (later King George VI) visited Gilwell on many occasions, and would join in singing one of the favourite Scout songs: "Alouette, gentille alouette, Alouette, je te plumerais..." accompanied by gestures. Unfortunately, he did not visit at the time that I was there.

The following year, with the church pack of Scouts and Cubs, I went for a summer camp in southern Ireland, near Linlithgow, on Lord Powerscourt's estate, situated at the foot of the Wicklow Mountains and not far from Dublin. I can't say that I enjoyed it very much, as discipline was firm, it rained quite a lot, and eating smoky food cooked over camp fires took some getting used to. The camp fire sing-song in the evenings was the highlight of each day. The Scout Movement was undoubtedly a good thing in helping to form my character, and at a later date it was a key element in helping me out of a difficult situation during the war.

At school I progressed well, and moved to the senior school in September 1932, where I successfully passed the examination for entry into Harrow County School. Before joining the school Dad arranged, with the manager of the shipping division, for Geoff and I to take a trip on one of the company's ships, the *Charlock*, bound for a port near Edinburgh to load Scottish coal. We boarded the ship in Dockland, sailed down the Thames into the estuary, and out to the North Sea. The captain, who wore a fine beard and had a waxed moustache, was a kindly person. He showed us to a cabin near his that had bunk beds, and told us that we would be eating with the crew. The ship's course was never far from land, and with a map we identified the towns as we sailed north. On the afternoon of the second day, after passing Berwick-upon-Tweed, our course changed

---

[1] Gilwell Park is set in 108 acres of woodland, north-east of London, on the edge of Epping Forest. Lord Robert Stephenson Smyth Baden-Powell (1857-1941), hero of the Siege of Mafeking (1899-1900), began the Boy Scouts Movement in August 1907 with the Brownsea Island Experimental Camp.

to north-west. The captain told us that we would be passing under the Forth Railway Bridge early the next morning and promised that he would wake us to see the sight. We did so, and stayed on deck as the ship made its way to Bo'ness dock to pick up the cargo of coal.

When we arrived the ship anchored, waiting its turn to tie up alongside the loading wharf. As the ship would be there for about three days to complete its loading, the captain took us to a coal mine and down to the coal face, where the miners, covered in sweat and coal dust, laboured away. We asked if we could see the renowned pit ponies, but were told that they were no longer used. After that he took us to Edinburgh to see the castle, and then to a grand hotel for lunch. Geoff and I were confused at the numbers of knives and forks beside our plates, and waited to see in which order the captain used them. They served a bowl of fruit for dessert with a small dish containing water and a slice of lemon. As I picked it up to drink, the captain smiled and told me that it was for rinsing my hands after peeling the fruit. The return journey to London took us a little over two days, where we tied up at East London dockside, and saw Pop waiting for us.

At the beginning of September 1933, dressed in a new green blazer with the school badge sewn over the pocket and wearing grey shorts, I enrolled at the Harrow County School for Boys' in Gayton Road, Harrow. The first thing that struck me on entering the main doorway for the first time was a cut-glass, coloured panel honouring an old boy of the school – Flight Lieutenant John Boothman, who had piloted the Supermarine airplane that had won the coveted Schneider Trophy for high-speed flying.[2]

I disliked the fact that I was put into 2D class where I was required to learn the German language, as I would have preferred French, of which mother had some knowledge, but on the plus side I soon made friends with Johnny Craft and Peter Morris. I was not bad in English, Maths, and Geography, but my favourite class-

---

[2]John Boothman, born in Wembley in 1901, won the race in a Supermarine S6B seaplane on 13th September 1931. He died in 1957. See website www.jeffreymaynard.com/Harrow_County/boothman.htm.

room lesson was in the Art class under 'Georgie' Neal. I was keen
on most sports – physical training, athletics, swimming and rugby
and, as they were also the favourites of Johnny and Peter, we often
trained out of school hours trying to beat each other. The highlight
of my athletics career happened in 1936 when, as a fourteen year
old, I represented the school in the half-mile event at the Inter-
School games at the White City, and I came a respectable fourth.

The school was divided into four 'Houses', and I was told that I
would be in 'Northwick', with my friends in 'Weldon' and
'Kenton'. With my background in the church Cub pack, it was natural that I joined the Northwick Scout patrol where, amongst others, I obtained proficiency badges for cooking, map reading and
hiking at Scouts pace (fifty paces walking followed by fifty paces
jogging in turn) that made it possible to cover long distances without tiring. Though I played rugby at school, my real love was football, and at the age of fifteen I was playing for a local team called
Beaufort F.C. (later to become Northwick Park F.C.) in the
Middlesex County Amateur League. Geoff played at centre forward,
whilst I played on the right wing combining with the right half. My
brother scored many goals each year, and I used to kid him by
telling him that he did no work and only hung around for the glory
of being top goal scorer. The team won a number of trophies as
league leaders, but more important was the Sportsmanship Trophy
that we were frequently awarded by votes of other clubs in our
league.

I was also keen on cycling, but the old 'bone shaker' that I possessed was coming to the end of its days, and I was keen to have a
new one, but I knew that we would not be able to afford it. Jimmy
Haines, who lived opposite our house, at number 43, and who
became a lifelong friend, proposed a solution. He had seen a notice
in the window of W.H. Smith the Newsagent in Kenton Road adver-
tising for boys to deliver newspapers. I found out that, as I was only
thirteen, before I could apply for the job I needed permission from
the school and a doctor's certificate. My parents dealt with this matter. Geoff and Jimmy applied with me and we were all taken on. We
were told that we would have to report at 6.30 am, including
Sundays, and sort the different publications into an order for deliv-

ery. Sturdy bicycles were provided by our employer, and each of us set out on our circuit of deliveries by 7.00 am, aiming to complete the round in an hour and be home for breakfast before going to school. It was tiring, but I had already worked out that if I stuck to it, the pay of five shillings a week would enable me to buy a new Raleigh bicycle with a three-speed gear and drop handlebars within twelve weeks. Three months later I had the pleasure of becoming the proud possessor of the 'bike'.

At home we had frequent visits from my maternal grandfather, Clement Brown, who was widowed and had moved to a house in Rayners Lane and for whom I had great affection. He had been a postmaster in Maidenhead, and was always interesting to talk with, particularly on the subject of his early life, telling me tales of his simple life in the 1860s under the reign of Queen Victoria and, later, King Edward VII, before the days of motor cars, aeroplanes, cinemas, wireless telegraphy and radios, that brought history to life. I don't know why, but he had a habit of calling me Jack. Perhaps he thought that it suited my character! He, like my paternal grandfather, had many children.

One thing that my father always insisted on was an annual fortnight's holiday by the sea in July. In the early days we boarded the Clacton train and changed onto a train with two carriages that puffed its way on a single branch line to the terminal at Brightlingsea. There we would walk to a boarding house, owned by a retired colleague of his. It had a large garden full of fruit trees, William pears, Cox's apples, Victoria plums, and an area of raspberry canes and blackberry bushes. With Geoff and my sister Barbara we were allowed to pick and eat some of the fruit, occasionally resulting in stomach pains from overeating. Brightlingsea, in the County of Essex, is situated on the Blackwater estuary not far from Clacton, and boasts a small beach by the lighthouse, about a mile from our 'digs'. However, across the estuary there were miles of sandy beaches below the marshes of St Osyth, but the only problem was how to cross the stretch of water. We found a fisherman who offered the use of his boat to ferry our family across. I don't think mother was over keen on stepping into a rocking rowing boat, so we only went there on a few occasions. The fisherman was a friendly type and offered to take my brother Geoff and I out with him at 6 am the following morning, when he would be collecting some lobsters from the pots that he owned. We did so, and enjoyed the experience, particularly the way he handled the creatures.

Most days we walked to the lighthouse beach or to a sea-water swimming pool nearby but, returning one day for lunch, I collected a new injury. Walking beside me Geoff was swinging his beach spade around his head and got too close; the metal blade of the spade caught me on the upper lip and made a nasty cut, but the local chemist closed it up with a couple of clips. Another incident that could have been more serious happened to my sister, Barbara. She was sitting on the edge of the swimming pool in her bathing costume and fell in. She couldn't swim and was floundering into deep water when my father heard her cries. He jumped in fully clothed and pushed her to safety, where Geoff and I pulled her out. Whilst Barbara was able to change back into her clothes, it was another matter for Dad, who told me to run back to the house and bring a pair of trousers and a shirt for him. I did so, but whilst the trousers were all right, I had mistakenly brought one of my brother's shirts. We had a good laugh!

My friend Jimmy Haines and I were interested in cars and motorcycles, particularly the latter, so that, when pocket money permitted, we went to Wembley Stadium to watch the Wembley Lions, a motorcycle speedway team, competing against teams from other towns in England on the oval dirt track. It was natural that, because of this interest in motorcycles, Jimmy bought a 1925 Calthorpe machine for the princely sum of five shillings. Even though it was only ten years old, I thought that it was really fit for the scrap yard, but we had agreed that it would be fun overhauling it and trying to make it work. This became our principal hobby over the next few months.

With wire brushes and cleaning materials we attacked the dirt and rust on the frame, wheels, petrol tank and handle-bars. The engine was removed from the bike frame and dismantled. The carburettor was stripped, cleaned, the float checked, the needle re-set and the unit re-assembled. The spark plugs were cleaned and the gaps checked and adjusted. The cylinder head was removed and the piston withdrawn, in order to replace the piston rings. The valves were reground by hand in their seating. Other mechanical parts were checked along with the dynamo. The clutch was dismantled to check the pads, and all seemed well except that, when it came time to reassemble it, we hit a snag. Not having the proper tool to compress the clutch spring we struggled, and it was not until we enlisted the aid of our friends that, with a broomstick, lots of laughter and a great deal of effort, the spring finally surrendered and the reassembly was accomplished.

When all of this work was completed, we concluded that, not only had we learned a lot about a combustion engine, but also that the Calthorpe even looked like a decent motorcycle again. The only question that remained was – would it work? As Jimmy's dad owned one of the few cars that now existed in our road, we 'borrowed' a few pints of petrol. Knowing that the kick starter would not function, the only way we could get the engine to start would be to push the bike and let in the clutch when enough momentum had been gained. We realised that we could not do this on the road in front of the houses, so we pushed it round to a quiet area in Bonnersfield Lane, behind Manor Road, that was basically not much more than a footpath but devoid of motor traffic. We decided to have our trial run there.

Our friends having joined us for the great event, Jimmy climbed on to the saddle of the bike and selected a gear with his foot, held in the clutch lever and, with a nod from him, off he went under the impetus of the gang pushing the bike. Many attempts were made with different mixture and throttle settings, until at last we were rewarded by the engine firing with a great roar. Jimmy throttled back with a broad smile on his face before setting off slowly down the lane in first gear. As he gained confidence he changed into second gear and increased his speed. Being satisfied that he could control the bike he stopped and invited me to climb up behind him on the mudguard.

I was just beginning to enjoy the experience when, rounding a slight bend in the lane, we nearly ran into a policeman who, holding up his hand yelled "Turn that damn thing off." Jimmy did so, and we watched as the 'Bobby' walked slowly around the machine commenting as he went: "Faulty silencer, worn tyre, broken mud-guard". Turning to Jimmy, still sitting on the saddle, he said "Now my lad, show me your driving licence". Jimmy remained silent as the policeman continued: "You could be in serious trouble". At that moment Jimmy noticed that the 'Bobby' was not wearing the customary blue and white striped band on his sleeve denoting that the constable was on duty. Unwisely he remarked, "You can't do anything to us as you are not on duty and, in any case, we are not on a public road." The policeman went red in the face and replied: "A policeman is always on duty and, though this is not a road, it is a public footpath where you could have injured anyone who happened to be walking up the lane." Jimmy quickly realised that he had made an error and, after saying that he was sorry, went on to explain that in his excitement at completing the renovation of the bike, he had only wanted to see if it worked. The 'Bobby' seemed mollified, but nevertheless cautioned both of us: "Until the faults have been rectified and the motorbike taxed and insured, you are not to take it outside the place where you live – don't forget I'll be keeping an eye on you."

In July 1937, I decided that I was wasting my time at school. Although I should have been sitting the Matriculation Examination in the following year, I had not been an assiduous student, and dreaded the thought of failure. Because of this, I had convinced my father that I should leave, arguing that as I liked drawing it would be better if I applied for an apprenticeship with an architect, rather than waste another year at school. To my surprise he agreed, and promised to write to Mr Randall-Williams, the headmaster, to tell him that I would not be returning to school for the new term at the end of August.

However, even though I went for several interviews, I was turned down as, I was told, my drawing experience was not enough and, moreover, they required someone with higher academic qualifications. To say that I was disappointed was putting it mildly, but as I longed to start earning money I decided that I would have to accept any job for the time being.

My father had a friend who worked in the city, and obtained a position for me in a wholesale garment warehouse in

Aldermanbury Street, some fifteen minutes walk from Broad Street station. I expected to have an office job but, on my first day early in October, I was told that I would have to start at the bottom and work my way up. 'Start at the bottom' was an apt description, as I was sent downstairs to the packing room, referred to by employees as 'the dungeon', to be taught how to pack parcels.

Apart from the working conditions, I had a forty-five minute journey by train and then a walk to get to my place of work. It meant that I had to leave home at 7.30 in the morning to arrive by 8.30 and then, like other employees, I had to sign my name in a book. This book was taken away at 8.35, and anyone who arrived late had to report to the manager. The work day finished at 5.30 in the evening, except for Saturdays, when the warehouse closed at 12.30 pm. Excluding a lunch break of one hour, this meant that I worked a forty-four hour week for the sum of fifteen shillings.

However, fate took a hand.

Playing football in icy conditions one Saturday afternoon early in November, I caught my foot in a rut and twisted my right knee, making it impossible to bend it without pain. A visit to the doctor confirmed that I had a torn cartilage, and I was given a medical certificate prescribing rest for two weeks. Hooray, I thought, at least I'll have a break from the dungeon. Pop, who had been a top-class amateur footballer, and had even played for West Bromwich Albion on occasions during the 1914-1918 war, decided that I should see an osteopath for treatment. As this didn't resolve the problem I was admitted to Great Ormond Street hospital for an operation. Seven days in bed in the hospital passed quite pleasantly but, when it was time to take the bandages off, I was able to see that I was going to be left with a scar nearly four inches long. After a few days at home I returned to work temporarily, as I'd decided that I would find another job.

In February 1938 I was taken on as a commission accounts clerk in the offices of the Hoover manufacturer at Perivale, in the suburbs of London. What a relief it was to be working in a large office with many teenage youngsters. In addition, the offices and factory were about ten miles from my home, so that I was able to enjoy cycling to work. It had the additional benefit of my not having to pay train or bus fares except that, when the weather was really bad, I used public transport.

It was there that I had my first experience of the female mind. Working at one of the desks close by me was Marjorie, a pretty blonde typist, with whom I had exchanged a few words and smiles until, eventually, I decided that it would be nice to take her out for an evening at the cinema. I was afraid of being refused, so I approached her friend Eileen and asked her if she thought that Marjorie would go out with me. She laughed, and said: "The only way you will find out is to ask her." Several days later, with my heart in my mouth, I plucked up courage and was surprised when she accepted my invitation to go to the Odeon Cinema in Leicester Square and have a meal with me afterwards. The following day, after finishing work, we took the underground train to London, where we enjoyed a good film followed by a meal at a Lyon's Corner House restaurant.

Unfortunately the service was slow, so it was nearly midnight before we arrived back at Hammersmith station. As it was so late I walked with her to her home and shook her hand and said goodnight, before returning to the station to catch a train home to Harrow, only to find that the last train had already left. Not fancying a ten mile walk home, I decided to call on my Aunt Doris, who lived just over a mile away from Hammersmith Broadway, where I arrived at about 1 am, and knocked on her entrance door. After a short delay, I heard her say "Who is it?", and once I had convinced her I was her nephew she let me in. After listening to the reason for the late call, she made up a bed for me in her lounge, saying that she would telephone my parents first thing in the morning. For many years after when I met my aunt, she would laugh and refer to me as the "dirty stop-out".

The sequel to this outing with Marjorie evolved over the next few weeks. On several occasions I asked Marjorie to go out with me again, but she always had a reason why she couldn't. Eventually I spoke to Eileen again, and asked her if she knew why, to which she replied: "She thinks you are a dead loss as you never even held her hand in the cinema, and didn't even kiss her goodnight." I thought, so that's what happens when you think that you are trying to behave as a gentleman!

One Saturday morning during that summer of 1938, in company with a friend, Frankie Grimwood, we cycled the eighty miles
from Harrow to Portsmouth. There we took the ferry to Ryde on
the Isle of Wight, where we intended to camp for the night. During
the evening we visited the town and, amongst the many things that
attracted our attention, was a poster announcing that Alan
Cobham's Flying Circus would be at a local field giving flying
demonstrations.[3] Frankie and I agreed that it was something that
we should not miss. The following morning, after a breakfast in a
local cafe, we cycled over to the field early, paid our entrance fee,
and hurried over to get a close-up view of the open cockpit, two-
seater bi-planes before they took to the air. When they eventually
did, we were amazed at the skill of the pilots giving their aerobatics display, and were sorry when the demonstrations were over.

As we were about to leave we heard an announcement offering
five-minute flights over the Solent for the price of five shillings.
Even though this was a quarter of my week's pay, it was an offer that
I felt I could not refuse, and Frankie was of the same opinion. We
joined a few others who were waiting for their turn, and eventually arrived at the head of the queue. I walked towards the aircraft,
was helped into the front seat by the pilot, and told to strap myself
in. Being a field with no runways, the pilot turned straight into
wind, opened the throttle, and off we went. As we lifted off the
field and climbed away I saw for the first time how beautiful the
town, surrounding villages and countryside looked from the air. We
circled over the Solent, seeing Portsmouth in the distance, before
returning to the airfield where the pilot made a near-perfect three-
point landing. I was so captivated by this experience that it left me
with a feeling that one day I must learn to fly.

It was about this time that, on one of my visits to Hendon aero-
drome, I saw for the first time one of the new planes to join the
RAF. The Hurricane, compared to the bi-planes that were currently
in service, was very impressive to look at and, moreover, the pilot's

---

[3] Sir Alan John Cobham KBE, AFC (1894-1973), a pilot during the First World War,
had started his so-called Flying Circus in 1932.

demonstration was out of this world. However the aeroplane that I most wanted to see was a Spitfire, a direct descendant of the Supermarine S.6 monoplane that won the Schneider Trophy outright in 1931 when piloted by Flight Lieutenant Boothman who, as I have mentioned, had been educated at Harrow County school, albeit a few years before my time. It gave me a more personal interest in this aeroplane but, unluckily, it did not make an appearance on the days that I was at Hendon, though I did see one in flight in the distance a few weeks later.

As the days went by, I was aware that there was more and more evidence of a deteriorating situation as Hitler continued his invasion of European countries. Despite this my father remained optimistic that Great Britain and France, working together, would find a solution and that there would be no war involving our two countries. By the end of August 1939, the situation had become more and more ominous, first with the occupation of the Sudetenland, and then with the invasion of Poland on 1st September. There was no doubt that the storm was about to break.

Chapter 2

THE DAY THE
WORLD CHANGED

I remembered quite clearly that on that fateful morning, I had been working on a trench at the bottom of the garden and was warm from my exertions. From time to time I had paused to survey progress as, for several weeks now, I had used some of my spare time digging a hole some 8 feet long and 4 feet wide. I had calculated that, if I dug it some 3 feet deep, I could assemble and submerge the corrugated iron sheets to form the Anderson shelter, which had been supplied to most households. With the earth that I had excavated, I had decided to cover the top to give added protection, feeling that it would serve the family well should there be war and the enemy drop bombs in our vicinity.

Just before 11 am I heard my mother call from the house "John, if you wish to hear a speech to be given by the prime minister over the radio, you had better stop work, wash your hands and come in." I replied "OK Mum. I'll be up in a minute." Despite the fact that I had been preparing the shelter, and that the family had received their gas masks, I couldn't imagine that there would really be hostile activities but, nevertheless, I sat down with my mother and

then, after the announcer's introduction, heard the solemn voice of
Mr. Chamberlain:

> "This morning the British ambassador in Berlin handed the
> German government a final note stating that, unless we
> heard from them by 11 o'clock this morning they were
> prepared at once to withdraw their troops from Poland, a
> state of war would exist between us."

After a pause, he continued: "I have to tell you that no such under-
taking has been received and that, consequently, this country is at
war with Germany."

I looked at my mother and could think of nothing better to say
than: "I suppose that I should get on with the shelter, though I
doubt that we shall need it." I had hardly restarted when I heard the
banshee wail of the air-raid siren that brought mother to the back
door calling out: "I am worried about your sister who is playing
with friends in the Kenton recreation ground and I want you to go
there and fetch her home."

Running down our road into Francis Avenue, over the iron foot-
bridge spanning the LMS (London, Midland & Scottish) railway
lines and into the park, I started my search and, whilst doing so,
thought of the time only a few years previously when the recreation ground had not existed and the ground was referred to as
'Bentley's field'. With my brother and friends, we had enjoyed playing in the rough grass or scouring the hedgerows for bird's nests to
find the different coloured eggs to add to our collection. On other
days when the field had been freshly mown, we used to play hide-
and-seek around the hay trusses, or climb into one of the trees that
surrounded a pond where, at thirteen years old, I was encouraged
by the older boys to smoke a cigarette.

Coming back to my present problem, I continued my search for
my twelve-year-old sister, and eventually found her playing behind
the tennis courts. I told her that mother had sent me down to take
her home as war had been declared. As we walked briskly towards
our home, I was relieved to hear the steady note of the all-clear
siren.

My brother Geoff, being two years older than me, had been training with the Territorial Army since 1938, and was immediately mobilised and sent to a camp. At the same time LDV units (Local Defence Volunteers – later to be called The Home Guard) were being formed all over the UK consisting, mainly, of 'old sweats' of the 1914-18 war, as well as youths of sixteen to eighteen years and men who were in reserved occupations. My next-door neighbour, Mr Constable, who had been a captain in the 1914-1918 war and was the commanding officer of a local unit, asked me to volunteer as company runner, with the responsibility of cycling to outlying guards stationed at strategic points with orders or instructions. As daylight shortened, riding a bicycle became somewhat hazardous. Moon-lit nights were not too bad, but on the nights when there was no moon and blackout conditions were in force, it was rather dangerous. Some of the 'oldies' who had been in the last war considered that these guard duties were a joke, as they had to share one rifle between three of them, and were supplied with only five rounds of ammunition and instructions that they were "only to be used in an emergency".

During September, I continued with the construction of the shelter, and was quite pleased with my handiwork. Parts of the shelter had been assembled and had been sunk into my excavation, with the top covered over with the surplus earth. I had also made some steps to get down into it, put in a fitted bench-seat in the interior, and had built a blast wall in front of the entrance to complete my effort. Although there had been one or two alerts during the month, it had not been necessary for the family to try out the 'comfort' of my handiwork.

About this time I had changed my job again, having found employment as a clerk with a coal firm in north-west London. Life took on a pattern, leaving home at 7.30 am, walking to Kenton station, catching a Bakerloo train about 8 o'clock and walking the mile to the office at Kensal Green. In the evenings, when I was not on duty with the LDV, I frequently went out walking with my friend Jimmy, sometimes ending up at the King's Head pub at the top of Harrow-on-the-Hill.

October arrived with no significant action in the Harrow area, but on the 17th the newspapers made me aware that the Germans meant business. A squadron of their bombers attacked part of the British fleet moored in the Firth of Forth, Scotland, and inflicted damage on the cruisers HMS *Southampton* and *Edinburgh*. In France there was little movement reported from the BEF (British Expeditionary Force), but I was particularly interested in the activities of the RAF squadrons who were frequently in action.

November came with ever-lengthening darkness, multiplying the problems of the blackout. With no street lights, and cars having had metal hoods fitted over their headlights to reduce the chances of them being seen from over flying enemy aircraft, crossing the road or even walking on the pavement was dangerous. My father bore witness to this when, patrolling as an air-raid warden, he walked into one of the red letter boxes on the pavement, and damaged a number of teeth.

Travelling on the train early morning and evening, it became obvious that the government was taking precautions against air raids on the prime targets of railway lines and depots. In the passenger trains, cotton mesh was glued over the windows to reduce injuries from flying glass as a result of bombs being dropped. With the long winter nights upon us, it meant that travelling both in the morning and evening was dismal, as the only illumination permitted in the carriages came from very low-powered blue lamps.

The papers reported that several air raids had occurred during the month in the Thames area and along the east coast, mostly confined to dropping the new magnetic mines to disrupt shipping. However, scientists soon devised a method of successfully neutralising this weapon.

The winter rains were quite heavy and, to my dismay, the shelter began to fill with water from seepage, and soon became unusable, but fortunately a new type of shelter was becoming available for use inside a house. It consisted of a strong angle-iron structure of table-top height covered by a steel plate and protected on the sides by wire mesh. The Morrison shelter (named after the Minister of Home Security) was designed to support the debris of a collapsing house. Because it took up a large space in a room, it became the dining table in many houses. Other types of shelter became evident – brick-built units with reinforced concrete roofs were constructed on the pavements of many roads.

The *Daily Express* newspaper printed maps of Europe and the North African area, which I had pinned up in my bedroom and, as events were reported, I was able to determine their location and mark the map with coloured pins. In France, it was still mainly the RAF who were in action, whilst the Allied ground troops continued to become bored with inactivity. At sea there were plenty of activities, with extensive reports in the papers of the naval battle unfolding in the South Atlantic, involving the three British cruisers HMS *Exeter, Ajax* and *Achilles* and the German pocket-battleship *Graf Spee*. The latter received so much damage in the action that it was forced to seek shelter in the neutral port of Montevideo, Uruguay. After the limited time that she was allowed to stay in port had expired, the captain sailed his ship out in the estuary where, to avoid capture, he had the sea valves opened, and scuttled the ship. Like all Britons I was proud of the Royal Navy.

Geoff, who was now a gunner in the 75th Royal Artillery Regiment, came home on leave for Christmas and, in his uniform, he was naturally the centre of attention. He was good looking with dark wavy hair and, in his smart uniform, he was assured of success with the girls – sometimes with complications. On one occasion, after he had returned on leave, he telephoned his latest girlfriend, Thelma, the daughter of a jeweller, and arranged to meet her. When he came home later that evening he told me a *faux-pas* that he had made. Apparently when he arrived at her house, her greeting was rather cool and, when he asked her what was wrong, she produced a letter that Geoff had written before coming on leave and said: "I think you should read what you wrote." Geoff did so and soon saw his error; the letter was addressed to "Darling Brenda", and he realised what had happened – he had written to two of his girlfriends on the same day, but had put the letters in the wrong envelopes! Turning to Thelma, he asked her if she had read the contents and she admitted that she had. Geoff responded by laughingly saying that he would forgive her for reading correspondence addressed to another person. I had to admire his resourcefulness, and he must have been forgiven as our family received Christmas presents from Geoff that had been purchased in the jewellery shop, managed by Thelma's father.

The New Year was welcomed in and my life continued in its usual pattern, including my addiction to following the progress of the war from the newspapers. In France the stalemate was continuing on the ground, but an increase of aerial activity was reported. More disturbing was the rumour that the morale of some of the Allied troops was being tested to the limit, in particular for the *poilus* of the French army who were cooped up in the Maginot Line fortifications.

During this period of inactivity in France, a group of comedians led by Flanagan & Allen[4] were putting on nightly shows in a theatre in London. In their repertoire of songs I remembered the opening bars of one of them, which related to the German fortifications similar to the French Maginot line:

'We're going to hang out our washing on the Siegfried Line,
Have you any dirty washing mother dear?
We're going to hang out our washing on the Siegfried Line.
If the Siegfried Line's still there.'[5]

Another song, relating to food rationing, started with these words:

'Run rabbit, run rabbit, run, run, run,
Don't give the farmer his gun, gun, gun,
For we'll get by without a rabbit pie,
So run rabbit, run rabbit, run, run, run.'

---

[4] Bud Flanagan was born Chaim Reuben Weintrop, later changed to Robert Winthrop. He took the name Flanagan from a sergeant-major with whom he had served in the Royal Field Artillery during WWI. Born in East London on 14th October 1896, the youngest of ten children of Polish immigrants, he died in Sydenham, London, on 20th October 1968. Chesney Allen, born in Brighton, Sussex on 5th April 1893, died at Midhurst on 13th November 1982. (http://www.turnipnet.com/crazygang/gang.htm).
[5] The Siegfried Line, a series of Nazi German defences stretching from the Swiss border to Aachen, was approximately 300 miles long and up to 20 miles deep in places. It was constructed by over half a million workers between 1936 and 1938.

One event reported in the press that made me proud to be British was the courageous action of the Royal Navy in releasing nearly three hundred merchant sailors from imprisonment on the German merchant ship *Altmark*. The sailors had survived the sinking of their ships by enemy raiders, and were being transported by the *Altmark* for internment in Germany. The British became aware of this, and intercepted the ship off the Norwegian coast. To avoid capture the captain of the prison ship sought refuge in Josing fjord. Undeterred, and despite protestations from the Norwegian government concerning neutrality, the destroyer HMS *Cossack* was ordered to enter the fjord, release the prisoners, and bring them home. This they did.

In February, Geoff came home on a forty-eight hour pass, now sporting the single chevron of a lance-bombardier on each sleeve. We went out together, sometimes playing billiards over Montague Burton's shop in Station Road, Harrow. On other occasions of course, he was off to see some girl or other. Reports from France during this period were mainly concerned with activities of the RAF and when, during a conversation with one of my friends, Frankie Grimwood told me that, having celebrated his eighteenth birthday, he had already made an application to join the RAF and had been accepted to train as a pilot, I vowed that, when I became eighteen, I would be following in his footsteps.

The news on 10th May, that Hitler had once again shown his treacherous nature by ordering the German army to attack across the neutral countries of Holland and Belgium and also eastern France, was difficult to believe. When the much vaunted Maginot Line was bypassed by German tanks and troops, who crossed the Belgian frontier and also the French frontier at Sedan, it was apparent that the Phoney War was over, and that the real battles were just beginning. The other item of great importance concerned the resignation of Prime Minister Chamberlain and his replacement by Winston Churchill, who was to head a National Government of all parties.

As the situation developed across the Channel, I followed the progress on my wall map. The pins showing the front lines were moved daily and, to my disbelief, within a short time they showed that the Germans had driven a wedge between the main French armies in the south and the British and Commonwealth troops in the north. By the last week of May, the British Expeditionary Force and a number of French and Belgian units had withdrawn to a Dunkirk enclave. After a heroic stand, and with the courage of the Royal Navy backed-up by the help of a flotilla of small boats manned by civilians, a third of a million soldiers, including many French poilus and some Belgians, were brought safely across the Channel to England.

Many of the returning soldiers complained that the RAF had let them down by not protecting them on the beaches. I couldn't believe that the air crews, whom I had come to admire and love, would do such a thing. It soon appeared that the ground forces had not appreciated what the pilots had really been doing until Churchill made a speech in Parliament confirming that the RAF had done a magnificent job, by concentrating their effort behind the lines and preventing many of the enemy bombers from reaching the beaches. He further stated that the RAF had brought down over 250 of the enemy aircraft for the loss of sixty British aeroplanes. Though it sounded good, I thought that probably these figures would eventually be corrected. Later I listened to Winston Churchill's invigorating words:

> "The British Empire will defend to the death this native soil.
> We shall fight on the seas and oceans, we shall fight with
> growing confidence and strength in the air, we shall defend
> our Island, whatever the cost may be, we shall fight on the
> beaches, we shall fight on the landing grounds and in the
> streets, we shall fight in the hills; we shall never surrender."

Such was the power in the delivery of his speech that I, like most of my countrymen I believe, felt proud to be British and was convinced that the Nazis would never succeed in landing in Great Britain.

Following the emerging stories from the newspapers I learnt that the French armies, despite being cut off from the British and Empire troops by the German tactics, had fought on for a while after the Dunkirk evacuation. By mid-June however, their government headed by Laval and Pétain were discussing armistice terms with Hitler. It resulted in an agreement between the two countries, under which the Germans would occupy about half of France including all coastal areas, and the French would be allowed to form a government controlling the rest of France, based in the town of Vichy.

Soon after this event, the newspapers reported that the French naval fleets were given the choice of either joining the British and Empire forces or sailing for a neutral port. If they did not take one of these choices, the Royal Navy would have no option but to immobilise the fleets to prevent them being taken over by the German navy. The French ships at anchor in Portsmouth and Plymouth had shown no resistance, and were taken over by British troops. However, the French fleet of warships anchored at Mers-el-Kebir near Oran on the North African coast presented a problem. It was reported that negotiations were being entered into for their surrender, but there was little trust on either side. It was complicated by the fact that the admirals, on both sides, were required to refer to their respective governments. It seemed that the French were prevaricating and unwilling to take a decision and, with delays in the exchange of messages between the Vichy and Whitehall, patience ran out. Eventually the British navy was ordered to open fire on their previous ally. It resulted in the sinking, or damaging of the major part of that fleet and the loss of life of many French sailors.[6]

By July, when most of the problems resulting from the capitulation of the French had been overcome, the war became more personal for me. Air raids became a little more frequent, and the sight of German aircraft being attacked by the pilots of the fighter squadrons excited me. By now I was counting the number of days

---

6 The British shelling of the French fleet, Operation *Catapult*, took place on 3rd July 1940, and resulted in the deaths of some 1,200 French sailors. The battleship *Bretagne* capsized (977 killed); the battle-cruiser *Dunkerque* was damaged (with the loss of some 200 lives); the battleship *Provence* ran aground; and the destroyer *Mogador* was also badly damaged.

until my next birthday in September, when it would be possible for me to volunteer for military service – in the air force, of course.

Around the middle of August I was busy down on the coal wharf at Kensal Green where I worked. Aerial activity was more intense with squadron after squadron of German Heinkel and Dornier bombers, easily recognised by the 'ron-ron' of their unsynchronised engines, flying at a medium altitude overhead, escorted by Messerschmitt fighters. To the noise of the engines was added that of the eight machine guns of the Hurricane and Spitfire aircraft that were attacking them, and of the Bofors anti-aircraft guns that were joining in the fray. Whenever an enemy aircraft was hit and started to plummet to earth, I cheered with the rest of the spectators. Hearing the sound of metal hitting the ground, I was told by an elderly man that it was either spent cartridge cases from the machine guns, or shrapnel from the ack-ack guns. He suggested that if I didn't have a 'tin hat' I would be better off in the office. Realising that this was a danger that I hadn't thought of, I hastened to follow his advice.

From this time on air raids increased in frequency, and I found that my evenings were now fully occupied with LDV duties of running messages to the outlying guard posts. From reports in the newspapers I realised that the German air force was making great efforts to put the airfields out of action, particularly those used by the fighter squadrons, in order to minimise the Luftwaffe's losses. For me, however, it was the enemy bombers that flew over at night which caused me most concern. Situated north-west of London, Harrow was not on the normal flight paths of aircraft coming from Occupied Holland, Belgium and France, but Northolt airfield was not far away, and the main railway lines were close by. Several bombs were dropped in the vicinity, but the main attacks were centred on London. The anti-aircraft balloons were some deterrent, but the main defence came from the anti-aircraft guns as, unfortunately, the RAF was poorly equipped for night fighting.

Under the barrage of gunfire, I was often out in the streets on my bicycle, despite the fact that cycling with a 'battle bowler' on was not easy. On many nights I was appalled to see the clouds over London reflecting the red inferno of the fires devastating Docklands and The City. The reports in the following day's papers gave some details of the damage, but I wondered how the people in the East End of London could stand up to such constant bombing, even though they had an occasional respite, when the weather was too bad for flying. During this period, my mother, sister and I, when not on duty, would spend the nights in Mr Constable's house next door, or vice versa, sleeping in the Morrison shelter. My father was not there, as he was out on air raid warden duties, and Mr Constable was at the headquarters of the LDV.

During the early weeks of September aerial activity became more intense. Daily air battles and dog fights were taking place over London and the Home Counties, with the most concentrated activity being on 15th September. I followed the newspaper reports avidly, hoping that one day I would be able to pilot a Hurricane or Spitfire. As my eighteenth birthday fell two days later, on the 17th, I knew that there was a possibility of accomplishing my dream of flying by signing up for military service and volunteering for the RAF, when I hoped to be accepted for training as a pilot.

Chapter 3

CALL OF DUTY

I woke at 7.30 am on Saturday, 21st September, and was pleased to see that it was a sunny morning, auguring well for my aspirations. Dressed in my sports jacket and grey trousers I went downstairs to where my mother was preparing breakfast.

"You act as if you have an appointment somewhere," she remarked. "Mum, perhaps you have forgotten that I am going to the recruiting office to see if I can join the air force."

Looking at me, she continued, "Are you sure that you must do this? With your brother already in the army, the house won't be the same without you."

"I know, but I've often told you and Dad that I want to join the RAF and learn to fly." Finishing my meal, I kissed mother telling her not to worry, collected my birth certificate, that I knew I would need to prove my age, and a few other items that I thought would be useful during my application interview.

I said goodbye, left the house and walked to Kenton station, and boarded the 140 bus for Edgware, where I knew a recruiting station was located. After asking directions, I arrived soon after 10 am, entered the reception area and approached a sergeant sitting behind a desk, who wrote down my name and a few particulars on a form before telling me to go to the waiting room. In there I found that there were many young men sitting around, most of whom seemed to be about twenty years old – the age of compulsory call up. Seeing a vacant chair I sat down beside a person who gave me a friendly smile. This led to an exchange of names – Stan Stillwell – John Misseldine. Stan told me that he was approaching his twentieth birthday, but had decided to volunteer in advance of his call up in the hope of being able to join the RAF and become a pilot or, if he failed, at least train to be a member of an air crew in another capacity. He added that if he had waited until he was twenty years old, it would have been the military authorities who decided in which service he would be enlisted.

I told this new found friend that I had not thought of that but, in any case, since the time that I had flown in an aircraft in 1938, I had one ambition, which was to become a pilot. Now that we were truly at war I felt that it had become a possibility, particularly as with the recent air battles over Europe and the UK and the requirements for air crew in the Middle and Far East, that the air force were left with a serious shortage of pilots. I felt that there would never be a better opportunity to obtain my 'wings', and perhaps one day fly Spitfires or Hurricanes.

Our conversation turned to the forthcoming interviews and the sort of questions that were likely to be asked. We agreed that, if both of us successfully passed this preliminary stage, we would keep in contact and prepare for the main interviews and tests that would come at a later date.

After waiting an hour, the names of twelve would-be airmen were called out, including both of ours. We were conducted down a corridor into a medical centre, where we were surprised to be told to strip and line up. The medical officer passed down the line, looking at our general physique, including the 'cough 99 routine'. Seemingly satisfied with this cursory appraisal, we were then told to put our trousers on again and wait for further individual tests and examinations. As there were several medical officers in attendance, the waiting period was not long before I was shown into an examination room, to be greeted by a smiling squadron leader medical officer.

"How old are you?"

"Eighteen, sir."

"Height, weight, we'll check that in a minute. For what trade are you volunteering?"

"Aircrew, preferably pilot, sir."

"Right. There are a few basic tests that I must do – heart, lungs, vertigo, colour blindness, eye sight and ear, nose and throat in particular – which will be repeated at greater depth at an RAF Station if you are selected to train as aircrew. So I suggest we get on with it."

When this was completed there were further questions on health, operations and illnesses, including those of antecedents in the family, all of which were noted on a form. At the conclusion, the medic told me that I was in excellent health and that I should return to the waiting room for an interview.

Stan, who had finished with the physical examinations before me, was waiting in the ante-room, where we waited before being called in separately for an interview with an officer.

"Where were you educated?"

"Harrow County School for Boys."

"What exams did you pass?"

"To Matriculation standard."

"Did you pass?"

"Not exactly, as I had to leave school before sitting the exam."

"What sports did you play?"

"Athletics, football, rugby, swimming and tennis."

Many other questions were asked, most of which I felt were not very pertinent. Having exhausted all the questions that he had on his list, the examiner said that he was satisfied, and that he was recommending that I should be sent to the RAF Headquarters at Uxbridge, for additional medical, psychological tests, and an educational assessment, with a final interview to determine if I was suitable for training as aircrew. He advised that I would receive a notification within a few days.

Joining Stan afterwards, I learnt that he had also been successful in his interview, and in consequence expressed the hope that our visit to Uxbridge would be on the same day. As by now it was about 1.30 pm we found a local snack bar and, whilst eating, made a date to meet and revise the subjects that might help in what we expected would be a very severe test.

During the following days we met at one or other of our homes, where we decided that a knowledge on the functioning of an aircraft engine and trigonometry, which might have a bearing on aircraft navigation, would prove useful. We had only revised for one week when, to my surprise, I received a letter from the Air Ministry ordering me to report to Uxbridge at 9 am on Friday, 4th October, using a travel warrant that was included. When I told my parents, they were astonished to learn that I was to report so soon, but father commented that, even if I was accepted, it would probably be many weeks or possibly months before I would be called up.

When I awoke on Friday, 4th October the sky was overcast, but I felt that it would be a marvellous day as I was convinced that, by the evening, I would be accepted for aircrew training, as I couldn't believe that it would be otherwise.

Leaving home early, I boarded a bus going to South Harrow station where I hopped on a train going to Uxbridge, arriving soon after 8.30 am. It took me about ten minutes to walk to the gates of the RAF Station, where, after presenting my papers at the guard room, I was directed to a waiting room that was full of recruits. They all appeared to be much older and more mature than me and, in particular, there was a number of strapping policemen. It made me wonder if the air force would consider me to be too young and immature to fly. Happily, Stan arrived soon afterwards and, in chatting with him, it dissipated my sense of inferiority, and I felt more at ease.

We had not long to wait before the first of us was called for the medical examination. Stan and I waited patiently until our turn came. Eventually my name was called and I was shown into a room and met the medical officer. After reviewing the initial report that he had received from Edgware, he commenced a series of tests. Amongst them was one for equilibrium, where I was made to sit on a stool that was revolved quite quickly for about a minute, and then asked to walk a straight line. He then made the normal tests on my eye sight, after which he gave me a card covered with a multitude of coloured dots and asked me if I could decipher a number contained within the dots. I looked closely and replied that I could see a number seven. "Good," said the doctor. "You are not colour blind." When the medical examination was concluded, I was told to return to the waiting area and, by midday, the rest of the twenty-four recruits had been seen by the medical officer and had joined me in the waiting room.

Soon after a sergeant came in and gave each of us a 'chit' that would enable us to get a meal in the airmen's mess. I feared the worst, but was pleasantly surprised to find the food quite appetising.

At 2.00 pm we were all sent to a classroom where, after sitting down at desks, the officer in charge, who looked like, and probably had been, a school master, distributed an examination paper covering a variety of subjects, telling us that we had one hour to complete our answers. The general questions covered basic mathematics – adding, subtracting, multiplying and dividing – and specific questions on the cycle of a four-stroke engine and on navigation: "An aircraft left point A flying at 150 mph, to point B at 100 miles to the North. (a) With zero wind how long would it take the pilot to reach his objective? (b) With a North wind of 20 mph, would it take him longer? (c) With a South wind of the same velocity, how long did it take him?" Other general questions were included in the paper, with the final request: "State in less than 100 words, the reason why you wish to join the RAF and to train as aircrew." As 3.00 pm approached I put my pen down and our papers were collected.

Back in the waiting room, we were all told that our tests and examinations were being appraised and that, for those who had passed, there would be a final interview with an officer who was a psychologist. He asked a number of questions and at the end of the session told me that, despite my lack of a Matriculation report, he considered that I had an IQ above the average and would recommend me for pilot training.

When my turn came, about 5.00 pm, I was accompanied by a sergeant into the office of a senior officer. Remembering the drills that I had been taught in the LDV, I marched in smartly and stood to attention before a group captain. He told me to relax, whilst he reviewed the file of the medical and examination results. Looking up, he said "I see that you want to be a pilot" and, with a smile, "I suppose that it is because of your previous flying experience." After questioning me at some length, he said that I would be inducted as aircrew/GD, and that the GD meant that, if at any time during the aircrew training course I failed to reach the required standard, I would be returned to general duties and be assigned to another suitable trade. He concluded by saying that after a period of basic military training and, providing I conformed to the discipline, I would be ready to start the initial training for aircrew where, he felt, I had a very good chance of being successful. Finally he asked me if I wished to take deferred call-up to arrange my domestic life or opt for immediate service. To this I replied, without hesitation, "Immediate service". The group captain smiled at the promptness of my answer before calling in a flight sergeant, and saying "I am attesting this volunteer as aircrew/GD, after which you are to escort him to the station warrant officer (SWO) for a leave pass enabling him to return to his home." Before I left, the officer shook my hand and said "You are now in the RAF. Good luck and happy landings."

The flight sergeant took the file containing my details, and accompanied me into the SWO's office. It was there that I made my first mistake, when I informed the SWO that I would like a 7 days' leave pass before reporting for duty. There followed a moment of stony silence whilst the NCO read the file. Looking up he said "Airman, you are now in the RAF so, first of all, stand to attention. Secondly, I am giving you a movement order for you to go to 9 Personnel Despatch Centre (PDC), in Blackpool. Thirdly, here is a travel warrant and, finally, you don't come in here and tell me how much leave you are going to have. Leave is a privilege, and I am telling you that you can only have forty-eight hours. Make sure that you are on the train to Blackpool on Monday." Somewhat cowed I turned to go, but at the last moment, not knowing if it was right or wrong, I thought that I'd better give a salute of some sort to mollify the warrant officer.

Before leaving the RAF Station, I hung around waiting for Stan who, when he finally appeared, told me that he, too, had been accepted and would be going to Blackpool. On the way home on the underground train, I realised that I could not give the necessary seven days' notice required by my employers in order to leave my job, but reasoned that they couldn't do much about it anyway as I had already committed myself. I also began to wonder what my parents would think when I reached home and told them that I was already enlisted in the RAF.

As it happened my mother, father and sister Barbara, now fourteen years old, were just sitting down to an evening meal when I entered the house. Pop asked me how I had got on, and when I replied that I had been accepted to train as a pilot, he said: "Good for you, but no doubt you will have to wait several weeks before being sent to a training unit." "Sorry Dad, but it's not quite like that. I have already been sworn in, and have to report to the Personnel Despatch Centre at Blackpool on Monday." Dad seemed to be at a loss for words, and mother looked sad, but my sister said that it would be great to be able to tell her friends at school that she had a brother who was going to be a pilot. The weekend passed slowly, albeit that I made visits to neighbours and Jimmy in particular, to say goodbye. Knowing that I would be kitted out on arrival in Blackpool, I only packed a few personal items.

Up early on the Monday morning and accompanied by Pop, who was on his way to his office, we boarded a train for Euston station, where I had arranged to meet Stan. He was there waiting, and we found the right platform to board the train for Manchester, where we could make a connection for Blackpool. Going north, away from the main targets of the Luftwaffe, the journey passed uneventfully, without any sign of air raids, and we arrived at our destination in the late afternoon. We reported to the Railway Transport Officer (RTO) with the other new arrivals, and were told that we would have to present ourselves at the dispersal centre warehouse the following morning to be kitted out. For the moment however he told us to climb aboard a 3-ton lorry that would take us to our accommodation in boarding houses.

The following morning we assembled and marched to the warehouse for the clothing parade. The first item that I received was a kit bag – 'airmen for the use of' – uniform, battle dress, greatcoat, shirts, tie black, underwear, socks, forage cap, boots, gym shorts, vest, and plimsolls. Knife, fork, spoons, plates, drinking mug, gas mask and cape (doubling as a ground sheet) quickly followed. The enigmatic phrase 'airmen for the use of' suffixed to all items made me smile. It was an odd way of describing things, I thought. After stuffing all these items in the kit bag, I then lined up with the others to get my 'dog tags', the serviceman's description of identity discs. One was fire resistant in a hard, red material, the other water resistant in a hard, green material, and both were die-stamped with my name and enlistment number, 1291166. After returning to the billet to change and deposit the rest of the kit, we took out our eating utensils and went to the mess hall for lunch. When we had finished eating we found that we had to line up to wash our utensils, before returning to the hall, where we were told to remain seated. Within a few minutes a pilot officer entered, welcomed us, and outlined the programme of basic training, followed by a lecture on hygiene, with a particularly graphic explanation on the dangers of contracting venereal diseases.

The days that followed developed into a routine. I was now part of a squad of a dozen recruits, and required to be on parade at 8.30 am for roll call, and then a march to the pleasure park on South Shore for a period of drill, right turn, left turn, about turn, etc, under the gaze and shouts of a warrant officer.

We had a pause at 10 o'clock to change into sports gear, for physical fitness training on the beach. At first, the unaccustomed use of many muscles was agony, but as the days went by this problem disappeared. Each Friday the routine was broken by Pay Parade. Lining up with the rest of the unit, I eventually arrived before the paying officer, came to attention, saluted as instructed, and said "AC2 Jack Misseldine 1166", the latter being the last four figures of my enlistment number. I put my hand out, received the princely sum of seven shillings and, after saluting again, took one pace to the rear, turned, and marched off.

Most afternoons were devoted to lectures, firstly on armaments covering the Lee Enfield rifle. Then the Lewis machine-gun with its rotating drum feed of bullets that in its heyday had been used in aerial warfare during the 1914-18 hostilities. Now it was relegated mainly to ground defence. More up to date were the Vickers machine-guns with which the new breeds of fighters were being equipped. The terminology of the components described by the instructor bewildered me at first – feed pawl, and feed pawl actuating stud were ones that came to mind – but I soon learnt to dismantle and reassemble a gun in a reasonable length of time. Other lectures covered various aspects of service life; the meaning of station standing orders (SSO), covering permanent rules and regulations on an RAF station and daily routine orders (DRO), covering the orders of the day, guard duty roster, movement of personnel and other information covering the next twenty-four hours.

Route marches entered into the programme after the second week. First a five-mile jaunt, lengthening gradually to ten miles as fitness improved; but worse was to come. We were taken on a route march with a Lee Enfield rifle at the slope, which I considered to be the ultimate torture. I thought: Is this how we learn to fly?

Once a week we had a shower parade. The usual 3-ton transport took the squad to Derby Baths at North Shore, basically for a shower, but, on completion of these ablutions, we were allowed half an hour to swim in the swimming bath. As nobody had a swimming costume and we were all males, it didn't matter. It was there that I learned the meaning of the laws of gravity. Diving from the top board, in all my nakedness, I discovered it was a painful experience if one didn't make a perfect entry into the water.

Life however, was not all 'square bashing' and lectures. The evenings were free and with Stan and other friends we would wander round the town. Apart from the nightly blackout, it was like any other peaceful, seaside town that I had known before September 1939. On one trip to town we stopped at a photographer's shop, where Stan and I had our picture taken together. Once a week we went to a local dance in the Tower Ballroom, where I made friends with a local girl. It was a friendship that nearly ended in disaster!

Having made a date one evening to meet her in a cafe on North Shore, we went for a stroll along the upper level of the promenade. The night was very dark, with no moon, and as we walked arm in arm we paused to look out to sea and also at the stars in a clear sky. Thinking that we were near some steps to descend to the lower promenade, and with my arm around the girl, I turned to descend. Unfortunately the steps weren't there, and we fell some 10 feet onto the promenade below, where I landed heavily on my backside, bruising the base of my spine. The girlfriend was not so lucky, having taken the brunt of her fall on her right ankle. Despite being in some pain, I carried her back up to the road, and somehow supported her to her home. I visited her a few days later and found that she was all right, but it ended a beautiful friendship before it had even started.

The basic training lasted four weeks and, at the conclusion, a list of postings appeared on the notice board. Reading down the list I found that I was destined for Jurby on the Isle of Man and, reporting to the orderly office, I received a movement order and travel warrant. Thus, on the 4th November, I took a train to Fleetwood, boarded the ferry boat to Douglas, the capital of the Isle of Man, and took another train, running on the rather ancient narrow-gauge railway line, to the RAF Station at Jurby. Arriving at Jurby and having 'made my number' with the orderly office, I was directed to a hut that I would share with some twenty-three other airmen. The corporal in charge assigned me to a bed and indicated a small cupboard in which I could keep my things. On learning that this was my first time in barracks, the NCO told me to look at the other beds and the way kits were laid out, as each morning there would be a kit inspection. He warned that the warrant officer, who would make the inspection, was a stickler for tidiness and organisation. The bed was a typical iron-framed army issue with a mattress in three sections, and which, I quickly learned, were referred to as 'biscuits'. To my disgust there were two blankets and no sign of sheets but, as the hut was warmed by a coal fed pot-bellied stove in the centre, I felt that I could survive the cold. I thought: "Ah well you are really in the Forces now!"

Next morning, we were roused at 7.00 am for a roll call parade in the square. After dismissal, I followed the other members of the hut to the mess for breakfast. Once this was over it was back to the hut to prepare for the inspection. The 'biscuits' were placed one on top of the other, with the two blankets folded neatly on top. Various items of kit were also neatly arranged with them. Soon after, the corporal gave the order: "Stand by your beds", and doing just that I waited, feeling that I had correctly prepared for this moment. To my dismay the inspecting warrant officer found fault, and warned me that, if it was not corrected the following day, I could look forward to "kitchen fatigues".

During the morning we were drilled on the square, followed by a two-mile march around the airfield. It was there that I saw aircraft for the first time since I had joined up, and recognised Fairey Battles and Handley Page Hampdens. That afternoon, with two other occupants of the hut, I was detailed by the corporal in charge to wash the floor. Others were sent to collect fuel for the stove, which was kept constantly alight during the day as it was noticeable that the weather was becoming colder. During the evening I wrote home but, with strict censorship, I was unable to tell them where I was stationed. The only address that I could give was an army post box number.

The routine seemed to be established until, on about the fifth day, I read the DRO and saw that I was on guard duty that night from 8 pm until 8 am the following morning. The routine was two hours on sentry duty patrolling the airfield in pairs to protect the aircraft, followed by four hours off duty in the warmth of the guard hut. For my first duty I 'copped' the 8-10 pm and 2- 4 am periods – 'the graveyard shift'. December came with an abundance of snow and freezing conditions that made me wear all of the warm clothes that I possessed, plus a scarf and a balaclava helmet when I was on guard duty, but even then it was difficult to keep warm. This led my companion and me to find shelter, on one exceptionally cold night, by climbing into a Hampden to escape the biting wind. We knew that we were taking a risk of being caught by the orderly officer, but reckoned that the chances were minimal. The routine of guard duties continued until the last days of December, by which time I was beginning to believe that I had been forgotten and that I would never get a chance to become a pilot. However, the monotony was broken by a Christmas lunch that, considering the rationing problems, was excellent.

On 29th December I read the DRO outside the orderly office, and found that I was posted to the PDC at Babbacombe in Devon. On reporting to the orderly room I was told that, as I was not required to arrive in Devon until the 3rd of January, I would be granted four days' leave. A movement order, ration tickets and a railway warrant to my home, as well as a warrant for the onward trip to Babbacombe, were handed to me. Arriving home unannounced, mother and father welcomed me with open arms whilst my sister Barbara admired me in uniform.

In the evening I called on Jimmy and we walked up Harrow Hill to the King's Arms, where we met other friends. An evening of drinking included a session of Cardinal Puff, a drinking game that required an applicant, seeking to be a member of this illustrious group, to complete an investiture ritual. The ritual demanded a coordination of mind and body, with the consumption of a pint of beer in several stages during the test. If the applicant made an error during the ritual, he was required to drink the remaining beer in his glass and recommence with a new pint. Many a 'novitiate' had gone home worse for wear without gaining membership.

On 31st December, my parents invited neighbours and friends of mine to their house to celebrate the New Year of 1941. It was a good party, with plenty of drink and food that must have used up most of mother's ration coupons. Sometime after we had toasted the New Year we started playing poker, happily with only penny stakes that lasted well into the early hours of the morning. The rest of my leave with the family was enjoyable, but I also spent some time going out with Jimmy, and seeing other old friends. I took the opportunity to visit my old school and stood in front of the stained glass window in the entrance hall depicting Flight Lieutenant Boothman; I felt that I had to do this, as I hoped that in the near future I would fly a Spitfire, a direct descendant of the aircraft that he had flown. Whilst there, I met some of my teachers with whom I had no rapport as a schoolboy but now, in uniform, I felt almost their equal and, to my astonishment, found that they were now quite human and easy to talk with.

Much as I enjoyed my first leave, I was more than pleased to be on my way to Torquay in Devon, knowing that at last I would be fulfilling a dream and start my real training on the road to becoming a pilot.

The train for Torquay was waiting beside platform four but, as it was not due to leave until 9.00 am, there was enough time for me to get a cup of tea from a NAAFI vehicle stationed in the forecourt. Fifteen minutes before it was due to leave I joined a crowd of airmen and boarded the train. I was lucky enough to find a seat in a carriage crowded with troops. The train left on time and, as I gazed out of the window, I recognised the stations that we passed through – Reading, Newbury, Hungerford, Taunton and Exeter – before eventually arriving at Torquay in the afternoon. Disembarking with the other airmen, I reported to the RTO who arranged transport to take our group to a requisitioned hotel at Babbacombe where I learned that they were also aiming to be pilots.

During the next month we fell into the routine of parading in the morning, followed by physical training (PT) and, usually, a route march. Some afternoons we had lectures, but frequently we were left very much to our own devices and walked down to the nearby town of Torquay, where our favourite haunt was a Milk Bar serving creamy Devonshire milk shakes. Some evenings we went drinking in a local pub in Babbacombe where, on one occasion when demonstrating the rules of Cardinal Puff, I failed miserably, and was in such a condition that I had to be carried back to our billet. The following morning I woke with a severe hangover and vowed that, in future, I would be more careful when playing the drinking game.

The days began to drag and, as usual, we all began to wonder if our service records, which should have followed us from our last unit, had been lost. Our anxiety was dispelled when, on 9th February, we read the DRO and found that fifty of us were being posted to 3 Initial Training Wing (ITW) in Torquay to start our initial training on the following Monday.

On reporting there I was detailed to A Flight with twenty-four other cadets, while the rest were assigned to B Flight. We were informed that we could now wear the white flash in our forage cap denoting a cadet under training as aircrew. Before hostilities had broken out the majority of air force pilots were regulars, supplemented by pilots who had been trained in university air squadrons and, as such, wore a distinctive 'A' (auxiliary) below the eagle on the shoulders of their uniforms. I was happy that, because of the shortage of aircrews, the requirements had changed. Most of the volunteers were a gregarious bunch, coming from many different walks of life, and I felt that I had as good a chance as any of the other cadets of completing the initial training successfully, and laying the ghost of my inferiority complex acquired at school.

Both Flights remained billeted at Babbacombe, which meant an early start to march down to the training centre on the quayside in Torquay. The classrooms and the mess room were in a building beside the harbour and, while the meals didn't appeal to everyone, I even enjoyed the corned beef, spam, whale meat, baked beans and scrambled eggs made from reconstituted dried eggs, that were all too frequently on the menu. Fresh fruit was a rarity, but we often had a tinned variety, so that, as I had never been fussy over food, I quite enjoyed the meals.

Over the next eight weeks, I studied hard and applied myself to every aspect of the training, and found that the lectures on the functions of the piston engine were no problem due to my experience with Jimmy and the motorcycle. Theory of flight was enlightening when it was explained that the shape of the upper side of the wing gave the aeroplane 'lift'. Navigation had always interested me, albeit on the ground, and as a Scout map reading was an essential skill when going on hikes in unfamiliar areas.

Probably the most arduous lessons were the signals sessions learning the Morse code. Though I progressed with other cadets to a level of sending and receiving twelve words a minute, we seemed unable to improve on it. The instructor told us that this was not unusual, as many recruits 'blocked' at about this point. In any case, we had attained a sufficient degree of expertise required by a pilot, who would only use it to be able to read and send recognition codes as all fighter aircraft were equipped with VHF communication.

Physical fitness was by no means forgotten as, apart from the early morning half hour of PT on the quayside, additional exercise was provided by marching the Flight up a hill to the signals classroom about a mile away. What made it more tiring was that we were required to do it at the RAF speed of 140 paces per minute. Twice a week the squad was taken on route marches, the favourite of which was to the village of Cockington. The drill sergeant, who was a decent type, allowed us a break of one hour when we arrived there, and we immediately discovered why. He had halted us beside a well-known pub, Cockington Forge, where our Flight and the sergeant made good use of this watering hole.

On other days we had sessions of 'square bashing' on the harbour quay. The Flight in which I was a member performed well as a unit, and as we progressed each airman took it in turns to command the squad. I soon learned that the trick of giving the orders for a manoeuvre was to ensure that it was given on the correct foot. For example, an about turn order had to be given when the right foot of each airman was just making contact with the ground, and with a shout of "left, right, left, right", the 180 degree turn was completed, setting the squad off in the new direction on the left foot. It reminded me of a story that my father had told me: An army squad was training on a similar quay and the newly appointed corporal was giving the orders. Trying to work out on which foot he should give the next order, the NCO hesitated, whilst the squad continued to march inexorably towards the edge of the quay. When only yards from the water's edge, an 'old sweat' shouted: "Corporal. Say something, even if it's only goodbye!"

At the beginning of April the lectures were finished, and we came to the crucial examinations and tests that were spread over a two-day period. After waiting an anxious twenty-four hours during which time our papers were assessed, the results were finally pinned on the notice board, and I was gratified to see that I was near the top of the class. On the final parade, those of us who had passed the tests were told that we were now promoted to leading aircraftmen, with an increase of pay to ten shillings and sixpence (52.5p per week). The following day, after a passing-out parade, we were given a pair of two-bladed propeller insignias to sew on the sleeves of our uniforms to denote our new rank. At the same time I had noticed that several of the airmen were now wearing a VR insignia on the shoulders of their sleeves, denoting a volunteer reservist. As I was one of these, I bought a pair of these patches and sewed them on at the same time as the 'Props'. Thus, on 14th April 1941, the first stage of my training was completed and, like the rest of our group, I expected to be granted some leave. To our chagrin, we were informed that our Flight was to leave the following morning for the PDC at Wilmslow in Cheshire to await posting to an Elementary Flying Training School.

Chapter 4

AN INTRIGUING
POSTING

The day after my arrival at Wilmslow I assembled with ninety-nine other would-be pilots, to be told by an officer that we were to be sent on leave for seven days. We were each given £5, and advised that, during our leave, we were to bring our civilian wardrobe up to date. He then went on to say: "When you return, you will be going by sea to an undisclosed destination for your training. It will involve a long sea journey and, so being, it is best not to speculate where, or mention the fact that you are taking civilian clothes. Any careless talk, or even a hint of where you might think you are going, could put your lives at risk on the voyage." Despite this admonition there was a great deal of discussion amongst us as to where our destination could be. Somewhere in Africa was the favourite bet, but why civilian clothes?

Arriving home I found that my brother was there on sick leave, with his leg in plaster; not due to enemy action, but simply a broken leg sustained when he was playing for his regimental team in a football cup final. I was pleased to see that once again he had been promoted and was now sporting the chevrons of a gunnery ser-

geant. Our parents and sister thought that it was great to be a complete family again. Geoff and I were often out together, that is when
he was not out with some girlfriend or other. Some afternoons we
went to our usual billiard hall, above Montague Burton's shop in
Station Road, Harrow, for a game. I will never forget the day when,
as we came out, we found that it was raining and, with Geoff's leg
still in plaster, he didn't fancy the mile walk home. Seeing a
motorist just getting into his car nearby I approached him and, as
a result of a brief chat, he told us to jump in, and took us home.
Arriving there Geoff asked me what I had said to the motorist.
"Nothing much. I only implied that your injury was sustained on
active service, though I don't think playing football really enters
into that category."

The days passed very quickly, during which time I bought a new
sports jacket and grey gabardine trousers that, together with my
other civilian clothes, I packed in a suitcase. On the final day of my
leave, 21st April, I said goodbye to the family and left home to go
to Euston station in London, to board a train for Wilmslow. Soon
after arriving, I wrote home. "I expect you are wondering why I
haven't given you an address where you could write to me but, as
we have been told that we will be moving on very soon, it would
be pointless. However, I will write every Saturday and Wednesday
until the time I leave so that, when you stop receiving letters, you
will know that I am on my way overseas, and that the next letter
will be from some 'unknown destination'."

On 25th April, our contingent of 100 would-be pilots assembled, and we were taken in the usual uncomfortable 3-ton trucks to
the station. There, we found that we had two reserved carriages,
which meant that we would travel in reasonable comfort. Passing
through Manchester, Preston and Carlisle, we crossed into Scotland,
eventually arriving at Glasgow Central station. Our reserved carriages were uncoupled and attached to a shunting engine that took
us on to Gourock station, where we lined up in columns of three
and marched to the dockside to board a ship. It was the Manxman,
which was a ferry ship normally used for taking passengers
between Liverpool and Douglas, Isle of Man. With the exception of
the dining room, the passenger areas had been stripped of furni-

ture and replaced by frameworks of wood, from which hammocks were suspended.

By 10 pm, soon after we had boarded and sorted ourselves out, we became conscious of the noise of the engines and shouts from the dockside handling crews, preparatory to departure. Shortly after, the engines increased revolutions and the ship moved slowly away from the quayside. By then most of us were busy having fun with the hammocks, which had an annoying habit of swinging away when one tried to climb into them. Peace eventually descended about 11 pm, except for the noise of the engines, which eventually lulled me to sleep.

The following morning, we lined up for breakfast and, as the ship was crewed by Royal Navy personnel, they produced the inevitable thick cocoa. After finishing our meal, we took our drinks on deck to chat and watch the coastline on the starboard side, in the hope of distinguishing land marks but, as it was hazy, we could see nothing but water. The ship was proceeding at speed and, looking at the watery sun, I realised that we were travelling in a north-westerly direction. By the evening of the 28th, after forty-eight hours at sea, the *Manxman* approached land, which I surmised could only be Iceland. This turned out to be correct when we steamed into Reykjavik harbour.

The usual transport was waiting at the quayside and, after climbing aboard, we were taken to an encampment of huts at Helgafell, some thirty miles from Reykjavik centre. The area was obviously volcanic, covered with rocks from previous eruptions and with hot springs near the camp evidencing the high temperatures underground. One of these springs had been engineered to supply hot water for ablutions, and also to a large concrete basin serving as a swimming pool.

Time dragged as, apart from PT every morning and some 'square bashing', there was little to do – not even a chance to visit Reykjavik, as it was out of bounds to military personnel. On some days, together with Eddie Thompson, Jack Reeves and Jimmy Mallinson, with whom I had become friendly on the ship, we hiked over the rock-strewn ground and climbed a small extinct volcano, whilst on other evenings we had a dip in the pool. It was almost too hot for comfort, contrasting with the cool air temperature. The main pastime in the evening was playing cards, reading or theorising as to where our ultimate destination would be. We did have one excursion by lorry that was organised to visit the RAF Station at Kaldadarnes, where a squadron of aircraft was based to operate long flights over the sea, in protection of the convoys of ships sailing to or from the Canadian or US ports.[7]

Three weeks after our arrival in Iceland, we were told to pack our kit and climb onto the lorries, to be transported back to the harbour. Awaiting there at the quayside was a medium-sized passenger ship that we were told to board and ordered to sort ourselves out four to a cabin – Jack Reeves organised matters so that Eddie, Jimmy and I were in the same cabin which was equipped with four bunks and was to be our home for the next seven days. Before we sailed we were assigned to lifeboat stations, where we were to assemble in an emergency. Looking at the lifeboat, I read the inscription *M.V. Circassia*.[8]

At dawn the following morning, 21st May, the ship left harbour and, once out into the Atlantic, worked up a good speed. I had expected to see signs of other ships that we would join and sail in convoy with, but as time passed it became obvious that we would be crossing the North Atlantic alone, except for the occasional glimpse of an RAF Sunderland flying boat. Talking to a sailor, he confirmed that the *Circassia* was classified as a fast armed merchantman and as such frequently sailed alone. Looking around I could only see two Bofors anti-aircraft guns and thought that, apart from its speed, the description was a bit of an exaggeration. Having an interest in navigation and discounting the zigzagging, I was able to

---

[7] 269 Squadron, with Anson and Hudson aircraft, was based at Kaldadarnes in varying strength from 1940 to 1943.

[8] The Anchor Line's MV *Circassia*, 11,170 tons, launched in June 1937, was requisitioned on 14th October 1939 as an armed merchant cruiser, and fitted-out with eight 6-inch and two 3-inch guns. On 5th March 1942 she was fitted-out as a troopship, taking part in all the major landings in the Mediterranean during 1942-44. On 25th April 1966 she arrived at Alicante, Spain for breaking up.

estimate, from a watery sun and my watch, that at present we were sailing in a south-westerly direction. Forty-eight hours later, I felt that it was more north of west, as it had grown noticeably colder.

Life on board developed into a pattern. Up at 7.30 am, wash, shave, make up the bunk bed and tidy the cabin before going to the dining area for an excellent breakfast. This was due to the fact that plying from North American ports, the ship was able to victual with food that was rationed or unobtainable in the UK. The mornings were occupied with boat drill followed by PT on the foredeck. During the rest of the day we were left to our own devices, but on occasions we were interrupted by the tannoy loudspeaker: "Practice. Practice. All passengers to lifeboat stations."

After lunch we frequently went on deck for a walk, but inevitably ended up in one cabin or another playing cards or just talking. Occasionally I would go to the mess room where pontoon was being played, but avoided being drawn into the game as, with a number of Americans returning to their home country, participating in the stakes was beyond my meagre pay.

One afternoon, in the cabin that I shared with my friends, Phil Smith and three of his friends joined us. Talk turned to girls and sex, with one after the other describing in lurid details their exploits under the sheets. Eventually Phil turned round to me to give my version. Reluctantly I started to give my thoughts but was interrupted by Eddie, who came over and with a smile whispered to me: "I think you had better shut up, as it is obvious that you have never been to bed with a girl." They all had a good laugh as they knew that I was only eighteen and, as the baby of the group, they did their best to cover my embarrassment, some of them going so far as to say that their own stories were not that true. Nevertheless, it left me with a determination to find out what this sex thing was all about if a suitable opportunity presented itself.

By 24th May, it had become much colder and, when I went up on deck for my usual after-lunch walk, I could see small ice floes near the ship and in the distance what appeared to be an iceberg. I assumed that we were further north than I had thought, and wondered if we were going to make a stop in some port of Greenland. During the night there were some strange noises that I concluded were coming from the ship brushing against the ice floes. With thoughts of the disaster that befell the Titanic a quarter of a century earlier, I hoped that we would not encounter an iceberg. The following morning, my fears were put at rest, as there was no sign of any ice and we seemed to be heading in a south-westerly direction.

Three days later we sighted land and the ship steamed into a harbour late in the afternoon where, on disembarking, we were told that it was Halifax, Nova Scotia. Transport was waiting at the dockside and, after a fairly long drive, we arrived at the personnel despatch camp at Moncton.

The following day the mystery of our ship's route so far north was resolved, when I bought a local newspaper and read of the exploits of the Royal Navy and its hunt for and destruction of the German pocket-battleship Bismarck. Looking at a diagram that traced the movements of the enemy ship, I realised that we had had a narrow escape. Apparently the German battleship had left Bergen fjord in Norway heading into the North Atlantic Ocean. From the route and time scale illustrated in the diagram, it seems that on 25th May the enemy ship must have been approaching the track of the Circassia. No doubt it was the reason why the captain took our ship on a more northerly route; otherwise we might have been a victim of the Bismarck. It was sad to read that during the Royal Navy's efforts HMS Hood was sunk but that, on 27th May, the same day that we docked in Halifax, the navy had prevailed, and had sunk the enemy ship.

The following morning, 28th May, we were woken up early and taken to the railway station, where our contingent of 100 cadets boarded two reserved carriages on a train bound for Toronto. The route took us along the southern shores of the St Lawrence River, until we crossed over it to pass through Quebec. Continuing along the northern shore we arrived at Montreal, and my first glimpse of a large Canadian city. Unfortunately we only stopped there for a very short time, so that we were unable really to appreciate the French architecture and influence in the city.

Having changed trains there, we continued along the banks of the river until we reached Lake Ontario, with its glorious forests making a magnificent backdrop to the lake. Arriving at Toronto fairly late, we were surprised to be greeted by a reception committee and brass band. Our stay there was short lived but my friends and I were able to visit the town, where the local inhabitants were very friendly and, noticing our British uniforms, often invited us for a drink. One of them went so far as to take three of us around town in his car to get a close look at the skyscraper buildings, something that none of us had seen before.

On the third day of our stop over, the mystery of our destination became clear when we assembled in the dining hall. An officer called for silence and said: "As you know, the United States is a neutral country but, despite this, you probably read in a newspaper that Prime Minister Churchill made an agreement with President Roosevelt to acquire some fifty of its old destroyers. What was kept a secret was that he also negotiated a way in which potential pilots could be trained in the USA under a scheme devised by General Arnold to train American pilots. The President had agreed that his country would make these facilities available to train pilots for the RAF on the understanding that these cadets would come as civilians. That is why you were instructed to bring civilian clothes."

He continued: "You will split into two contingents of fifty, one of which will go to a place in Texas and the other to California on a train leaving tomorrow afternoon. You are to dress in your civilian clothes, and I would remind you, gentlemen, that, as you are the first group to train under this scheme, your conduct must be exemplary. Any person failing to live up to this standard will be taken off the course and sent back to the UK."

The following morning we attended a clothing parade to obtain lightweight khaki uniform shirts and trousers, gym shorts, socks and black shoes and were informed that these could only be worn when on the air base. To complete our preparation for entry into the USA we collected visas enabling us to remain in that country for a period not exceeding four months.

The day after, I packed my kit bag with my blue uniform and other items that I would not require until we reached our destination, whilst a change of underwear and small items for the journey went into a suitcase to go with me. Late in the afternoon, dressed in my sports jacket and trousers, I paraded with the others and, looking around, was amused at the variety of attires the others had chosen. We were told that we would be leaving that evening and that our kit bags should be stacked together in two piles, one for the California group, the other for Texas, ready to be loaded into a goods van at the rear of the train, whilst we would be taken by bus to the main railway station. It was getting dusk when we arrived there, but everything was well organised and in no time we had boarded reserved carriages on the waiting train.

The train left on time, but by the time we stopped at the US border near Detroit for the immigration formalities, it was quite dark. Settling down as the train gathered speed, I was pleased to find that the seats had obviously been designed for long distance travel; they reclined to a comfortable position enabling one to sleep. It was not long before the rest of the occupants settled down and all was quiet, except for the occasional snore from some unsociable people.

I awoke early the following morning, to find that we were in Chicago, where apparently there was going to be a delay and, with true American hospitality, arrangements had been made for the group to be taken on a tour of the city by coach. Contrary to my impressions, gathered from the films I had seen at cinemas in England, it was not a town of sordid streets and gangsters, but a beautifully planned city with skyscrapers even taller than those in Toronto. Returning to the station I realised that our carriages had now been coupled to another train which, I was told, was the famous Chieftain that ran from the Atlantic to the Pacific. In order to cope with such a long trip over a variety of terrain, the motive power was provided by two very impressive large steam engines.

Soon after 11 o'clock the long train pulled out of Chicago Central, heading through the State of Illinois. Through the window I could see that it was cattle country, evidenced by the stockyards near some wayside stations that I saw from time to time. Leaving Illinois behind we crossed the northern part of Missouri, with its fields of grain and cotton and herds of cattle, until we reached Kansas City, where we had a half hour stop and were able to take the opportunity to stretch our legs.

During the night we continued on south towards Oklahoma, until I awoke in the morning to see a changed landscape of miles and miles of wheat fields, and other crops. Things were going well and then Eddie reminded me that it was time for lunch, and we wandered through the coaches until we found the dining car, where our group was scheduled to eat at midday, with the rest of our party an hour later. After lunch, we explored the facilities on board, passing through several other carriages until we found a lounge bar and an observation car, from which one could get an excellent view of the countryside. Better still, we found a carriage equipped with individual shower cubicles – something which would have been unheard of in British trains. Returning to the bar, we met some American servicemen and, as conversation progressed, they realised we had an English accent and, eventually, we admitted that we were RAF cadets. Learning this they asked for a souvenir of our meeting, suggesting an exchange of a button off their tunics for one of ours with the RAF wings embossed on it. We told them that it was not possible as we were civilian guests of their country.

Continuing our journey through Oklahoma, I saw a number of odd-shaped tents that our American friends told me were tepees of an Indian settlement. Later on in the afternoon we entered the state of Texas, with its flat ranges stretching as far as the eye could see. It seemed fairly barren but nevertheless must have had some vegetation to sustain the herds of cattle that I could see. I also saw some odd-looking contraptions that our American friends explained were called 'nodding donkeys', whose purpose was to pump oil from the wells over which they were situated. Soon after midday we arrived at Fort Worth, where we were told that we would be staying for about three hours, during which time the group bound for a flying school in Texas would leave the train.

With three hours to spare, Eddie, Jimmy and I started to walk towards town, until we saw a large man wearing a broad-brim Stetson hat standing by a car. As we went by, in an accent reminiscent of the cowboy films that I had seen, he said "Heh! You young Britishers, I'll give you a lift into town in my little old automobile." A modest description for a luxurious six-seater Cadillac with bull's horns fixed above the radiator that made me think that he must be connected with the cattle business. Talking nineteen to the dozen, he confirmed this, and then insisted that we should visit a nearby stockyard containing hundreds of cattle, many of which belonged to him. He then took us on a quick tour of part of the town and on to visit the manager of the town's airport, before returning us to the station to continue our journey. Before parting company I asked him how he knew that we were British before even speaking to us. He replied, "I know most of the people in this town, and in any case considering the way you are dressed, you could only be British."

Leaving Fort Worth, the train continued in a southerly direction, passing through Austin and San Antonio during the night. The tracks then gradually turned towards the west, running beside the Rio Grande river for a while and then into open country, before cutting back to follow the river again until, early in the morning, we arrived in El Paso, New Mexico. Here we halted for a change of crew, giving us a short time to get a feel of a Mexican border town. It was a colourful place, quite different from the other American towns we had stopped at or passed through.

For the last section of our long voyage, we crossed into Arizona, a state producing a mixture of agricultural crops such as cotton and maize, but with extensive areas of desert. Finally we crossed the border into California, with the train climbing through the Sierra Nevada Mountains. At one point a third steam engine joined the two engines pulling our train, to assist it over the steepest climbs, until we finally descended to pass through a barren area, and arrived at Los Angeles station on 3rd June 1941.

At the railway station our group was met by Squadron Leader Reynolds, who was to be our commanding officer, and also a number of reporters. It seemed that, despite the fact that our reason for being in the USA should have been confidential, the press had somehow obtained information that this group of 'civilians' were actually RAF cadets, who had come to the States to learn to fly. The reception made our group feel rather guilty, as we realised that we were getting reflected adulation that rightly belonged to the air crews who had been in action in France, and, alone, had defended the skies of Great Britain since the previous June. The exploits of the fighter pilots in September the previous year, which was already referred to as the Battle of Britain, were apparently well known by the Americans.

A bus for us, and a lorry for our kit, was waiting outside the station, from where we were driven to our barracks in Glendale. 'Barracks' was hardly a fair description of our accommodation, as it had previously been a country club and gaming establishment, complete with swimming pool, tennis courts and gymnasium. We were intrigued to find that there was even a sliding wall, behind which there were gaming tables and where, in the days gone by when gambling was prohibited, the equipment had been hidden.

Once settled in, our group was introduced to the drill sergeant, after which the squadron leader outlined the programme of the course. "This establishment is known locally as the Polaris Flight Academy, and is ostensibly a civilian flying school, but in fact the RAF designation is No. 2 British Flying Training School."

"Starting tomorrow, you will have a callisthenics (PT) session each morning before breakfast and, for the next few days, there will be lectures, details of which will be published on the notice board each evening covering the following day's subjects, after which you will start your flying course. In order to simplify the organisation of flying, you will be split into A & B Flights, with five airmen detailed to each instructor. Work hard and I am sure that you will succeed. Good luck."

Chapter 5

FLYING AND FUN IN THE USA

Having passed a peaceful night in my new home, I woke early the following morning and, after washing and dressing, went with the rest of the group to breakfast. We then trooped over to look at the notice board, where details of our allocation to Flights had been pinned. My name appeared under A Flight, together with those of Eddie Thomson, Jack Reeves, Gordon Lambard, Jimmy Mallinson, and twenty others making up the complement of twenty-five.

Over the next three days we attended lectures on the Stearman PT-13B, our primary training aircraft. Our instructor described the biplane, its controls, instruments, take-off, approach and landing speeds, ending up by emphasising the need to be careful when using the individual toe-brakes on the rudder pedals. We also covered the basic principles of a radial engine that was easy for me to understand, resulting from the dismantling and rebuilding of the motor bike. Navigation lessons brought a surprise to me; the needle on a compass does not point to the North Pole, but to the Magnetic North Pole, a fact that added the word 'variation' to my aeronautical vocabulary (the angular difference between the two poles that varies in different parts of the world). Another was 'deviation' (the errors of a magnetic compass in an aircraft when flying on different headings).

The latter had to be charted on the ground with the aircraft in a flying position. Aeronautical maps were something new, showing contours and altitudes of high ground, location of aerodromes and airfields, roads, towns, villages, railway tracks and other information. Meteorology was fascinating, learning to distinguish between the different cloud formations, their dangers and the effects of winds. However, I realised after the first few days of lectures that we had only touched on the subjects, and that there would be plenty of hours' study going into more details of each one.

As the first weekend approached we were told that we were free until Monday morning, except that if we left camp we had to be back by 11 pm each night. With the facilities on the camp – swimming pool, tennis courts, etc, – we had options but, if it came to visiting the town, the big question was, where to visit and by what means?

The problem was resolved immediately after breakfast on our first Saturday morning, when we saw that a number of cars had arrived in front of our barracks. It seemed that the newspaper articles concerning our arrival from the British Isles, printed in the *Los Angeles Times*, had aroused the interest of many Americans of UK descent. Having followed the events in Europe since 1939, many of them had arranged for food parcels to be sent to relatives and friends, and it was some of them who had come out to befriend and entertain the young men who had come from war-torn Britain.

One of them, Archie Wallace, asked if anyone came from his home country, Scotland, and Eddie Thompson, who originated from Paisley, was soon in conversation with him and his wife Joanne. I was standing near Eddie at the time, and he introduced me to them, after which we set off in Archie's rather ancient car to their home, where Joanne had already prepared lunch. They then took us on a trip to discover the coast at Long Beach, and then back to their home for an evening meal, before returning to our barracks.

Monday, 9th June was a memorable day. Our Flight was taken by bus to Glendale airport, where our instructors were waiting in front of a line of primary trainer aircraft Stearman PT-13 biplanes. They were not dressed in uniform, but we felt that most of them were Army Air Corps pilots or ex-pilots, with the exception of one or two who looked like the 'Barn Storming' veterans who gave flying demonstrations up and down the country. Our group of five airmen was introduced to Mr Wise, to whom we had been assigned for the first stage of flying lessons. Each of us was issued with a lightweight flying helmet equipped with a Gosport speaking tube and earphones for talking to, and receiving comments from, the instructor. This type of aircraft was not equipped with modern radio communications.

Having been issued with parachutes and shown how to operate them, each of us was taken up for a short flight of twenty minutes to gain air experience. When my turn came, I put on my helmet, climbed into the rear cockpit, connected the Gosport tube, and checked with my instructor that we were in contact. We taxied out, but had to wait a while at the end of the runway as, being a civilian airport, there was plenty of passenger traffic arriving and departing. Eventually, my instructor was given the green light from the control tower, turned on to the runway, opened the throttle and took off, commenting all the time on what he was doing. We flew around for a short while until coming in to land for a near-perfect three-point landing.

Once everyone had experienced his first 'joy ride', we were told that, because of the amount of traffic at Glendale airport, as and from the following Monday our flying lessons would take place from an airstrip near the village of Newhall, where we would have the sole use of the airfield. Normally flying would take place in the morning, whilst ground lessons would occupy the afternoon. However on the 10th and 12th June I had two further flights of about forty minutes from Glendale, where I was allowed to take control of the aircraft and experience the effects of the ailerons, elevators and rudder with shallow turns.

On 16th June, after the usual early-morning callisthenics and breakfast, a yellow bus arrived at 8.00 am to take us to Newhall. Arriving there we found that the instructors had flown the aircraft from Glendale, and were ready to start our training in earnest. As

Newhall was merely a grass airstrip with just a small building serving as a control tower and no radio contact with aircraft, we were assembled near the building to be instructed on the method of air traffic control. A signal square was located in front of the building with a wind sock to indicate the direction and strength of the wind, and some planks of wood painted white, that could be laid out to show whether a pilot should fly a left-or right-hand circuit and the direction in which he should land. We were told that, on arriving back at the airfield after a flight, we should fly across it at an altitude no lower than 1,500 feet to confirm the direction of landing and strength of the wind before letting down to 1,000 feet and joining the circuit on the upwind leg. At the end of the runway, there was a vehicle manned by an individual, whose job it was to control the landing aircraft and fire a red Very light if he considered that an aircraft was on a bad approach, or that the runway was not clear.

Having assimilated this essential information, each of us in turn climbed into the cockpit in front of the instructor for a thirty-minute lesson on controlling the aircraft on the ground: using the throttle to control the speed, and the individual foot pedals to govern the direction or braking of the aircraft. These brake pedals had been designed so that the bottom portion controlled the rudder in the air and the top portion operated the sensitive braking system on the ground. Before the morning was over we saw what could happen when one of our group, who was taxiing too fast, pressed the top of both pedals too hard at the same time. The result was that the aircraft came to an abrupt halt, ending up on its nose.

During the next two days, with Mr Wise instructing, I flew away from the airfield to practise straight and level flying. It required co-ordination of the stick and rudder, and at first I found that, whilst concentrating on keeping the wings level, I would fluctuate on the altitude, or vice versa. When this happened Mr Wise would react harshly, by moving his dual control stick quite violently, which, being linked to my joystick, caused my knees to receive some hefty knocks, which I found was annoying. Later, when talking to other pupils, I found that they had suffered the same treatment from their instructors.

On the Thursday, I was introduced to medium turns, followed on the Friday by demonstrations of how to climb, glide and stall the aircraft, at first by following my instructor through the movements, and then taking control to practise them myself. By the end of the week I had logged four and a half hours of flying and, because of the intensive ground instruction each afternoon in a classroom that did not have air-conditioning, I felt pretty tired.

In discussing amongst ourselves the way that we were being taught to fly, most of our group agreed that we should say something about the harshness in the way our faults were corrected. Fortunately an opportunity arose when a well-known British film star of that era – John Barrymore – invited all the cadets and the instructors to a meal in a restaurant, with the object of consolidating Anglo-American relations. In this convivial atmosphere, many of us found that it was a good moment to discuss our feelings with our tutors. The evening was a great success, with most of us doing justice to the alcohol, particularly Tommy Lee and I.

On Saturday, Archie and Joanne Wallace collected us after breakfast, and Eddie and I spent the day with them again. They invited us to stay overnight, as they had plans for the Sunday. When we told them that we were under orders to be back at our base each night, Archie said: "Never mind. We'll come over and pick you up early as we have arranged to meet my brother-in-law, Tom, who works in the motion picture industry." True to his word Archie collected us at 8 o'clock, and drove us over to meet Tom Martin, his wife Agnes, and daughter Ruth, who took us to the studio where he worked, showing us the sets of films in the making and, afterwards, driving us to Beverly Hills to see the magnificent homes where many of the stars lived.

As usual Monday dawned with a bright blue sky, and our faithful bus was there at the usual time to take us to the Newhall airfield. The instructors concentrated on teaching us the principles of take-off and landing. When my turn came I spent forty minutes with Mr Wise trying to follow his advice and apply the lessons I had learned in ground school. I felt that my approach to the airfield and judgement of height when coming in to land were reasonable, but my instructor gave the impression that he was not satisfied. This worried me, even more so when the following day I was told that

I would be required to repeat the previous day's exercises with the chief flying instructor (CFI), Mr Theobald. He spent an hour and a half with me, firstly demonstrating a normal approach and landing and then a touch-and-go exercise, in which he made a normal approach and touch down but, instead of braking to a stop, opened the throttle to take off again. Having done this he told me to take over the controls in the air, complete a circuit, land and then taxi back to the beginning of the runway to take off and complete another circuit and landing.

It seems that the reason the CFI gave me a check flight stemmed from the reports that he had received from my previous instructor. At all events he must have been satisfied with my check flight as, the following morning, he advised me that I had been transferred to another instructor, Mr Lee, whom I had met at the party. Tommy was a jovial character, and I felt much more relaxed as we took off for the morning's flying lesson, during which he first checked my approach and landing. Satisfied with this he took control and told me that he would demonstrate the drill required when forced to make an emergency landing as a result of an engine failure on take-off. Essentially, he said, as soon as you are airborne select a likely area within your forward vision where it would be possible to make a forced landing. He emphasised that on no account should a pilot try to turn back to the airfield as, with no height and very little speed to play with, the plane would undoubtedly stall and crash. He then handed the controls over to me to practise several simulated forced landings.

Friday evening brought a surprise when Eddie received a phone call from the famous film star, Ida Lupino, a descendant of a very famous English theatrical family. When Eddie had put the phone down he told us that Tom, who was working on the film in which Ida was the star, had spoken to her about the English cadets.[9] Hence the phone call, during which she extended an invitation to him and four of his friends to a party at her beach house in Malibu on the following Wednesday. Eddie had to tell her that we were not

---

[9] Ida Lupino, born in Camberwell, London, on 4th February 1918, died in Los Angeles on 3rd August 1995.

allowed to leave the barracks during the week but, on learning this, she promised to organise a party on a Saturday evening in future.

Tom Martin contacted Eddie and suggested that he would like him and a couple his friends to come to his house for breakfast and make the acquaintance of his family. As a result of this conversation, on Sunday morning, 29th June, Tom arrived early and, with Eddie and another friend, Larry, we were driven to his home in Glendale. His wife Agnes and daughter Ruth greeted us on arrival and took us in to their large family room. Sitting down for breakfast we talked about food rationing and, when we mentioned how strictly eggs were rationed in the UK, Agnes asked us how many eggs and slices of bacon we could eat? Seeing that we were hesitating to reply, she proposed that she would keep frying until our hunger was satisfied. We did manage to restrict ourselves to four eggs and six slices of bacon each, eaten under the amusing glance of their daughter. When we had finished, there was a knock on the front door, and Ruth went out to come back with her friend whom she introduced as Lois. Tom then suggested that the seven of us should get into his spacious car, for a trip through the San Bernardino Mountains to Lake Arrowhead and Big Bear Lake. There we walked around the lake admiring the scenery and, after having lunch, descended to the coast at Laguna Beach for a relaxing afternoon of swimming and sunbathing.

There was no flying on the Monday or Tuesday, just a full day of lectures. One particular incident that I remember from that day was a discussion started by our engineering instructor. At the end of a lecture on a radial engine he suddenly posed the question: "What makes an aircraft fly?" After hearing the replies, he smiled and posed another question: "Could an aircraft fly without a propeller?" After the laughter had subsided he continued, "Your engineer Frank Whittle not only believes that it is possible, but he has already designed such an engine, and went on to describe a Jet engine.[10]

---

[10] Frank Whittle, later Air Commodore Sir Frank, OM, KBE, CB, FRS, Hon FRAeS, born 1st June 1907, died 9th August 1996, had taken out a patent for the design of his jet engine in 1930.

Like many of the students, I was able to understand the principle, but still could not imagine that an aircraft could really fly without a propeller.

The following day was again devoted to take-offs and landings, during which time the first of our group went solo. Naturally we congratulated him, albeit with some chagrin, as most of us had hoped to be the first. Several others followed suit during the course of the day, but I had to wait until the following day, Thursday, 3rd July, for an unforgettable experience. As I went out to my aircraft, instead of Mr Lee I saw the CFI sitting in the rear seat and, after I had climbed into my cockpit, he told me to taxi out, take off and complete a circuit of the airfield before landing. Having done so he told me to return to the beginning of the runway, where he climbed out and said, "Well done. You can now do a circuit by yourself."

I carried out my checks and obtained the green light from the ground controller before taking off. Climbing to 1,000 feet, I completed the circuit and turned onto the final approach for my first solo landing. Happily, all went well, and I made a good touchdown. Ecstatic at this achievement, I let the aircraft roll and, in my elation, opened the throttle and took off again for another circuit and landing. This second attempt was not quite so good, but I was satisfied as I taxied back to the dispersal point. There I was greeted by a very annoyed Mr Theobald. "I told you to do one landing, and I won't stand any cadet who disobeys my orders. If it happens again you will find yourself in trouble." Somewhat chagrined I joined my friends, who at least had the decency to congratulate me and confirm that I was the eighth cadet to 'go solo'.

4th July, being an American national holiday, was something new to us, but a group of us went down to Little Venice and joined in the fun. The fact that we were joining in a celebration of the defeat of the British by Union Forces and the signing of the Declaration of Independence in 1783 did not enter our heads. In any case it seemed rather incongruous considering that they were now helping to train British 'warriors'.

The following evening, a coach was laid on and the whole of our contingent were taken to Charles Laughton's place, where the great actor had laid on a party for our benefit. Many famous ex-patriot British actors were present, including Deanna Durbin, Robert Cummings, Vincent Price, Edward G. Robinson and Ida Lupino, with whom I had a conversation during the course of the evening. She said that she had already spoken to Eddie and that she hoped that I would be one of his friends who would be coming to her house on Malibu beach. The party that we were at was going with a swing, and I was really enjoying it until I was foolish enough to demonstrate the ritual of Cardinal Puff with tots of whisky. It soon had disastrous effects, and I don't remember much, only that I was carried out to the coach for the return journey, and suffered a gigantic hangover the following day.

Back to work on Monday, 7th July. 'Work' can hardly be the correct description of learning to fly, particularly as I was reliving the thrill of my first solo four days before, something which I am sure all pilots remember all of their lives. To have been in total command of an aircraft for the first time, is more than a milestone in a person's life. During this week the training began in earnest. Tommy Lee took me up for forty-five minutes of stalling and spinning. We flew away from the airfield, climbed to a safe height and, with the nose up, Tommy cut the throttle until the speed of the aircraft dropped, the controls became sluggish and the nose dropped suddenly in a stall. Pushing the stick forward and putting power on, my instructor held the aircraft steady until we had gained flying speed and full control again. After demonstrating this twice, Tommy went one stage further by going through the same procedure as before, except that he kicked the rudder bar as we stalled and the next thing, I realised, we were in a spin. Letting it rotate several times he then put on the power or, as he said, "poured on the coals", pushed the joystick forward and applied opposite rudder. The world stopped spinning and we made a clean recovery.

On a second flight, the same day Tommy showed me a manoeuvre which he called "eights across a pylon", designed to develop co-ordination of the hands, feet and brain. He picked a point on the horizon – a mountain top – and proceeded to drop the right wing with the stick and rudder, centralising the rudder at the bottom and pulling gently back on the stick. As the nose of the aircraft rose through and above the horizon, with left stick and rudder, he took the nose of the aircraft across and through the point on the horizon that he had picked. Letting it continue down to the left, he again centralised the rudder pulling back on the stick until the nose passed through and above the horizon; right stick and rudder until we crossed through our aiming point for the second time. I realised that in fact we had described a figure of eight with the nose, but wondered how long it would be before I achieved such a skill?

During this week I was tasked to carry out take-off and landings by myself, commonly known as 'circuits and bumps'. This was followed by another session of 'eights across a pylon' with the difference that Tommy made me do it myself and, to my satisfaction, after nearly an hour of repeating the exercise, my instructor gave me the thumbs-up. More spinning and stalling with Tommy, and then two days of solo flying practising spinning, stalling and 'eights', completed the week's flying.

At the end of this week an unfortunate accident occurred when returning to Glendale in the bus. Stan Young was sitting in a window seat on the near side of the bus and, because it was hot, had the window wound down with his arm resting on the window sill. As we were coming down a gradient, an overtaking car cut back in front of our bus, and our driver had to pull sharply to the right very close to the side of the road. It was bad luck that we were passing a telegraph pole which, though the driver avoided hitting it with the bus, passed so close that Stan's arm, resting on the window ledge, hit it. This threw his arm back against the window supports tearing some flesh off and, worse, causing a compound fracture of the lower arm. He was taken straight to hospital, where the doctors operated and set his arm in plaster, advising our CO that, though it would take time, they expected that he would make a full recovery. For Stan the worst news was that he would not be able to fly for some while, but the CO promised him that he would be included in a later course.

About this time I received my first letter from home, which I am afraid was cut about somewhat by the censors. Nevertheless, enough of it remained to give me news of my family. It made me realise how lucky I was to be living in comparative luxury, whilst they must still be suffering from air raids and continual rationing. Apart from replying to the letter, I spent most of the morning writing up notes on the lectures that we had had during the week, until Tom arrived soon after lunch and took Larry and me down to Long Beach for a swim.

During the third and fourth week in July, the amount of ground instruction in the classrooms increased, and additional hours were spent in the air. As the confidence of the students increased, we were introduced to more and more manoeuvres – slow rolls, snap rolls, and our first experience of looping, which was far simpler than I thought. After one demonstration by Tommy, I climbed back to 4,000 feet for safety, pushed the stick forward and, with plenty of throttle, attained the required speed, pulled back on the stick and held the aircraft straight with the rudder. I climbed past the vertical position until we were upside down and, as the aircraft came round into the second half of the loop, I throttled back as the speed increased and eased off the back pressure on the stick as I completed the manoeuvre. I also learnt a variation that consisted of completing the first half of the loop and, when the aircraft was upside down, half rolling into a normal flying position but going in the opposite direction.

Another variation that Tommy demonstrated was what he called the Immelman turn; after completing the first half of a loop, instead of a half roll recovery, he rolled a quarter of a turn and pulled the stick back into a tight turn that almost blacked out my vision. I thought that it seemed like a good exercise which would be useful in combat if an enemy aircraft was on my tail. Another was a very tight turn that required a lot of top rudder pressure to avoid the nose dropping. Amongst the instruments in the aircraft was one that had 'a needle and ball', to indicate if a turn was being made correctly – too much or too little application of the rudder would cause the tell-tale needle and ball to slide one way or the other. Needless to say, when carrying out these steep turns, the instructor would watch the instruments, give advice or make caustic comments.

It was during the last week of the month that the last of the cadets went solo. Jim McGowan had been having some difficulty in landing the aircraft but, after many additional hours and with the persistence of his instructor, he finally managed to fly the aircraft alone. The same evening, to mark the occasion, we decided to throw him in the swimming pool, where we saw him floundering around and going under. We thought he was having fun, until we realised that it was not pretence and he was in danger of drowning. Several of us jumped in and pulled him out and, when he recovered somewhat, he remarked, "You might have asked me if I could swim, or at least have thrown me into the shallow end."

A letter from Frankie Grimwood, who was himself shot down in 1941, arrived during the week, reminding me of our flight in the Isle of Wight. He, too, was overseas, in Canada, and had started his training well before me, so that he was approaching the conclusion of his course, whilst I had only reached forty hours of flying and had a lot more to learn.

The end of the month came with yet another party organised by the film colony. This time it was at a restaurant located in Olvera Street in the Mexican part of the city, where we were treated to very spicy food and an excellent floor show of Mexican dancing and singing. Whilst we were there, we wandered down the street and discovered a print shop where, on the front page of what purported to be a local paper called Hollywood Star News, they would set up any title that we wanted. As a bit of fun I had them print a headline "Misseldine an RAF flyer dives a P-38 at 600 mph". (The P-38 was a twin-boomed fighter plane known in England as the Lockheed Lightning, and 600 mph was a speed far in excess of any current fighter plane). I thought that it would be fun to send home to my parents.

Through Tom and his connections with the studios, we had met the manager of a radio station, who asked Jimmy Mallinson and me to come along to the studio to watch a live broadcast as part of the audience. What we hadn't realised was that it was a chat show, and we suddenly found ourselves escorted to the stage and interviewed whilst they were still on the air. When the broadcast of the show was finished, he asked the audience to stay and invited them to ask us questions about life in the British Isles under German air raids. Most of these were easily handled, but we were astonished at a question from one of the audience who was about our age, when he asked us why the British had not helped the American soldiers to fight in the 1914-18 war!

Saturday, 2nd August, was another eventful day. Ida Lupino had kept her promise and had sent a car for Eddie Thompson, Jimmy Mallinson, Jack Reeves and myself to be taken to the party at her house on Malibu beach. There were plenty of her friends from Hollywood there, including Vincent Price. Around midnight he said that he fancied a swim in the sea, and challenged me to go with him for a 'skinny dip'. As I had had a few drinks during the evening, I took him on and we slipped away from the party, stripped off on the beach and had a fantastic swim in the darkness. Eventually we made for the shore, only to be surprised by a number of the guests standing on the beach, who had realised what we were up to and had come down carrying torches, which they were shining in our direction, and were laughing at our predicament. As it was warm, we stayed in the sea until they had dispersed before getting out and dressing. The party continued until, at about 2 am, we said our goodbyes to our host, climbed into her limousine and were driven back to our base.

There was no flying on the following Monday and Tuesday as we were revising the subjects we had learned in ground school, for a test on the Wednesday. Most of us were quite happy that the questions presented no real problems, and the majority of us received satisfactory pass marks. Once that was over with, we resumed our normal routine of flying on the Thursday.

More and more time was spent flying solo, practising all that we had learned to date, with occasional checks by Tommy and more practice on instrument flying. For this, a hood was placed over my cockpit, so that I could not fly visually and, after my instructor had taken off and the airplane had gained a safe height, he told me to fly straight and level for two minutes, holding the altitude and heading. When I had done this for about five minutes, he then instructed me to make a rate-one turn to port through 90 degrees and then to starboard to get back on course, whilst maintaining the same altitude. I found that it was a challenging exercise demanding a lot of concentration on the instruments, ignoring bodily sensations. On the rare occasions that there were a few cumulus clouds in the region when I was flying solo, I flew over to them and into them for blind-flying practice. It was also fun to fly just over the top, to enjoy the sensation of speed.

Navigating cross-country flights to the Mojave Desert region became a more frequent exercise, usually requiring a landing at Palmdale airstrip before returning back to Newhall. To do so, we were required to prepare a flight plan calculating the necessary compass headings taking into account any wind, and an ETA that we knew would be checked by observers at Palmdale and Newhall. Although basically flying on compass bearings, it required constant checks with land marks, in order to make any necessary corrections to stay on track.

On 14th August, Tommy took me up for night time take-offs and landings, and after demonstrating the procedure told me to try a landing. I was surprised to find that it was not too difficult, as the runway landing lights helped in judging the angle of approach and 'hold off' for touch-down.

The hours of flying were building up, and we were all approaching the seventy hours that would graduate us up to a basic trainer, the Vultee BT-13A. This was a monoplane with a fixed undercarriage and a more powerful engine than the Stearman. We were told that our time in Glendale barracks and our flying from Newhall would terminate on the 15th, when we would move to real barracks and to War Eagle airfield[11], five miles west of Lancaster, California in the Mojave Desert and with a hard runway that was

---

[11] War Eagle was used by the US Army Air Forces as a training field. War Eagle Field, which opened in 1941, was the site of a contract flying school, Polaris Flight Academy, which was one of four schools operated by the Cal-Aero Flight Academy, with its headquarters at Glendale's Grand Central Air Terminal. There were two other auxiliary landing fields associated with War Eagle Field: Liberty Field and Victory Field. Liberty Field was located eight miles north-east of War Eagle Field. The location of Victory Field has not been determined. In 1944, the name of the Polaris Flight Academy was changed to Mira Loma Flight Academy. The facility was closed in 1945, at the end of World War II.
From http://www.militarymuseum.org/WarEagleField.html.

nearing completion.

This meant that there was no flying for a week during which time we were transferred by bus to our new location. Whilst we had flown over the area on some of our cross-country flights, I had not realised how barren it was. It was primarily a desert but interspersed with plenty of tall cactus plants known as Joshua trees. On seeing these monsters, a thought crossed my mind that a forced landing in this territory could be disastrous.

Arriving at our new home, we found that the accommodation was excellent. The entrance to the airfield was impressive with a motive over the main door 'War Eagle Field', flanked on either side by RAF pilot's wings. For accommodation, there were individual bungalows divided into eight spacious rooms, each of which had been designed to accommodate two people. I paired up with Eddie, whilst Jack and Jimmy took the room next door. The dining room was comfortable with a recreation room next door, equipped with a milk bar and soda fountain, where we could also buy chocolates and sweets ('candy' as we were told to call them).

Having settled in, we had a couple of day's instruction in the classroom covering the various aspects of the Vultee that was to be our next 'steed'. We were assigned to an instructor and, luckily, Eddie, Larry, Jimmy, Jack and me, found that we were to have the same individual, Mr Behrens. After introductions, he took us over to one of the aircraft that had an enclosed cockpit covering the trainee pilot and instructor, instead of the open cockpit that we had become used to. Standing on the wing, I could see that the aircraft was equipped with VHF radio for contact with ground control and easier communication between instructor and pupil. Before climbing into the cockpit to identify the instruments and layout of all the dials and switches, Mr Behrens spent the rest of the morning explaining the handling differences that we would find, compared with our previous aircraft. In the afternoon, and after a short wait, it was my turn for my first flight in a monoplane. My instructor taxied out to take off on a graded strip, as the main runways had not had their final tarmac surface laid. During our climb up to altitude, Mr Behrens commented on the effects of the controls and invited me to try them, after which he took control again and demonstrat-

FLYING AND FUN IN THE USA 69

ed stalls, spins and a simulated forced landing, before returning to
the field. During the afternoon, we attended ground school, mainly confined to the correct methods of using the VHF radio and the
normal phrases that were to be used to avoid confusion in transmission.

The following day, I climbed into the aircraft with Mr Behrens,
who demonstrated a take-off and then flew out of the circuit to
give me some experience of handling the aircraft in the air.
Returning to the airfield after landing, he told me to take over and
to taxi slowly round the perimeter strips to get the feel of handling
the aircraft on the ground. Satisfied that I was controlling the BT-
13 adequately, he then told me to taxi to the threshold of the runway, take off, make a circuit and come in to land, followed by a second take-off with a 'touch and go' exercise. Having completed
these, Mr Behrens told me to taxi back to the dispersal, where he
climbed out and said, "OK, it's all yours. I want you to do a take-
off, do two 'touch and goes' and one final landing, then return to
the parking area." I thoroughly enjoyed the experience and was
pleased to find that, being a heavier aircraft and a monoplane, it set
down more easily on landing, whereas the previous biplane tended to float a little before setting down. Over the next two days this
exercise was repeated, with occasional flights with my instructor,
improving my techniques, by which time I realised I had now
passed through a landmark of fifty hours solo.

It was no secret that RAF cadets were in the area training to be
pilots, particularly as the RAF wings were noticeable at the entrance
to the camp. In consequence, it was not long before we received
many invitations to different local events, amongst which was one
from the Canadian Legion, who were holding their field day later
in the month, and in preparation for the opening of the soccer season. They were keen to arrange that the RAF should field a football
team to play against a team from the Douglas Aircraft Company,
billing it as: "The team that makes aircraft versus the pilots who fly
them." Our drill sergeant took charge and, with the inclusion of
some cadets from No. 2 Course, he was able to find enough football players to create a reasonable team. From then on, part of our
daily PT included exercises to get the potential players match fit and

identifying the positions to which the players were most suited. A few practice matches were arranged, sometimes early in the morning but mostly in the evenings, to avoid the hot sun.

The latest invitation from Hollywood stars came from Mary Pickford, the wife of Douglas Fairbanks Junior, who invited quite a large number of us over to her home, 'Pickfair', for an afternoon of relaxation. On Saturday, 6th September, she arranged for a coach to collect us from War Eagle Field, Lancaster and, after a ninety-minute drive, we arrived at her home. There we were pleased to see that she had thought of everything, including the presence of a number of starlets and college girls to keep us company. The house was beautiful, as indeed was the garden, and had a magnificent swimming pool. We had a marvellous time, culminating, at the end of the day, with many of us receiving invitations from some of the college girls to meet them again. Jack Clarke, Eddie, Gordon and I made a date with Nedith Heinzberger and some of her friends to meet them the following weekend at the Wiltshire Palms for a swimming party.

At Lancaster, the training continued on the Vultee, repeating much of what we had learnt on the Stearman, but with more emphasis now on flying correctly using the instruments – airspeed, altitude, compass heading, climb and descent, turn and bank indicators, as well as watching the engine temperature, oil and fuel gauges. Navigation exercises were more frequent but, as most of the flights were over desert areas, it was not difficult to fly a correct course. The surrounding mountains in the far distance acted as check points and helped considerably. However, we were warned by our instructors that navigation would not be so easy when flying over the UK or Europe, with its patchwork of green fields, comparatively flat countryside and small towns and villages that looked alike from the air.

On Sunday, 19th September, two days after my nineteenth birthday, Eddie, Larry and I went to the Wiltshire Palms to meet Nedith and her friends to celebrate the occasion. As Lancaster was some seventy miles from Hollywood, we had hired a cab to take us there. It was a hair-raising ride through the San Bernardino hills by a driver who took corners at speed with the tyres squealing. When we suggested that he slow down a bit, he said that, as airmen, we should be used to travelling fast and, in any case, he was well insured. Happily, we did not have to book him for the return journey as Nedith had promised that she and her girlfriends would arrange transport back to base. The day passed well, until it was time to leave late at night, when Anne Brown in one car, and a friend in another, drove us back to camp. On the way, Anne offered to let me drive the car, but I had to confess that, though I could pilot an airplane, I had never driven a car.

The following Saturday was the day of the challenge soccer match. Transport by coach had been arranged by the organisers for the team and supporters, and we arrived to find that our hosts had thought of everything including brand new shirts. As we knew that the Americans preferred their own game of football, we had not expected many spectators, even though we were aware that there were quite a number of British expatriates living around Los Angeles. To our amazement, when we trotted out on to the field, we were greeted by applause from a large crowd of spectators in the stadium. We were told later that there were over 5,000, the largest crowd they had ever had for an opening match of a season. Our team played well enough, but we lost by four to two even though Bill Utting played brilliantly and scored both goals. Considering the fact that we had not played together before, we all felt that it was a creditable performance.

By the end of September I had completed some thirty-three hours on the Vultee, of which fifteen were solo, and it was time to move on to the last stage of our flying training with the North American AT-6. Before doing so, however, we were required to have two sessions of night-flying with the Vultee under the supervision of an instructor, in the vicinity of the airfield, with particular emphasis on take-offs and landings.

The North American AT-6, known as the Harvard in the RAF, was more powerful than the Vultee, but was slightly more complicated as, amongst other features, it had a retractable undercarriage. We noted that when the engine was running, the Pratt and Whitney Wasp engine driving the propeller had a distinctive rasping noise of its own.

It was at this point of our training that we were introduced to mnemonics as a memory aid. We had already become accustomed to the routine of walking around the aircraft for an external check but, because of the increased complexity of the Harvard, we were taught that, after climbing into the cockpit, securing the safety harness and before starting the engine, we were to say UMPFF as we made our cockpit checks. Undercarriage locked down; Mixture control lever fully rich; Pitch of propeller fully fine; Fuel quantity and fuel pump on; Flaps up. Soon after take-off it was UMPTF – Undercarriage up and locked; Mixture; Pitch and Trim adjusted; Fuel checked.

After several flights with the instructor demonstrating take-offs and landings and instrument flying, on 3rd October I was told to take off on my first solo flight in this aircraft and to fly around for an hour to get confidence in it. During this period I appreciated the way the aircraft responded to stick and rudder and enjoyed the additional speed, before coming in to make a good three-point landing.

Being far away from Los Angeles, we were only able to visit the city when we received invitations and transport was arranged to get us there. However, even though there was little to do in the small town of Lancaster, we did, on one occasion, receive an invitation from one of the American staff on the base, to go to a barn dance in his home town of Willow Springs. In fact it was in a small village, only a mile or two from the base, where most of the men were employed in a gold mine. We went there one Saturday evening and were able to participate in the barn dances as the steps were being called out by a local, dressed as a cowboy. The country-style music was played by a small band of musicians using banjos and violins. The dancing finished at midnight, when some of the men went off on the night shift but, such was the hospitality of the folk, and particularly the wives, that they said that, as it was late, they could find us beds to sleep in that night. We weren't quite sure what they meant but, in any case, we had to refuse as we had to be back in camp for flights in the morning.

An interesting sequel to our getting to know Joe, an American civilian employed at War Eagle Field, was that a few days later he came to see us when we were having a coffee in the canteen, and showed us a song he had written, dedicated to the RAF, the music of which, I still remember:

'The Wings of England are spread across the sky,
The Wings of England are still flying high,
The Wings of England are like the lions roar
That sounds like England, since days of yore,
Thumbs up every lad, every son, every dad,
Keep a watch through the darkest night,
Thumbs up, give a cheer, for there's nothing to fear
Whilst the RAF's in flight.
So Rule Britannia, as in the days gone by,
For you and I, will never, never say die
Whilst the Wings of England fly.'

At times, most of us felt a little guilty of the semi-luxurious life that we were enjoying, particularly when reading details of the bombings and reduction of rations that our families were enduring in the UK. However, we knew that in a short time our training would be finished and that we would be returning home to take an active part in the war, with all its dangers.

The flying training still continued with a considerable amount of practice in aerobatics to increase our ability to control the aircraft in difficult situations. We were also called upon to improve our navigation, particularly dead reckoning and the use of the 'blind flying panel' of instruments. It included cross-country night flights to specific points of a triangular course under a hood. Low flying in a specified area and formation flying with up to six aircraft increased, making us realise that the end of the course was approaching, and that we were being prepared for the final stage of training on combat aircraft, when we returned to the UK. By the end of the month we had all completed 150 hours flying, of which ninety were flying solo, signalling the end of our elementary flying training in the USA.

We had our last round of parties in Los Angeles with the girls, said goodbye to Archie, Joanne, Tom and Agnes and returned to the camp for a last ceremony. For once we were dressed in our best blue uniform, and paraded in front of the CO and CFI. He congratulated us all on finishing the course and presented each of us with the coveted pilot's wings and a small brass plaque awarded by The Polaris Flight Academy. Later our log books, containing all the details of our flights, were returned to us with the final assessment of the CFI on our abilities as a pilot. I was pleased to see that I was considered 'above average'. We were all interested to know whether we would be posted to fighter squadrons, but were told that we still had one more hurdle to cross before a decision would be made in the UK. This would not take place until after a short familiarisation course at a Service Flying Training School (SFTS).

The following day we packed our kit and, dressed as civilians, were taken by the school bus to Los Angeles railway station. As we had managed to phone the girls to tell them the time of our departure, we were pleased to see them waiting to wave us goodbye. Though we had been fortunate enough to have been entertained by film personalities, our real friends had been the girls, amongst whom was Ann W. Workman. She and I had become close friends and, during the moments of farewell, I promised to keep in touch by letter; even discussing with her the possibility of my returning after the war with the thoughts of a long-lasting relationship and, maybe in time, marriage.

I don't remember much of importance that happened on this return trip, except that we took a different route. Our first stop was at Salt Lake City, in Utah, where we had enough time to leave the train and have a quick look at the centre of town, then on through the night passing through Cheyenne in Wyoming, before stopping at Omaha in Nebraska for a short while. The journey continued on to Chicago, where the train joined the same tracks that we had passed over, nearly five months previously, en route to Toronto where we transited overnight. Here we were able to obtain our sergeant's stripes and dress in our uniforms, before continuing on to the transit camp at Moncton in Nova Scotia, where we arrived on 3rd November.

We were confined to camp for the next seven days, until we were transported to Halifax to embark on a large troopship, together with other aircrew who had trained in Canada and a large contingent of Canadian soldiers. On 11th November our ship left harbour and joined others to sail in convoy, escorted by warships, to England. We docked in Liverpool harbour on 18th November, and reported to the RTO, who gave us warrants to travel by train to the Personnel Reception Centre (PRC) at Bournemouth. It was strange to be on British soil again with its damp and cold climate, so different from the unending sun that we had experienced in California.

The train was crowded with a mixture of soldiers, sailors and airmen, and the journey was tiring as I was unable to find a seat, and had to pass most of the time sitting on my kit bag. The discomfort was exacerbated when the train was held up for quite a long time at one stage, due to an air raid being in progress. Changing trains in London, our group eventually arrived at Bournemouth. We reported to the PRC where we were allocated billets in private houses and told to return the following morning. There we found that our ranks had been confirmed, with the exception of a few who had been commissioned pilot officers. I felt disappointed as, like most of our group, I had hoped that on attaining my 'wings' I would be commissioned, even though it was known that the chances were less than ten to one. However, I realised that, whilst at the beginning of the war, there were career RAF pilots, supplemented by RAFA pilots trained as auxiliaries in university air squadrons, all of whom were commissioned, the influx of civilians from all walks of life training as RAFVR pilots had necessarily created NCO pilots and aircrews.

We were hoping that we would be able to visit our families and, to our delight on the following morning, we were issued with a pass for seven days' leave, return railway travel warrants and emergency ration cards. It was great on arriving home to be with the family again, where my sister Barbara bombarded me with questions about my stay in California and in particular the contacts with the film stars. Even Pop wanted to know more about Charles Laughton, whom he maintained was the best of all actors. Unfortunately, as I had not been able to forewarn my folks of my arrival, brother Geoff was not present, having been unable to obtain leave.

Chapter 6

TAKING TO THE SKIES IN THE UK

Arriving back at Bournemouth after my leave, I found that, apart from occasional sessions of drill and PT, our group was left to its own devices. Most of the time, we spent walking around town, going to the cinema or dancing in the evening. It was during this period of waiting that we heard of the Japanese attack on Pearl Harbor and, because of this, the USA had become our allies, not only in the Far East but also in Europe.

The waiting period to continue with our next stage of training seemed unending, as we were all eager to get in to the air again. Eventually, some fourteen days later, we were relieved to read a list of postings on DRO. I found that, with a few others in our group, I was to report to 9 SFTS at Hullavington. Arriving there on 16th December I settled in the customary barrack room and spent the day making new friends and finding my way around the camp. The following morning, I reported to the stores to obtain British flying gear, Sidcot suits, leather flying helmet equipped with earphones, an oxygen mask incorporating a microphone, fur-lined flying boots, leather gauntlets, silk inner gloves, and a white rollneck pullover. The last visit was to the parachute hangar to sign for this piece of equipment.

The thought of the poor flying weather that I was not used to did not please me and neither did the fact that I was to be checked out on a Miles Master Mk III, an aircraft that I was unfamiliar with and different to those which I had flown in the USA. Whilst waiting for the weather to clear over the next four days, along with the other members of the group, we spent our time with the instructors going through cockpit drills. In addition we had spells on a Link trainer – a dummy cockpit, mounted on pistons and God knows what else, to simulate flying. It was a sensitive beast, difficult to control, but obviously had its use when flying was not possible.

Two days before Christmas I had a ninety-minute flight in a Master III and further flights after Boxing Day, with three different instructors. Due to bad weather there was no more flying until 4th January 1942 when, having completed the mandatory five hours with an instructor, I was allowed to go solo. Though the cockpit lay-out was different from those of the American aircraft, I had adjusted to flying this British plane and found that it presented no problems. However, navigation did, as the patchwork quilt of small farms and villages were so different to the wide open spaces of California.

On 7th January, flying was once again cancelled due to bad weather, which continued until the 12th. On this day we were informed that our time at Hullavington was at an end, and that we were to be posted to an operational training unit (OTU). Owing to the very short time that our group had been at Hullavington, and the limited amount of flying that we had been able to have, the only remark that the CFI made in our flying log books was 'Insufficient time to assess'.

Like the other pilots on this course, I spent an anxious time wondering if I was to complete my final training as a pilot in Bomber, Coastal or Fighter Command. To my relief, the following morning, on reading a list of our postings, I found I was posted to 53 OTU at Llandow in South Wales for conversion onto Spitfires. We were informed that as we were not due to report there until 20th January we would be granted leave. This was good news, as I had not been able to spend Christmas at home with my family. Even so, though I enjoyed being at home seeing the family, friends and a new girl-friend, I was more than anxious for the time to pass quickly and get to Llandow where, at last, I could lay my hands on the controls of a Spitfire.

The journey down to Wales was uneventful and when I arrived at Bridgend station, transport was waiting to take several other trainee pilots and me to Llandow airfield. As I drove through the gates I noticed that it had a concrete runway, but that it was not ideal, having a slight rise in the centre that made it difficult to see the other end of the runway when on the ground. Reporting to the orderly room, I was allocated a bed in barracks off the edge of the airfield and a bike to get from there to D Flight dispersal, from where I would learn to fly a Spitfire. After settling in and getting to know the other occupants of the hut, we cycled around the camp locating the sergeants' mess, ante-room, camp cinema and the NAAFI (a canteen restroom run by the Navy, Army and Air Force Institute).

The following day after collecting a parachute from the stores, I reported to D Flight dispersal, where I spent the morning receiving instruction on the Spitfire. In the afternoon I sat in the cockpit familiarising myself with the controls, which were quite different to those in American aircraft. Whereas the control column (joy-stick) had been simple in the previous aircraft, the Spitfire, having a very compact cockpit, had a more complicated one, articulated in the middle to avoid banging against the pilot's knees when moving it sideways to control the ailerons. It had a spade grip that includ-ed firing buttons for the machine guns and camera gun, as well as a lever connected by a Bowden cable to operate the differential brakes. This controlled a system whereby, when operating the lever with pressure on the left rudder pedal at the same time, it applied braking to the left wheel for turning in that direction, and similar-ly on the right hand side. With the rudder pedals centralised and the brake lever applied, equal pressure would be provided to both wheels to bring the aircraft to a standstill. A bit tricky!

It was the first time I had sat in a single-seat aircraft and, as there would be no dual instruction, it meant that I would have to fly solo right from the start. Knowing this, my fellow students and I studied the pilot's notes and memorised our lessons in mnemonics for the 'drills of vital actions'. Added to this were the lectures covering the fuel system, take-off, cruising and landing speeds, use of the pitch, air screw and mixture controls, and the trim tabs of the elevators and rudder. Amongst a host of other information given to us was that the Spitfires were MkI and were not equipped with an automatic hydraulic undercarriage retraction system. This meant that after selecting 'up', by moving the selector lever on the right hand side through a quadrant to unlock the gear, it was necessary to manually operate a hand-pump beside the pilot's seat to raise the undercarriage.

The weather on the 23rd was quite clear and, with Flying Officer Mileham checking me, I took off in a Master III to do a couple of take-offs and landings. After this, he took control and flew around the countryside to give me an idea of the topography. Unfortunately, for several days after this flight, the weather turned sour but on 2nd February, I was able to fly solo on the Master to improve my knowledge of the area, and identify reference points necessary to complete the required circuit when coming in to land.

During the following two days, with other cadet friends, I studied the pilot's notes for Spitfires – Air Publication 1565E and 2280 A, B & C – until the moment that I sat in the cockpit with an instructor, Flight Lieutenant Corbet, standing on the wing of a Spitfire to observe my actions. I then went through the primary cockpit checks of vital actions – UFLF (Undercarriage locked Down; Flaps Up; Landing Lights up; Fuel contents) – and then the start-up procedures – FTMPR (Fuel lever cock On; Throttle half-inch Open; Mixture control Rich; Propeller speed control Fully Fine; Radiator shutter Open) before starting the engine. Having completed these procedures and checked with the mechanic beside the 'trolley ack' (an external accumulator unit) that all was clear, I switched on the two ignition toggles, pressed the starter button and operated the Kigas priming pump as the engine was turning over. As soon as it fired, I screwed the priming pump into the locked position, and let the engine turn over on low revs for about thirty seconds, before moving the throttle to fast tick-over to warm up. During this period I checked temperatures, controls and brake pressure.

Having satisfied my instructor on these drills I was told to taxi round the perimeter track to obtain experience on ground handling. With the cowling over the engine being long, the forward vision on a Spitfire is limited and, even with the cockpit hood open and looking out of the side, it was still necessary to weave in order to ensure that there were no other aircraft or vehicles obstructing the perimeter taxi tracks.

The following day, 5th February, I was detailed to fly the Master III and complete four take-offs and landings and return to dispersal. Having parked the aircraft, my instructor said: "Today's the day you will never forget, as you are now ready to have your first flight in a Spitfire." Having said that, he told me to climb into Spitfire Mk I, K9799, taxi out, take off and spend an hour away from the airfield at a safe height, familiarising myself with the handling of the aircraft.[12] Fortunately it was a good day for flying as the weather was clear, with only a few cumulous clouds drifting around the sky. Having completed the drills for start-up, and with the engine warmed up, I turned the aircraft to a safe direction and signalled to the crew that they should sit on the tail. This was a necessary procedure in order to keep the tail down for the next checks. With the pitch control of the air screw in fully fine, I opened up to maximum boost in weak mixture to check the operation of the constant speed propeller control. Then, at maximum boost in rich mixture, I tested the magnetos in turn, ensuring that the drop in revolutions on each of the magnetos did not exceed 150 rpm. Having completed these checks I taxied out, following a number of other Spitfires round the perimeter track, to await my turn to take off. Before turning onto the runway I completed the final drill of vital actions – TMPFFR (Elevator Trim one division down, rudder Trim fully star-

---

[12] K9799 was from the very first production order of 300 Spitfires (K9787-9999, L1000-1096). Originally on the strength of 19 Squadron on 17th October 1938, K9799 went to 222 Squadron at RAF Hornchurch on 31st August 1940. It was damaged in action with the enemy on the afternoon of 2nd September 1940. Repaired, K9799 went to 53 OTU, before being 'struck off charge' on 18th August 1944.

board; Mixture control rich; Pitch control fully fine; Fuel cock lever on main tank and contents checked; Flaps up; Radiator fully open). I was now ready for the great event.

Checking with the control tower, I was given permission to take off and turned onto the runway with the canopy open. I tightened the friction nut on the throttle before pushing it forward and felt the engine revolutions increase until the instrument showed 2,700 rpm. It was a great experience feeling the power of the 1,000 hp Rolls-Royce Merlin engine, and the rapid acceleration of the airplane. With the control column pushed slightly forward, the tail came up into the flying position and in this attitude the aircraft, reacting to the torque of the propeller, started a minor swing but, as I had been taught, with the use of the joystick and rudder pedals, I was able to hold the aircraft down the centre of the runway until flying speed was obtained. I eased back the control column to climb at a speed of 140 mph before switching my left hand from the throttle to the control column, in order to release my right hand to select undercarriage 'up' and operate the manual pump. After pumping vigorously, the undercarriage warning light on the instrument panel showed red, confirming that the landing gear was fully retracted.

Turning out of the circuit, I closed the radiator, adjusted the throttle, mixture and pitch settings to climb to an indicated airspeed of 170 mph and, after a quick check of the instruments and gauges, turned north to fly over the hills and valleys of the Rhondda, noting any obvious landmarks as a check on navigation. Climbing up to 5,000 feet, I went through some simple manoeuvres, gradual turns increasing to very steep turns to get the feel of rudder, aileron and elevator. I then climbed to a bank of clouds where, flying just above the surface of them, I simulated an approach to landing by reducing the power, holding the nose up and watching the speed drop to below 100 mph. It allowed me to experience the nose-up attitude and to get the feel of the aircraft flying at low speed.

After about an hour, I turned south towards the coast, knowing that the airfield was a short way inland, and approached Llandow. I called up on the radio and was told that I would be number three to land. The controller advised me to be well aware of other aircraft in the region, and several minutes later he confirmed that I could join the circuit on the up-wind leg. From the experience that I had gained in the Miles Master, I picked out the reference turning points that I had registered for the cross-wind and down-wind legs. Then, looking to my left, I could see that I was in the correct position flying down wind parallel to the runway and that the aircraft in front of me had landed, leaving me clear to continue my approach.

Preparing for the landing, I opened the cockpit hood, reduced the speed to 140 mph and completed my checks of vital actions – UMPFF (Undercarriage down and locked; Mixture rich; Propeller fully fine; Flaps down; Fuel checked). In addition to this, I tightened the Sutton safety harness and gave a quick check on the engine instruments. By this time I had turned onto the cross-wind leg preparatory to turning into the final approach. In fact these two legs blended into one. Because of the long nose of the aircraft, we had been taught to make this approach in a wide turn to maintain a sight of the runway before straightening out onto the axis of the runway. Reducing the speed to 95 mph as I approached the boundary, I pulled the throttle further back to 85 mph as the aircraft crossed the threshold and the first yards of the runway. Gently nursing the aircraft with stick and rudder, I touched down slightly too fast and bumped a little before the aircraft settled down. Though I had not achieved the ultimate of making a perfect three-point landing, I nevertheless felt satisfied. With the limited forward vision on the ground I hoped that I was not going to run out of runway, but this worry was unfounded as, with judicious use of the rudders and braking system, I brought the aircraft to a standstill with plenty of space to spare.

Taxiing rapidly to a turn-off point on the runway, I lifted the flaps to avoid damaging them, and carefully made my way back to dispersal. Running the engine at 850 rpm for a short period, I pulled the slow-running cut-out and held it until the engine stopped. After turning the fuel cocks, magneto switches, and radio off, I unfastened the harness and climbed out of the cockpit, happy that my first flight in a Spitfire had ended without incident.

As the 6th and 7th of February were a weekend, my new-found friends and I had passes to leave the camp. A visit to Bridgend on the Saturday convinced us that, as there was little activity in the place, we would be better off by taking the train to Swansea and spending the afternoon there.

It was about this time that we heard a story concerning the station commander, Group Captain Ira 'Taffy' Jones. Apparently he assembled the pilots of a previous course to castigate them for not getting their wheels up quickly enough after take-off and, being an ace pilot from the 1914-18 war and with many hours of flying in the RAF since, he announced that the following day he would show them how it was done. True to his word, he taxied out on the following day, with most of the pupils watching, and roared down the runway until the aircraft hit the bump halfway down. As he became airborne he quickly selected undercarriage up but, unfortunately, he had failed to appreciate that it was the bump that had made the aircraft airborne and that, in fact, he had not attained sufficient flying speed. Lacking flying speed, the aircraft settled back onto the runway on its belly. I was never able to find out if this was fact or just romance.

Another story that circulated concerned his achievements in the Great War when flying with the RFC, the predecessor to the RAF. In those days the airframes were mostly of wood and canvas, with a weak point in the strength of the fixed undercarriage and, as 'Taffy' was renowned for his heavy landings, he frequently damaged or broke this structure. Eventually he was ordered to report to headquarters where the CO was alleged to have reprimanded him for damaging some forty aircraft on landing. To this Ira, who had an impediment in his speech, was reputed to have replied "Th... th... that may be t..t...true, b...but I have sh...sh shot down f...f...forty two" and, with a two-finger gesture said "So I'm t...two up". Again, I don't know if this is fact or fiction.

Unfortunately Group Captain Ira Jones's autobiography *Tiger Squadron* gives little information beyond 1941, but there is a germ of truth in the above stories (somewhat apocryphal no doubt). On 6th August 1918, having just shot down two Hun aircraft and narrowly surviving a similar fate at the hands of seven of their comrades, he "crashed on landing, turning head over heels". No sooner had he extracted himself from the wreckage than he, and his fellow officers, were ordered to present themselves for inspection by their sovereign, King George V. His Majesty stopped in front of Jones and spoke with him for five minutes or so. Though Jones did indeed have a pronounced stammer – "My stammering was very bad while I was speaking to His Majesty, but he didn't seem to mind" – he was able to inform King George that he had so far brought down thirty-five of the enemy, twenty-four actually shot down with a further eleven out of control. More victories were to be gained before war's end, and his overall tally was twenty-eight aeroplanes destroyed, three kite balloons, and ten 'probables'.

Jones was to meet King George again, at an investiture at Buckingham Palace, when he was presented with no fewer than four awards – the DSO, MC, DFC and Bar. He had already won the Military Medal but, having been commissioned 2nd Lieutenant (with a seniority date of 2nd August 1917), he was awarded the Distinguished Flying Cross and Bar, the Military Cross, and the Distinguished Service Order (on 2nd November 1918), the citation for which read as follows:

Lieut. (T./Capt.) James Ira Thomas Jones, MC, DFC, MM.
Since joining his present Brigade in May last this officer has destroyed twenty-eight enemy machines. He combines skilful tactics and marksmanship with high courage. While engaged on wireless interception duty he followed a patrol of nine Fokker biplanes, and succeeded in joining their formation unobserved. After a while two Fokkers left the formation to attack one of our artillery observation machines. Following them, Captain Jones engaged the higher of the two, which fell on its companion, and both machines fell interlocked in flames. (MC gazetted 16th September, 1918; DFC gazetted 3rd August, 1918; Bar to DFC, 21st September, 1918; MM gazetted 10th August, 1916.)

So young-looking was 'Taffy' Jones – and he was only 5 feet 3 inches tall, too – that, when on leave in Cardiff sporting his array of medal ribbons, he was arrested by a hawk-eyed policeman who was simply unable to believe what he saw!

As to the story of some forty crash landings, Jones himself wrote: "I have never left the ground without uttering a short prayer for a safe return, but the unsafeness of my landings had become an RAF legend. In point of fact, I have crashed twenty-nine times."[13] James Ira Thomas Jones, born 18th April 1896, survived them all, only to die in hospital before his time, on 29th August 1960, following an accident six weeks earlier. His family say that he tripped over a doorstep, others that he fell off a ladder.

What was true was that an event took place in the sergeants' mess. Whilst officers were not allowed to fraternise with the WAAFs, there were no such restrictions concerning NCOs and, as such, the girls virtually had a standing invitation to the occasional parties in the sergeants' mess. On occasions the CO of the station would drop in informally to have a drink with the NCOs and, on this particular night, he stayed rather longer than usual, with a glass of alcohol always in his hand. By midnight the party was still in full swing, even a little rowdy, with many of the sergeants having paired off with WAAF partners. I had no partner and, feeling tired, I left to return to my bed in the barracks. The following morning a scandal arose, when a rumour went around that our station commander had slept there overnight on the floor. At a later date I did hear that he had been retired, in RAF jargon given his 'Bowler Hat', but whether the events in the sergeants' mess were part of the cause of this, I do not know.

The weather was not good for flying on the following Monday, but things had brightened up by the Tuesday when I was scheduled to carry out a sector reconnaissance and, on the following day, practise turns, slow rolls, loops and other aerobatics during the day. On the Thursday morning, with an instructor flying another Spitfire, two of us were detailed to join him in the air to practise formation patterns, with Gordon, a friend, flying on the port side and myself flying on his starboard side. At first it was open forma-

---

[13] Taken from *Tiger Squadron*, p.12 (Time Life Education, July 1994)

tion, followed by close formation, with our mentor coaxing us to get closer. To my surprise it was not that difficult as, though the three of us were flying at over 200 mph, our relative speeds were virtually zero and, with careful use of the throttle, it was fairly easy to maintain station. The same afternoon, I was told to go to an area that had been designated for practising forced-landing procedures, then more formation flying on the following two days with an instructor, this time flying in line astern slightly below the aircraft in front in order to avoid his slipstream

It was when I landed on the 13th that I learned that there had been an accident involving one of the students who had had an engine fire when about to land. Fortunately he had been able to make a forced-landing in a field not far from the airfield, and escaped without injury. In our next class in the lecture room, we discussed this incident with the instructor, who remarked that the pilot had been lucky. We realised what he meant, when he went on to say that, in the previous six months, there had been nineteen major accidents resulting in the deaths of a number of students learning to fly at Llandow. He then went on to enumerate the major causes. Two had spun in after becoming disorientated when flying through cloud. Two more had spun in from unknown causes. One had spun in during a dog fight. There had been four incidents of flying into hillsides when flying through low cloud. Yet another two had crashed into the sea when failing to recover from air-to-sea firing practice. Two more had collided in mid-air, and two others had collided when low flying. There were three other fatal crashes of which the causes were unknown. He summarised by saying: "Trust your instruments, particularly your altimeter when you are in cloud, and ignore any body sensations which give misinformation. Apply the correct procedure for recovering from a spin, and you are ninety-nine per cent certain to come out of it, but above all keep a constant lookout for other aircraft to avoid collisions. When you go to the firing range, which has a target in the sea, don't attempt to dive at too great an angle or stay too long in your dive in an endeavour to get maximum hits. Until you have gained more experience, it is no shame to pull out of the dive early – there is no future for you if you leave it too late."

On the 15th I was detailed to fly the Master III with Pilot Officer Shackleton as safety pilot to be checked on instrument flying and, once again, the dangers of flying were brought home to me. A pilot flying Spitfire P7994, and landing before us, burst a tyre, which caused the aircraft to slew off the runway onto rough, frozen ground, where it turned over.[14]

There was no further flying until the following Tuesday when, after practising more formation flying, I was told to go to the air-to-sea firing range to feel the effect of firing the eight Browning guns. It was quite an experience and, needless to say, I took the advice that we had been given and pulled up from the dive on the target at a safe height.

During the week I was introduced to a new but vital discipline involving the airfield ground control unit using 'direction finding' equipment. This required a pilot to transmit on the VHF radio, so that the controller could identify the position from which the transmission was coming and give vectors (directions) to the pilot. It required the pilot to fly accurately on instruments and obey the instructions received from ground control implicitly. I was glad to add this discipline to my repertoire as, apart from its use in giving directions to a pilot to intercept an enemy aircraft, I realised that if caught in bad weather, or becoming lost on a return from a sortie, it would be invaluable in helping me to get back to base and, in extreme conditions, line the aircraft up for a final approach and landing.

The last days of the month concentrated on air-to-air firing approaches, mainly quarter attacks, using the camera gun as evidence, as well as practice dog fights. For the latter, a pair of us would climb to 10,000 feet and try to get on each other's tail. Lacking experience, but with plenty of enthusiasm, both of us were turning in ever tightening circles to achieve this end, when

---

[14] Spitfire Mk IIa P7994 was repaired. Handed on to 277 Squadron, it was shot down by flak off the French coast near Boulogne on 25th November 1943 on an air-sea-rescue operation. The twenty-two-year-old pilot, Flight Sergeant Raymond Powell, was killed.

both of us went into high speed stalls ending in vicious spins. After several rotations and using the recovery procedure of stick forward and engine power, I straightened out to see the other Spitfire that was still in a spin, pass within feet of my nose. It brought to mind the admonitions of the instructor, when he lectured us about the crashes that had occurred in the previous six months. I realised that we had escaped a mid-air collision by the skin of our teeth, and that, though flying was fun, it could also be extremely dangerous.

Our time was mainly taken up with lectures and flying, but we had a good social life on camp as, apart from the bar and activities in the sergeants' mess, we had Entertainment National Services Association (ENSA) concerts, and even, on one occasion, a show put on by WAAF and RAF amateur entertainers.

The first week in March was a wash-out as far as flying was concerned but, with improved weather on the 7th, I was able to get fourteen more hours in the air. One of the exercises was a height climb, where I managed to climb, staggering over the last few feet, to an altitude of 31,000 feet, from which height over the Bristol Channel I could see the coastline of Devon and Cornwall. Our group was now nearing the end of the course and expected to be posted to a squadron before the end of the month. In consequence, additional lectures concentrated on aircraft recognition, not only of the enemy's aircraft but also RAF & USA planes. In the height of battle, errors were still being made in identifying whether an aircraft was friend or foe, leading to a few pilots shooting at each other, sometimes with disastrous results. Errors of identification were not confined solely to pilots, as Allied aircraft were sometimes shot at by army or armed merchant ship gunners. However, radar stations on the ground were able to tell the difference, when Allied aircraft were fitted with an Identification Friend or Foe (IFF) automatic radio transmission system.

On 8th March we had the first fatal crash of an aircraft from our course, involving the pilot of Spitfire L1014. The inquiry assumed that he became disorientated in cloud, probably lost control, and spun out of the cloud to crash at Skirrid Fawr, near Abergavenny. To our horror the group captain made us all file past the coffin, with the idea of hammering home the dangers of flying improperly. It was traumatic, but perhaps he was right, as I never forgot the lesson.

The following week we had an exercise on airfield defence. A mock attack was arranged with a local army unit, and a large number of us were picked to fly and locate 'the enemy' in sectors that were allocated to each of us. The sectors were small, and we spent most of our time practically flying in circles to make sure we avoided other aircraft that had strayed out of their designated zones. When we felt we had spotted something, the drill was to fly low over the area to investigate the situation. Low flying is fun, but not under those conditions, a fact that was proved when more than one aircraft returned with telephone wires attached to the wing. To sum it up, it was a shambles.

On the 17th I was allocated to fly Mk II Spitfire P7602.[15] It was a later version which had been designed to start without external assistance from a 'trolley ack', as it had been equipped with a Koffman starter. This was a device in which six cartridges were placed in a drum connected to the engine and, when 'fired' from the cockpit, caused the engine to rotate, during which time, by use of the primer fuel pump, the engine started. I found it quite temperamental, and only got the hang of it after using four cartridges. Once the engine was started, I taxied out and took off to rendezvous with an aircraft towing a drogue, for air-to-air firing practice. I had been told to be careful, and only make quarter attacks with appropriate deflection as in clay pigeon shooting, and not to follow through into a stern attack, as the tug aircraft would have been in danger. I know that I expended some 1,200 rounds of ammunition with reasonable results.

This was my last day of flying at Llandow and, with a total of thirty-three hours on Spitfires, I was deemed ready to join a squadron. With a total flying time in training of nearly 200 hours and a good assessment on my proficiency, I felt confident of my abilities. However, I did recall a remark, made by one of my

---

[15] P7602 had seen active service on 66, 609, 313 and 417 Squadrons before joining 53 OTU with effect from 15th February 1942. It was finally struck off charge on 1st June 1945.

American instructors: "When you have completed 200 hours flying, you will think that you know all about flying and, when you have 400 hours flying in your log book, you will believe that you know all about flying BUT, if you achieve 600 hours flying as a pilot, you will realise that you still have much to learn. In the air you must expect the unpredictable. Remember – there are old pilots and bold pilots, but not many old bold pilots."

On reading DRO the following morning, I saw that I was posted to an auxiliary fighter squadron. A last rip-roaring party in the mess, and it was time to collect my movement order, railway warrant, and a leave pass. The thought of spending seven days at home with the family, before being required to travel north, was very pleasant but I wondered what my life was going be like once I had reported to 611 Squadron at Drem airfield, near Edinburgh, on 24th March 1942.

Chapter 7

SHOT DOWN

On the morning of 24th March, I left home to board a train at King's Cross station for my journey north to Edinburgh. The route took me through Peterborough, Grantham, Newcastle, across the border into Scotland until, just after dark, and to my surprise, we stopped at the small station of Drem. Leaving the train, I reported to the RTO who told me that there was a 3-ton lorry waiting that would take me, and the other airmen who had arrived on the same train, to the airfield.

Having checked in at the guardroom I was allocated a room to share with another sergeant pilot, David. Though I was hungry, it was too late to get a meal at the sergeants' mess, and I had to make do with the few sandwiches that were left in the packet that mother had thoughtfully provided.

The following morning I reported to the adjutant of 611 Squadron, who extracted the file he had received from the OTU at Llandow. With this in his hand he took me in to see my CO, Squadron Leader Douglas Herbert Watkins DFC. After saluting him, he told me to stand at ease, and invited me to sit down. He wel-

comed me to the squadron and, after looking at my log book, com-
plimented me on my assessments, and was very interested to learn
about the flying training in the USA as I was the first pilot he had
met who had undergone this 'different' training. He then explained
that the squadron had only recently come north, as the majority of
his pilots had been posted overseas or to other squadrons and, apart
from himself and the flight commanders, there were only two other
pilots on the unit who had any experience of combat. It was for
that reason the squadron had been sent to Drem to reform, and he
felt that I could take a leading part in the rebuilding of the squadron.
He then told me that for the rest of the day I was free to deal with
the formalities, including drawing a parachute from that section,
and then make myself known in the sergeants' mess and ante-room.
He concluded by telling me to report to Flight Lieutenant Dwight at
B Flight dispersal at 9 am the following morning.[16]

Up bright and early, I was pleased to discover that the breakfast
was more than adequate and, with David, obtained transport to take
us and our parachutes to B Flight dispersal. There I found we had a
fairly large hut furnished as a rest room with some easy chairs and
a small office, where I introduced myself to the flight commander,
Flight Lieutenant Dwight. He explained that, apart from intensive
training, the squadron would be semi-operational, mainly carrying
out convoy protection patrols over the Firth of Forth and its
approaches, as well as intercepting any German bombers or reconnaissance airplanes that approached the east coast of Scotland. He
continued by saying that regulations required him to check out my
flying abilities and, therefore, I was to climb into Spitfire Mk Vb FY-
N (AD115) and carry out a series of circuits and landings. He
briefed me on the runway in use, the direction and strength of the
wind, and gave me a call sign, advising me not to forget to contact
the control tower on leaving dispersal.

---

[16] Watkins joined the squadron in 1938 and saw action in the Battle of Britain. He
took command of the squadron in November 1941, by which time he had three
aerial victories, his DFC being gazetted on 29th April 1941. He claimed a fourth
victory over Dieppe on 19th August 1942, before relinquishing command of the
squadron in September 1942 to Squadron Leader H. T. Armstrong DFC.

Walking out to the aircraft, I was met by an 'erk', the RAF slang for ground crew. Donning the parachute, I climbed into the cockpit, adjusted the seat height and the rudder pedals, and was helped to strap on the harness by the friendly airman. When all was ship-shape, he climbed down and went round to the trolley-ack that was plugged into the side of the aircraft near the engine and which gave auxiliary power for starting the Rolls-Royce Merlin engine. Having completed the start-up checks, I gave the 'thumbs up' to the airman on the trolley-ack indicating that I was ready to start. As soon as the engine was running smoothly, he and another airman went to the rear of the aircraft and sat on the tail, whilst I ran up the engine, tested the magnetos and noted that all instruments were reading normally. This concluded, I throttled back and ensured that the pair of airmen who had been sitting on the tail had come in to view. (This was a necessary precaution as on one occasion, a pilot had taxied out for take-off with an airman still on the tail.) Having come round to the front, they then ducked under the wings to pull the chocks away from the front of the wheels. All was ready.

Drem airfield did not have a hard runway, but there were well marked take-off and landing strips on the field. Having contacted the tower, who confirmed the runway in use, direction of wind and barometric pressure reading, they gave me clearance to taxi out. Arriving at the threshold of the runway, after last minute checks, I turned into the friendly wind blowing straight down the runway and took off. Climbing to 1,000 feet, I completed the circuit, making mental notes of ground features that I used for the turning points. On the final approach, I was a little high, so side-slipped to lose altitude and came in for a three-point landing. Taxiing back under the approval of traffic control, I repeated this exercise five times before returning to dispersal to get an "OK" from my flight commander.

After lunch I returned to dispersal, where I had been allocated FY-Q (BL618), and was briefed for an hour of local flying at 3,000 feet to get to know the sector. Edinburgh was easy to see in the distance, and other elements like the Bass Rock, the Forth Bridge and small towns along the coast were noted. The following day I was detailed to fly FY-N to Turnhouse airfield, an alternative airfield to be used in the event of Drem being closed for any reason. After landing there and checking in with flying control, I returned to Drem. Further sector reconnaissance flights were made over the next two days, culminating in a dusk landing familiarising myself with the distinctive Drem approach and landing lights system.

During April I flew every day, sometimes two or three flights, mostly in FY-D (AB382), which I had now come to look upon as my personal aircraft, and so, with the help of the ground riggers, trimmed the aileron tabs to suit my style of flying. I was learning all the time. Plenty of formation flying, in pairs or a flight of four, including flying through clouds, which I discovered was not that difficult in tight formation and, most exacting of all, in squadron formation. Dog-fighting practice with another member of the squadron became a regular thing, using the cine-camera so that results could be analysed. Cannon and machine-gun testing, and occasionally air-to-air firing of machine-guns on a drogue towed by another member of the squadron in another Spitfire, was also carried out regularly. Low flying practice over land in a designated area or over the Firth of Forth was where I really appreciated the sensation of the speed of a fighter aircraft.

My confidence in my ability as a pilot was shaken on 15th April, when I was flying as No. 2 in a flight of four aircraft. After completing a number of exercises we returned to the airfield and approached to land in formation, until, on the final approach, we received a red flare and the leader aborted the landing. We had all lowered our flaps preparatory to landing and, as he opened up the throttle, he warned us to be careful when lifting up the flaps in a 'go round again' situation, reminding us that a Spitfire tends to sink during this operation. Having climbed away, we made another approach, and still received a red flare. Finally, it became apparent that the reason for the red flares was that we were not landing in the right direction, a fact confirmed by the windsock visible in the signal square in front of the control tower. Eventually, the leader abandoned the exercise of landing in formation and, somewhat distracted by the 'cock up' he had made, I took my turn to come in to land. My approach was good, and I landed quite safely, only to find that the aircraft undercarriage suddenly collapsed. A glance at the

undercarriage selection lever, confirmed that, probably due to the
fact that my concentration had been disturbed by events, I had not
ensured that the lever had returned to the 'idle' position after
selecting 'down'. Even though the wheels had come down, the
bevelled locking pins had not engaged. The following morning, I
was called in to see Wing Commander P.W.Townsend, who admon-
ished me for my carelessness and endorsed my log book.

Peter Wooldridge Townsend, born in Rangoon, Burma on 22nd
November 1914, was educated in England. In July 1935, graduat-
ing from the RAF College, Cranwell (which he had entered in
September 1933), he served on several squadrons before being
posted to the command of 85 Squadron at Debden on 23rd May
1940, by which time he had already been awarded the DFC (30th
April 1940). He scored several victories in the Battle of Britain,
though was shot down into the English Channel on 11th July 1940,
and was wounded in the foot in an engagement with the enemy on
31st August. Awarded a Bar to his DFC, he eventually rejoined 85
Squadron, which converted to a night-fighting role. Having been
awarded the DSO on 13th May 1941, he was posted to HQ 12
Group as wing commander: night operations. In April 1942 he was
posted as station commander, RAF Drem, Scotland, but two months
later took command of 605 Squadron at RAF Ford, on the south
coast of England.

In his autobiography, *Time and Chance*, Peter Townsend briefly
mentions his time at Drem where, with 611 Squadron, he began to
regain his verve for flying: "I flew again, as of old, with daring –
fast, hard and low. Regrettably, I once flew, with a Polish officer as
passenger, through the local telephone wires.... back in my office,
a telephone call was waiting, from the regional post office chief.
'One of your blasted pilots has flown through my telephone wires!'
he exploded. 'I'm sorry,' I replied. 'Please leave it to me. I shall have
the pilot severely disciplined.'"[17]

After the war, as an equerry to King George VI, he and the King's
younger daughter, Princess Margaret, fell in love. Wishing to marry,

---

[17] Taken from *Time and Chance* (William Collins Ltd, London, 1978)

the decision was made that, were the princess to proceed with the marriage, she would thereafter forfeit any royal entitlements, and he was swiftly appointed as air attaché in Brussels. In October 1955, though the flame of love still burned brightly between them, Her Royal Highness and Peter Townsend made the decision to call it a day, and this was officially announced on 31st October. Peter died in France, 19th June 1995.

Three days later, I had another 'incident'. Squadron Leader Watkins informed me that on the following morning I was to fly with him and the station commander on an army co-operation exercise, entailing a surprise attack on an anti-aircraft gun site just inland from the coast. Soon after dawn we took off in Vic formation, with my CO flying on the starboard side of Wing Commander Townsend, and me on his port wing. Heading out over the Firth of Forth, we dropped to about 50 feet above the water, and hugged the coast until we turned inland, where my leader ordered me into the echelon starboard position on No. 2's wing. As we approached the coast crossing over a low hill, my leader peeled off into a diving attack on the gun position, with No. 2 following suit and myself bringing up the rear. Turning sharply to port after the attack, we reformed into Vic formation as we flew low out over the estuary, where the leader decided to make another attack, but this time from the opposite direction.

Though I was aware that we were now flying into the rising sun, over calm water with a hint of mist, my main concern was to keep in good formation on the wing commander. Approaching the land again I was ordered into echelon starboard, and I crossed under and into my position flying slightly lower than No. 2. Almost immediately I felt the aircraft shudder and instinctively pulled up and away to gain altitude realising that, as we had been flying very low over the water, I must have touched the sea with my propeller. The engine was labouring but, by reducing the throttle and putting the airscrew into fine pitch, I found that I could maintain altitude, albeit at the reduced speed of 120 mph. As I approached the airfield I called for an emergency landing, made a short circuit approach and lowered the undercarriage, noting that the green light came on. I delayed lowering the flaps until the last minute in case I had to attempt to go round again.

As I came across the boundary, I could see the fire truck and ambulance in attendance, but I touched down smoothly without incident and braked to a halt. I used throttle to try to move the aircraft off the runway but the aircraft refused to budge, so I pulled the idle cut-off to stop the engine. The ground crew, fire tender and ambulance arrived as I released the safety harness and climbed out of the cockpit. With the engineering officer, who had come out with the fire engine, I walked around to the front of the aircraft to look at any damage. About six inches of the propeller tips had broken off, and it was apparent that it had been caused by contact with water. The officer remarked: "You were lucky that the airscrew was a laminated wooden Rotol version that broke off at the tips, otherwise I am sure that, had it been the De Havilland metal version, you would probably have been dragged into the water." After he had landed, the wing commander came over to see me and explained that, due to the reflection on the water flying into the sun, he must have misjudged our height. I thought it decent of him, as I had expected to be blamed for a flying error.

During all this flying training, as part of the 'work up' of the squadron, we had to take our turn on stand-by in case of enemy activity. This meant sitting at dispersal in full flying gear with the Mae West life-jacket on, and the parachute ready on the pilot's seat in the aircraft.

At the end of the month, I had my first experience of flying at night in a Spitfire, FY-D (AB382). The problem was that the exhaust ports became white hot and reduced even more the forward view, so that greater care had to be taken in zigzagging when taxiing on the ground to avoid any obstacles. However, once airborne, it presented no real problems as most of the flying was on instruments under the guidance of ground control. I was told to fly at Angels 5 (5,000 feet) and given a vector to fly but, nevertheless, I was able see where I was from the reflection of a nearly full moon on the water in the estuary. At one moment, as I neared Edinburgh, I became intrigued by what seemed to be silver boats floating down the river, and decided to fly over and investigate. As I got closer, I soon realised that it was an optical illusion and that the 'boats' were static barrage balloons. It was my forward speed that had given me the impression of their movement.

After forty-five minutes I set course to return to the airfield and received corrections of my course from ground control. As I reduced altitude I thought I could see the runway lights on my starboard side, and turned towards them advising airfield control that I had the runway in sight. Almost immediately ground control called me and told me to maintain height and gave me a course to fly that was about 20 degrees off my heading. I wondered why, but nevertheless followed their instructions and prepared for ground control approach (GCA). All went well, and I picked up the Drem circuit markers enabling me to turn onto final approach and see the runway lights. At the last moment the threshold of the runway was illuminated, and I was able to make a reasonable landing. After parking the aircraft in its dispersal bay, I went over to the control tower to find out what the lights were that had led me to believe I had seen the airfield before being re-directed. It turned out that these were a dummy string of lights in a remote area that could be switched on to fool any enemy aircraft. As luck would have it, they had been testing them at the moment that I was in the area.

On 3rd May, I had a stupid accident, nothing to do with flying, rather a little 'horse play' that went wrong. With some of the other pilots in the dispersal hut we were fooling around and I chased after one of them who, to escape me, climbed out of a window. As I went to follow him he shut the window just as I put my right hand on it to climb out. As bad luck would have it, my hand hit the glass, which broke, and opened up a three-inch cut on my wrist. Over at the medical centre the doctor used eight stitches to close the wound, commenting that I had been lucky, as I could easily have severed a tendon. However, he said that I would be off flying for a week.

When Squadron Leader Watkins heard this, he said that there was no point in my hanging around for a week and that I could go on seven days' leave. I obtained the leave pass and travel warrant and could have left on the overnight train, but I decided to wait until the following morning as the sergeants' mess was having a dance that evening to which the WAAF girls had been invited. With my

arm in a sling, I received sympathetic looks, and had no difficulty
in getting a partner, even though, with my arm across my chest and
touching the breasts of my partner, it made it a little difficult to
concentrate on dancing.

I finally arrived home unannounced the following afternoon and
despite my explanation as to why my arm was in a sling, there were
some who preferred to believe that it must have been suffered 'in
action'. I spent several evenings with Jimmy at the Red Lion pub at
Harrow-on-the-Hill, where what they chose to believe was good
for a few free pints. I felt guilty during my leave for, even though I
had an emergency card for rationed goods, mother fed me with
good meals that I knew she was subsidising from the family rations.

Returning to the squadron on 9th May, I landed in trouble two
days later. As a reciprocal arrangement from the exercise that we
had carried out in attacking the anti-aircraft gun positions, the station commander had invited the ack-ack unit to send over a number of their personnel, to have a flight and view their gun emplace-
ments from a pilot's point of view. As luck would have it Squadron
Leader Watkins detailed me to use the squadron Tiger Moth,
N6930, for this exercise.[18] Despite my protestations that I had
never flown this type of aircraft, having trained on American aircraft in the USA, the CO replied: "Anyone can fly a Tiger. Just do a
circuit or two to familiarise yourself."

Having done so, and realising that the Tiger Moth was indeed a
simple aircraft to fly, I loaded my first soldier and took off to fly
over his battery location. Returning, I did this trip three more
times, during which I became more and more confident in handling the aircraft. Before the fifth 'squaddie' climbed in, I was
approached by his mates, who told me that my passenger was a
'big-head', and asked me to do some aerobatics and try to make
him sick. After take-off, I flew the routine trip but, on the return,
climbed to what I thought was a safe height, even though I felt that
the altimeter was unserviceable, and I started some aerobatics –
loops, slow rolls, rolls off the top, Immelman turns and, finally,

---

[18] Tiger Moth II N6930 survived the war, and was struck off charge on 30th March
1950.

pulling the aircraft into a stall followed by a spin. Throughout this, I was continually being given the thumbs up by my passenger, and I finally gave up trying to make him ill!

Having lost my bearings during these activities, I made a medium turn to discover my whereabouts, and was surprised to find that I was over the middle of the airfield. Dropping down into the circuit I landed and taxied back to the dispersal ready for my next passenger. As I came to a stop, two of my sergeant pilot friends came up to the aircraft and told me that, under the instructions of the station commander, I was under arrest. At first I thought it was a joke, but they insisted that it was not, and that they had orders to take me to the station warrant officer (SWO). There a military policeman (MP) escorted me to my room, where I was told that I should stay until the following morning, when I would be taken before the station commander. Needless to say I passed a sleepless night.

The following morning an MP arrived and took me to the SWO, who knocked on the wing commander's door and, after receiving an answer, told me to take my forage cap off before marching me into the office. Standing to attention, I heard the warrant officer read out the charges:

> "Performing aerobatics without authorisation;
> Performing aerobatics within the vicinity of the airfield;
> Endangering one of HM aircraft;
> Risking the lives of pilot and passenger;
> Endangering livestock and property within the vicinity of the airfield."

As I listened to the charges I envisaged the worst – no more flying and possibly reduced to the ranks.

"What is your explanation?" asked the wing commander.

"I am not familiar with the aircraft, having flown it for the first time yesterday and did not notice that the altimeter was unserviceable. I was also carried away by a request to 'take down a peg' the soldier who was a passenger on my last flight, and thought that I was in an authorised region where I could carry out aerobatics safely. During the manoeuvres, I must have drifted with the wind and was unaware that I was over the airfield until I looked around to land."

"Hmm! What do you mean when you say the altimeter was unserviceable?"

"There was no second hand on it to show altitude in hundreds of feet."

"That is normal in a Tiger Moth."

"I didn't know that, as my only training on light aircraft was a Stearman PT-13B in the USA, which had two hands on the altimeter, one for thousands of feet, the other for hundreds of feet."

"Sergeant, I find your explanation plausible, but a little romantic, so that, under the circumstances, I reprimand you, a fact that will be noted in your records."

(I wondered if the incident of low flying over the water under his leadership had any bearing on his leniency.) Having been marched out, the SWO followed, and told me to put on my forage cap and return to see the station commander.

On entering, saluting and standing to attention, Wing Commander Townsend said "At ease, sergeant. I have read Squadron Leader Watkins' report on your flying which has been above average and, for that reason, I have been very lenient with you. However, it is essential that you pay heed to your position relative to the ground and, most importantly, keep a sharp eye out for other aircraft in your vicinity. If you don't, you will not last long in combat." Little did I realise then that this understanding wing commander would, at a later date as a group captain, become a close friend of Princess Margaret.

Squadron Leader Watkins told me that, as far as he was concerned, it was an episode of high spirits, from which he felt sure I had learned a lesson and, to prove it, told me that he considered me "operational". That being so, I was to lead a section on convoy protection patrols. Occasionally I was involved in a 'scramble' to intercept high flying Focke-Wulf Condors on reconnaissance intrusions, but only once did I get within sighting distance after chasing well out over the North Sea. Unfortunately, with fuel running low, I had to return to base. During the month we had many discussions covering tactics, aircraft recognition and a variety of other pertinent information.

Further evidence that Squadron Leader Watkins had some confidence in my abilities came later in May. I was asked to report to his office and, after a long talk with him, he told me that he had recommended me to be commissioned as a pilot officer and that I was to report to 13 Group Headquarters in Newcastle for an interview. The following day I was given a travel warrant and went by train, arriving at my destination just before lunch. I was able to get directions from the RTO as to the location of 13 Group Headquarters, where I was told that my interview would be at 1500 hours. Returning after lunch, I was escorted in to see the group commanding officer. After saluting him he told me to sit down in front of his desk. He referred to my service record, which he had in front of him, and asked a number of questions, being particularly interested in the training I had received in the USA. After about twenty minutes, he leaned back in his chair and said: "I think that you have the making of a good officer. BUT you are rather young and inexperienced and, for your own good, I will defer my decision for three months." I was somewhat disappointed, but at least I had some hope in the near future.

By the end of May I had flown nearly seventy hours on Spitfires with the squadron which, with the thirty-three hours at OTU, brought my flying hours on this type of aircraft to just over 100.

On 1st June I had my last scramble from Drem airfield and, after climbing to 27,000 feet without sighting an enemy aircraft, I was recalled to base. Soon after landing, I was told to start packing my kit as the squadron would be moving south by a special train the following day. It seemed that at Fighter HQ they considered 611 Squadron had 'worked up' to full operational standard, and was ready to be transferred to Kenley airfield in 11 Group.[19] It was from this airfield, amongst others in the south-east, that squadrons were now operating aggressive sweeps over northern France, with the

---

[19] RAF Kenley, south of Croydon, Surrey, was a long-established airfield, having been opened in 1917, during the First World War. Kenley, due to its location, was to play a significant part in the Battle of Britain.

object of forcing the enemy into combat.

A special train had been arranged to take the whole squadron south, and we arrived at Kenley on 3rd June. The first two days at our new home were devoted to familiarisation of the sector in the south-east part of England, but on the third day, in talking with 'Chiefy' Frank, the flight sergeant in charge of the ground crews, I mentioned that my parents lived only about an hour away. He suggested that, as he had a motorbike, he would willingly drive me over if we could get overnight passes. The passes were obtained without any problem, under the condition that we were back by 8.00 am.

I phoned my mother, who was delighted to learn that I would be coming home to stay overnight with a friend. We arrived in Harrow about 6 in the evening and, after spending the evening chatting with my parents and sister, we went to bed soon after 10.00 pm telling them that unfortunately we would have to leave early the following morning.

As we were in the middle of the long summer days, it was a pleasure to get up and set off at 6 am. With fairly clear roads we made good time and in fact, on a good stretch of road near Croydon, 'Chiefy' opened up the throttle to a speed of 65 mph. Sitting on the pillion seat, I saw two pretty girls walking on the pavement who were probably on their way to work, and waved to them as we went by. In doing so, I turned my head and noticed that we were being followed by a police car, and shouted at Frank to slow down. However, the police car overtook us, and the driver signalled us to stop. Getting out of the car the officer approached us and, with a smile on his face, said, "It was fortunate that you saw the young ladies, as we were catching up with you to book you for speeding." When I explained that I had been home on twenty-four hours' leave and was due back at Kenley by 8 o'clock he let us go after warning Frank to keep his speed down.

The following morning, 7th June, I read on the notice board that I was detailed to lead a section flying an anti-intrusion patrol between Shoreham and Beachy Head with take-off scheduled for first light on the 8th. Flying W3330, the patrol on the 7th passed without incident, but on returning to base I found that I had to repeat the patrol in the same area at midday; it was also uneventful.

After lunch Squadron Leader Watkins came over to B Flight dispersal hut and informed us of the pilots who were designated to take part in the 'sweep' the following morning, and that I was to be in Yellow Flight on the port side. I spent most of the afternoon checking out the spare aircraft that I was to fly, as mine was in the hangar undergoing routine maintenance.

I had already flown the aircraft during the morning, and found that it was tending to fly one wing low and so, knowing that the next flight would be over enemy territory, I asked the fitter mechanic to make a minor adjustment to the aileron trim tabs. I did a further test flight and found that the aircraft flew better but, during the flight, I found that radio reception had deteriorated. The radio mechanic made some adjustments, and a final test flight confirmed that this problem had also been rectified.

During the evening I played cards with some of the other pilots before going to bed fairly early, wondering what my first flight over enemy-occupied territory would be like, and blissfully unaware that on the following day I would come face to face with the deadly realities of war.

The morning was sunny and warm as I made my way to the sergeants' mess for breakfast; a meal of bacon and eggs – standard fare reserved for aircrew taking off on a mission. It was a luxury that was appreciated as, at that time, the ration for civilians was only one egg a month.

As soon as I had finished eating, along with eleven other pilots of 611 Squadron, I assembled in the briefing room to learn details of the day's operation. There, the briefing officer announced that it was to be 'Circus 191' with four other Spitfire squadrons, escorting an RAF squadron of twelve Boston (Douglas A-20) bombers on a sweep over northern France, penetrating forty miles inland south of Calais. The route had been planned to take us near to major enemy fighter bases in the St Omer region of northern France, with the objective of enticing them into combat. The pertinent information concerning the operation concluded with this advice, "If you are unfortunate enough to be shot down, it is your duty to try and avoid capture and to escape from France." He then went on to give some details, of which I remembered, particularly, that a downed pilot could possibly be able to obtain help from the master of a convent school in a small village not far from Montauban in south-west France, which had been reported as a safe house. "Alternatively," he continued, "an attempt should be made to reach the Pyrenees and cross into neutral Spain with the help of *contra-bandiers* (men who smuggle items from Spain to France). If this is the route that you take and are successful in crossing the frontier, it is certain that you will be arrested by the Spanish police and be sent to prison. However, you will be allowed to contact the British Consul in San Sebastián or Barcelona, who will arrange for your release and repatriation."[20]

As we left the briefing room, we were issued with a survival pack containing, amongst other things, a map of France printed on a handkerchief-sized square of silk, concentrated food tablets, water purification tablets, a compass that could be assembled from two trouser buttons, and a sum of money in French francs.

I returned to our squadron dispersal hut where my commanding officer, Squadron Leader Watkins, detailed the flight position for each pilot. I was designated to fly Yellow 4 as 'Tail-End Charlie' (see diagram) with the responsibility of guarding the squadron against an attack from the rear until we reached the target area. I was not too pleased as, if we went into combat, I would be paired-off with Yellow 3 to cover his tail, whereas I had hoped to be the lead of a pair, particularly as my air-to-air firing practice results had been very good.

Yellow Flight	* 4✈	3✈	2✈	1✈
Red Flight	4✈	3✈	2✈	1✈
Blue Flight	4✈	3✈	2✈	1✈

Departure was scheduled for midday and, by taking off in formation 'Vics' of three, 611 Squadron were airborne and formed up on the squadron leader in a very short space of time. Keeping below 500 feet to prevent radar detection, we joined up with the other

---

[20] The Bostons were from 88 Squadron, their target being the oil tanks at Bruges. 88 Squadron lost no aircraft on Circus 191.

squadrons and crossed the coast to the west of Dover where, along with the other formations, we commenced a rapid climb to our designated operating altitudes, during which time I tightened the mask over my face and turned on the oxygen as we passed through 11,000 feet.

> "June 1942 was a month of blazing hot weather with clear blue skies, a brassy sun and limitless visibility ideal for the circus operations. On 8th June Finucane [Squadron Leader Brendan E., DSO, DFC & 2 Bars] led the Kenley Wing, 602, 611 and 402 Squadrons, on a diversionary sweep for Circus 191 against Bruges docks and flew along the French coast from Ambleteuse and then inland to St Omer to draw German fighters away from the main attack. He was leading with 611 Squadron with Bocock leading 602. Warned by John Niven of FW190s crossing the wing's track below – 'I ordered the wing to attack making sure that the wing above were in a position to cover us.'"[21]

Two of the squadrons forming the 'wing above', the Hornchurch Wing, were 64 and 122 which, in the ensuing dog fight, suffered the loss of four Spitfires. Two pilots were killed and two were rescued from the English Channel. Of the Kenley Wing squadrons 602 lost one pilot killed and one aircraft badly damaged. This latter aircraft, Spitfire BM385, belonging to Sergeant W.W.J. Loud (later wing commander DFC & Bar), was found to have no fewer than fifty-nine bullet holes in it.

It was on this operation that Squadron Leader Finucane, unofficially the highest-scoring pilot in Fighter Command with thirty-two victories, was to score his last combat victory, though claiming only a 'damaged'. Born on 16th October 1920, he was killed in action, still not yet twenty-two years of age, on 15th July 1942, having been promoted to wing commander only days earlier, on 21st June, the

---

[21] Paddy Finucane: *Fighter Ace*, p.171 (Doug Stokes, William Kimber & Co Ltd, London, 1983). Flight Lieutenant Eric P.W. Bocock DFC was commander of B Flight, 602 Squadron. Niven was Pilot Officer John Brown Niven DFC.

youngest in Fighter Command. He has no known grave, and is commemorated on the Runnymede Memorial.

We crossed the French coast near Boulogne with 611 Squadron now flying at a height of 16,000 feet (Angels 16) and with me guarding the rear as 'Tail-End Charlie' to warn of any attack coming from the rear. Though I was occupied with this task, I had to maintain formation with the rest of the squadron, keep a check on the aircraft instruments and relate any landmarks that I could see with the map on my knees so that, if I became separated from the squadron, I would be able to navigate my return to the UK avoiding any dangerous areas. In addition, I was preparing the aircraft for possible contact with enemy aircraft by going through the routine of unlocking the safety catches on the armament, switching on the camera control, tightening the safety harness and mentally preparing myself.

As we swept round to the south of St Omer, I became aware of many aircraft climbing up from below but, before I could transmit a message on the VHF radio, I heard Squadron Leader 'Paddy' Finucane shout "Bandits 9 o'clock low". This was immediately followed by my CO ordering our squadron, call-sign 'Panther', to attack in sections. The flight leader of Yellow section responded immediately, peeling off with his No. 2 following him. My Polish section leader, Pilot Officer Felc, Yellow 3, followed suit with me guarding his tail. We dived towards a large formation that I identified as a mixture of Me 109s and Focke-Wulf 190 fighter planes, and my leader headed for them. For the first time I saw tracer bullets being fired in anger, streaming from the more powerful machine-guns of an enemy aircraft. They were passing at an oblique angle well to the rear of us and didn't seem dangerous. Nevertheless, I called my leader to warn him, only to find that he had decided to climb rapidly away.

I then made a fatal error.

I was torn between either trying to reform with my leader or take the classic evasive action of flying in a tight circle to turn and face my enemy. However, it was too late. The enemy pilot had attacked, and hit. The first I knew of his presence was the flames erupting in the cockpit. I knew there was a grave and immediate danger of the fuel tanks exploding, trapping me and sending me to my certain death.

There was only one option open to me – BALE OUT.

We had had lectures by instructors in the USA and the UK on the use of a parachute but no practical training. They had talked to us about the best methods to exit from a single-engine fighter plane, many of which had very tight cockpits, especially the Spitfire. The instructors emphasised that by constantly going over the procedure in one's mind, when the time came to abandon the aircraft, it would become a reflex action. They must have been right for, though it was difficult to see with the flames beginning to scorch my face, wrists and flying gear, within seconds I had detached the oxygen mask, disconnected the radio plug, released the safety harness, pulled back the canopy hood and somehow managed to get out of the aircraft that was now virtually out of control.

Hitting the clean air and breathing more freely, I searched for and found the D-ring attached to the rip-cord and pulled hard to open the parachute pack. Nothing seemed to happen for an age, but a sudden jerk and the fact that my right flying boot had decided to make the descent to the ground by itself, made me realise that the 'umbrella was up'. I imagine that I must have been at about 12,000 feet, with a wonderful view of the countryside occasionally obscured by a few clouds drifting below. I seemed to be floating with little sense of descending. This euphoric feeling disappeared quickly as I lost altitude, and I began to wonder what sort of reception awaited me as I neared the ground. Would the German soldiers be waiting and, if so, would they shoot me whilst I was still in my parachute? On top of this I was concerned over the problem of landing with only one boot!

After an age, though probably about ten minutes, I got the impression that the ground was rushing up towards me and, worse, I seemed to be heading towards a line of electric power cables. To avoid them I pulled on one side of the shroud lines connected to the parachute, as I remembered being told that by using this method one could steer the parachute. How effective it was I don't know, but I did miss the power lines and, following the classic rule of flexing my knees and rolling sideways when I touched the ground, the landing was thankfully not as severe as I had expected.

I had come down in the middle of a field, expecting to see the field-grey uniforms but, nevertheless, released the harness of the parachute, bundled it up, and together with my Mae West life jacket, helmet, goggles, and gloves I headed for a ditch, where I buried the items. Luckily there was still no sign of approaching soldiers, but I was aware that many civilians had arrived. They seemed friendly enough and, to my surprise, one of them gave me a bottle of beer and a loaf of bread.

Wondering what I should do, I was relieved when a young man approached me and asked: "RAF?" I nodded and, pointing to himself, he said "Georges", and went on, in faltering English, to ask me if I wanted to hide from the Germans or give myself up to them for medical treatment. With visions of spending months or even years in a prisoner of war camp, I replied "Escape". He then pointed to a copse of mature trees that he called le fanque, some 500 metres away, and indicated that I should hide there. He turned to the villagers and told them to go home, before he joined me walking to the trees. Once there he told me to find a spot to hide and that, all being well, he would come back after dark. As he left, I penetrated into the wood, and found a suitable spot beneath a large tree, where a pile of leaves had accumulated, on which I laid down to rest, thinking that, if I heard footsteps, I would hide under the foliage.

I knew that I was about fifty miles away from Calais, and wondered if I should try to reach the coast but, realising that the main forces of the Germans would be there, I knew that there was no point in heading in that direction. In any case, I thought, my new-found friend Georges had promised to come back if he could, so I would wait to discuss the possibility of escape with him.

Chapter 8

ON THE RUN

Coming back to reality as darkness fell, I suddenly heard the rustle of leaves made by someone walking slowly through the wood and, fearing that it was a German soldier, I remained still under the cover of the leaves. The sound of footsteps became louder as the person approached, and then stopped not far from my hiding place. I heard someone whistling softly, followed by a single word – "Jacques".

Reasoning that, if it had been an enemy patrol I would have heard the sound of more than one set of footsteps and that, in any case, it was unlikely that they could have known my name, I felt that it must be Georges, and moved quietly in the direction of the sound until I was able to recognise his friendly face. I approached him to shake his hand. As he responded he handed me a pair of old shoes that I put on, after which he indicated that I was to follow him through the wood.

We eventually reached a narrow lane, and continued walking, avoiding most of the main roads, though on several occasions we had to take cover behind hedges or in ditches when we heard the noise of an approaching vehicle that, because of the curfew, was undoubtedly a German patrol. After walking for nearly an hour, we crossed a field and arrived at a walled garden, where Georges whistled a few bars of a tune. When he heard someone on the other side continue the refrain he immediately climbed to the top of the wall and then gave me a helping hand to join him. As we dropped down the other side I could see a man standing there, accompanied by a girl of about my age. They shook my hand, and hurried me over to a chicken coop at the bottom of the garden, where they had already installed a deck chair. They indicated that I should rest there, keep quiet, and pointed to some bread and milk that they had placed in my 'accommodation'. Before he left to climb back over the wall, Georges assured me that he would return as soon as possible. The man and the girl, his daughter, left to return to their own house across the road.

Sleep was a long time coming, and my thoughts turned to the problem of what to do if the German soldiers searched the garden and found me. I knew that I would have to convince them that I had made my way here on my own, and deny that I had been helped by anyone. I also realised that if Georges was unable to return, I would eventually have to leave my hiding place, try to avoid capture for as long as possible and, hopefully, progress to the safe house in south-western France or attempt a crossing of the Pyrenees.

I slept fitfully, but as soon as I was fully awake I opened my escape kit and took out the silk map to try and locate exactly where I was, and then considered an alternative plan to get back to England. I was a competent swimmer, and it crossed my mind to head north for the coast, no more than sixty miles now, and swim out into the English Channel in the hope that one of the RAF air-sea-rescue launches might pick me up. I quickly realised that it was a foolish idea and discarded it, as well as another romantic idea of finding a German airfield and high-jacking a German plane. I concluded that the only realistic possibility of escape was to wait and see if Georges had any ideas.

Though it was early in the morning, my thoughts were interrupted by the sound of someone approaching and, looking out, I was happy to see that it was a young girl walking towards the chicken coop carrying a bucket, and recognised her as the same person who had shaken hands with me the previous night. When she had entered, I could see that she had feed in the bucket for the hens, and also that she had brought some more milk and bread. She then went to the hen roosts and extracted a freshly laid egg and offered it to me but, as I was averse to eating raw eggs, unfortunately I had to refuse it.

The day passed slowly, but I was happy to see her again in the evening, when she said a few words in French. Unfortunately, with my very limited knowledge of the language, I could only gather that she was the daughter of the owner of the garden and that her name was Yvonne. Once she had left and I settled down, my thoughts turned to my family in England who would be unaware of the fact that I had been shot down. Undoubtedly they would soon be receiving a telegram from the Air Ministry announcing that I was missing in action. It would certainly be followed by a letter from the station chaplain and my squadron commander, 'Dirty' Watkins, with more details. I could only imagine the distress that my parents and sister would feel when they received this news.

When Georges arrived with Madame Perel-Ferment to collect me around 11 pm, I was pleased to be on the move, even more so when I discovered that they had brought me some better footwear that was far more comfortable than the pair that Georges had brought to me in the wood. I had no idea where we were going but had total confidence in my helpers as the three of us set off for the home of the lady. For most of the journey we walked down minor roads, keeping an eye open for any sign of German patrols until, about an hour later, we arrived at her cottage near Haverskerque.

By now it was past midnight and I was surprised to find, on entering her home that apart from her husband, their three children were still up. Nevertheless, Monsieur Perel accepted that I could sleep in the house overnight, but insisted that I must leave early in the morning and hide in the adjacent wood. The following morning Madame Perel-Ferment brought me a shirt and a suit that, I believe, belonged to her sixteen-year-old son and, knowing that it would be foolish to be seen in my scorched battledress and white roll neck pullover, I dressed in these clothes. Even though the trousers were a bit short and the jacket was too small, I knew that being caught in civilian clothes would be risky and, as a precaution to prove my identity if I was captured, I kept my 'dog tags' (identity discs).

After a breakfast of ersatz coffee and a slice of bread, I left the house and made my way to the fringe of the wood, where I lay down behind a bush in a position from which I could see the house. As the morning wore on under a hot sun, I was plagued by mosquitoes that seemed to concentrate on the raw flesh of my burns. Whilst I was lying there I realised that it was 11th June, my sister Barbara's birthday, and that it would undoubtedly be a sad affair for her and my parents. I knew that by now they would have been notified by the War Office and the CO of my squadron that I was missing in action and that in all probability they would be hoping to receive news that I had been taken prisoner, rather than that I had been killed. Little could they imagine that I was alive and lying in a wood in France thinking of them!

At midday one of the children brought me something to eat, after which I must have dozed off for a while. Awaking, I saw in the distance a girl standing beside two bicycles at the front of the cottage, and a few minutes later Madame Perel-Ferment emerged and made her way towards me. She took me by the hand, and we returned to her place, where she introduced me to the girl, Marcelle, and told me that she was a friend. I was to ride one of the bicycles and follow her at a safe distance to the nearby town of Aire-sur-la-Lys, where I would be looked after. Before we left she applied some sort of powder to my facial burns in an attempt to make them less obvious, but I felt like a clown, with ill-fitting clothes and a whitish face!

Marcelle set off on the other bicycle with me following some fifty yards behind, taking a route along country lanes that passed through the hamlet of Tanney and the village of Thiennes, where we turned onto the towpath along the bank of the Aire Canal. We cycled on to the outskirts of Aire-sur-la-Lys, where we crossed the canal over the lock gates connecting it to the River Lys, and entered the town.

There, for the first time, I saw a German soldier, who was standing guard. Conscious of my appearance, I turned my face away from him as I rode past, expecting to be stopped at any moment.

Thankfully nothing happened, and I continued to follow Marcelle through the centre of town into the rue d'Arras. As we approached what appeared to be a butcher's shop, I saw my guide dismount and wheel her bike into an entrance beside the shop whilst making signals for me to do the same. On entering, I was greeted in a typical French fashion by her parents, Monsieur and Madame Caron-Dupont, who led me into their kitchen behind the shop, where they gave me something to eat and drink. Later they took me up to a bedroom on the first floor that I was to share with their fifteen-year-old son, Albert, indicating to me that I should not show my face at the window and only leave the room when they invited me to come downstairs. Later Albert fetched me to go down to the evening meal with them, after which I was glad to go back to the bedroom and sleep in a comfortable bed, remembering the nights that I had spent with clucking companions in the hen house.

The following morning, 12th June, Monsieur Caron called me down to the kitchen, where I found a man waiting. He introduced himself, in English, as Doctor Lambrecht, and began treating my burns with a liquid that, I was told later, had been supplied by a local pharmacist named Monsieur Kerleveo. The doctor said that he had great admiration for the resistance being put up by the British and, because he had been a prisoner of war during the 1914-1918 war and had no love for 'les Boches', was glad to be able to render such service as he could to help a pilot of the RAF. He said that he would return periodically to continue treatment until my burns were healed. To avoid any suspicion that his frequent visits might arouse, he, Monsieur and Madame Caron would say that it was Albert, their son, who was undergoing some medical treatment.

To pass the time I amused myself by sketching and trying to learn some French with the help of young Albert. His father, who had a wicked sense of humour, enjoyed visiting me when he was not too busy in the shop, and I remember one morning in particular, not long after I had arrived, when he pulled back a corner of the bedroom curtains and asked me what I saw on the opposite side of the road.

"A hotel", I replied.

"Et le nom de l'hotel?"

Looking closer I saw the name and replied, "l'Hotel d'Angleterre".

He laughed and said "Il n'y a pas des Anglais. C'est le Quartier General des Boches" – "There are no English there. It's the Germans' headquarters."

He told me that the Germans were billeted across the road – a fact that sent a shiver down my back, until I realised that I was probably in quite a safe place. I was now many kilometres from the village where I was shot down and, whilst the search for me had no doubt spread out, they would hardly expect me to be hiding on the doorstep of one of their headquarters.

The days drifted by in the safety of the Caron-Dupont's home, punctuated by the visits from the doctor until, after nearly a fort-night, he seemed satisfied that the burns had dried out without infection, though my face and wrists still had a number of scabs. He said, "It's now time for action that may hurt a little, but I'm sure that you will feel better afterwards." Without wasting any time he proceeded to lift off the scabs with a kitchen knife that he had ster-ilized. He was right on both counts – it did hurt, but I did feel bet-ter!

During this time Marcelle used to come in with a young man who I thought was her boyfriend, until I found out later that both of them had connections with an organization based in Brussels that had helped soldiers who had been left behind at the time of Dunkerque. He was introduced to me as Albert Mestdagh, a Belgian by birth, and though he spoke some English and my French was practically non-existent, ironically our main means of conversing was in German, a language that I had some knowledge of from my school days.

When the doctor considered that the treatment was finished and that the tell-tale signs of burns had largely disappeared, Marcelle and her brother, Albert, insisted on taking me to meet a friend of theirs in the living room at the rear of a baker's shop a few doors away. The business was owned by the parents of their friend Regine Caux and, in order to try and raise my morale, they had organised a small party with some of their young friends. I can't say that I really enjoyed it, as I was conscious of the fact that, even though the burns on my face had healed quite well, I did not feel comfortable and, moreover, I thought it was risky as the house was not far from the Hotel d'Angleterre. However, I certainly appreciated their efforts after so many hours alone in the bedroom.

Towards the end of the month Albert, the Belgian, visited again and said that he had obtained an identity card that had been forged using a photograph that had been taken at the party. He asked me if I had a plan of escape, and I told him that I thought that I could get help from a place not far from Montauban. Though he seemed genuine, I didn't go into any details, as we had been warned that the Gestapo were devious and used many tricks to get information out of prisoners and, also, I was not absolutely sure where the place was. He then said that he would like to accompany me, as he wanted to join a Belgian parachute regiment.

On 29th June 1942, when my burns were healed and scars were hardly noticeable, the Belgian and I felt that it was time to make a move. The Caron family provided us with a small attaché case filled with a few necessities and food. I thanked them for looking after me and, when saying goodbye, made them understand that if I escaped back to Britain or, even if I were captured and sent to a prisoner of war camp, I would return to visit them when hostilities were over.

Just after 7 am we set off walking through the back roads of Aire-sur-la-Lys to the railway station where, with some of the money from my escape kit, Albert bought tickets and we boarded the local train to Arras. Whilst we were waiting there for the mainline train to take us to Paris, an individual approached and spoke to Albert. To my surprise, Albert opened the case and presented the person with a *saucisson* from our provisions. I wondered if it was a bribe or just a gift to a friend or beggar. The train arrived more or less on schedule and we were lucky enough to find two seats in a crowded compartment. Though my burns were practically healed, I was conscious of my appearance and felt that people seated nearby were looking at me with suspicion. After a stop at Amiens the train eventually drew into the terminal at Gare du Nord in Paris where, as we descended, a cold shiver ran down my back when I saw the number of German soldiers on the platform. As we approached the exit, it became evident that the guards stationed there were examining nearly every passenger's papers. With my false identity card, I became nervous as we got nearer to the guards, until Albert rose to the occasion by bumping into some people in front of us. In the ensuing argument that distracted the guards, I was able to slip by without producing my papers by mingling in the centre of the queue.

Descending into the Metro underground railway system, Albert bought tickets, and we took a train to the suburb of St Denis. Leaving me in a local park, he went off to see a contact, where he hoped we could stay the night.

I was getting a little restless as time passed by without a sign of Albert, but he turned up late in the afternoon, and we boarded a bus to Montparnasse. Alighting there, he took me to the house of a man who, I believe, was a member of a religious order. Though I slept quite comfortably, I nevertheless woke early and, with Albert, walked to the mainline station, where my companion bought tickets for us to travel to the town of Tours. The journey passed uneventfully, and when we arrived at Tours Albert signalled me to follow him off the train. We passed through the ticket barrier without incident and walked down the street, passing several German soldiers, who again gave me an odd feeling. After Albert had made some enquiries, we walked to a bus stop. When a bus arrived showing its destination as Esvres, we boarded it, and eventually arrived at the destination. At Esvres we found that there was a train that ran on a single-track branch line to St Branchs. There we would be able to make a connection with a train that would pass through Rouvre, a village that Albert apparently knew was not far from the Demarcation Line.[22]

Arriving at Rouvre we left the station and walked out of the vil-

---

[22] Following the Franco-German armistice in June 1940, France was divided into two main administrative areas – Occupied France, controlled by the Germans, covering the north and west coasts, and Unoccupied France, administered by a 'puppet' French government from the town of Vichy, basically the south and south-east of the country. Dividing these two areas was the so-called Demarcation Line.

lage until we came to a country lane leading to the south. After walking down this lane for a while, we caught up with a group of six people. Albert started to talk to them as we passed, and they came over and shook my hand, saying "Pilote Anglais". Once again I was perturbed by the fact that my companion had revealed this information to the group, but he explained to me that they were a family – father, mother, grandmother and three children – who were intending to cross into the unoccupied area, and had told him of a good place where this could be accomplished.

We quickened our pace and left the family well behind, until we came to a large field of wheat from where we could see, in the distance, what seemed to be a fairly important road. Albert said we must cross it to get into Vichy France, but that we had to be careful as there were most likely Germans patrolling the area. We entered the field and, as a precaution, dropped to our knees and started to crawl. Having covered some 500 metres, we lifted our heads above the crop to assess the situation, and saw a couple of Germans some distance away walking up and down the road. We felt that by observing the pattern of their patrol it would be possible to cross over to Unoccupied France.

However, to our consternation, we both saw the head of a person in the wheat field not fifty metres away. Part of my flying kit had been a sheath knife, a souvenir from my days as a Boy Scout. I always carried it when flying, to use in case of the inadvertent inflation of the dinghy pack that, with the parachute, formed a cushion in a Spitfire. Albert asked me to give him the knife, as he was going to see who the mysterious person was and that, if the person was unfriendly, he might have to use it. The minutes ticked by with no sign of him, so I decided to follow his tracks through the wheat to see if all was well. To my astonishment I found him sitting beside an individual who turned out to be a farmhand, who had paused to eat his lunch. However he was able to give Albert some advice on crossing the Demarcation Line. We moved off and, on approaching the road, noted that the soldiers we had seen were now some distance away, and had their backs turned to us giving us the opportunity to make a dash across and hide behind some bushes.

Looking back up the road we could see that there had been no

Above left: The Misseldine family, May 1946. Back row (l-r): The author, Mauricette; Barbara (sister); Captain Geoffrey Misseldine (brother). Front (l-r): Gladys (mother); Edward (father); Muriel (Geoffrey's wife) and son David.

Left: Mother and sister Barbara, at home, circa 1944.

: How fashions change. Aunt Doris's wedding Bert Brown, 29th September 1934. Aunt Doris ebrated her 100th birthday on 21st February 09.

Above right: The author with brother Geoffrey (left), in the garden of their Harrow home, probably circa 1930.

Top: B Flight, 1 Squadron, 3 Initi
Training Wing, January 1941. Jac
Misseldine is second row, sevent
from left.

Above left: Iceland, 26th April–20t
May 1941, en route to transit
camp not far from Reykjavik.

Above right: M.V. *Circassia*, on whic
the author and fellow cadets sail
to North America, 20th–27th M
1941.

Left: Iceland, May 1941. Rugged
terrain near the transit camp.

Top left: War Eagle Field, near Lancaster, in the Mojave Desert. It was still under construction when the author and the other cadets arrived there on 15th August 1941.

Top right: Joshua trees, Mojave Desert, near the airfield. No place to land.

Above left: The impressive entrance to War Eagle Field, 1941.

Above right: Barracks at War Eagle Field, Lancaster, California, USA, August 1941.

Left: Arrival at Los Angeles, 3rd June 1941. The author halfway back on right against the wall.

No. 2
British Flying Training School

GLENDALE, CALIFORNIA

* *

NO. 1 COURSE
June 14, 1941

Bottom Row,
Left to Right:
FRANCIS LEACH
JOHN R. BROCKBANK
T. EDGAR JENKIN
L. R. GORE
J. G. CLARK
DESMOND J. SMITH
DOUGLAS A. HINE
CHARLES W. M. SAUNDERS
D. J. HAWKINS
J. H. REEVES
RON W. SHEPHERD
J. E. MISSELDINE
KEN. WARREN
W. G. LAMBERD
O. F. LODGE
E. V. HONER

Center Row,
Left to Right:
STANLEY R. YOUNG
ERNEST BUGLASS
JAMES R. MALLINSON
W. HUGH HUGHES
TREVOR J. A. MARSDEN
C. G. WALLER
DAVID R. P. BOOTH

DOUGLAS V. HAMER
LAWRENCE LOWERY
DONALD J. ROONEY
R. G. MacINNES
GEORGE I. CLAY
P. G. ASHMORE
G. MOSES
E. L. PORTER
G. B. BLUNN

Top Row,
Left to Right:
WILLIAM R. GUILFOYLE
RONALD R. WILLAN
ALFRED W. UTTING
J. McGEOWN
HARRY P. COLLINGS
L. R WRIGHT
PHILIP S. SMITH
ED THOMSON
DON F. HUBBARD
ANDREW P. PATERSON
GUY H. RAPSON
ALAN B. WILSON
A. EATON
WILLIAM A. WRIGHT
J. ETCHELLS
J. HORSLEY
J. K. MANN

Top: No. 1 Course, No. 2 British Flying Training School, Glendale, California, USA, 14th June 1941. The author fifth from right, front row.

Above left: What happens when you brake too hard!

Above right: Primary trainer: Stearman PT-13Ps, Newhall airstrip, June 1941.

Bottom left: The author on first solo, 3rd July 1941, at Newhall airstrip, near Los Angeles, USA.

Above: Jim McGowan, last of the group to go solo, getting a ducking. Barracks in the background.

Middle: Vultee BT-13B inter-mediate trainer, August 1941.

Bottom: Conciliation party, July 1941.

Top: Advanced trainer: North American AT-6 (Harvard), October 1941.

Middle: Over the vast prairies of Canada.

Bottom: Advanced trainers just over the US border. North Dakota below.

Top: Party at 'Pickfair', the home of Douglas Fairbanks Junior and of Mary Pickford (in white on the author's left).

Above left: With Nedith Heinzberger and Jack Clark, Wilshire Palms Hotel, LA. What a way to fight a war!

Above right: The author with Hollywood film star Ida Lupino on Malibu Beach.

Far left: Ida Lupino at her house on Malibu Beach.

Left: Jack Reeves with the author's close friend Ann Workman, September 1941.

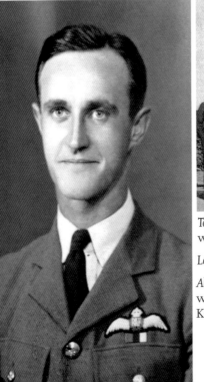

Top: At Drem with 611 Squadron. The author first left on wing. Squadron Leader Watkins, centre front.

Left: The author, flight sergeant pilot, October 1942.

Above right: 7th June 1942. The author (fifth from left), with another pilot and ground crew, 611 Squadron, Kenley.

Shots of 611 Squadron on the ground and airborne from RAF Hornchurch, Biggin Hill and Redhill, 1942.
Photos courtesy of *Aldon Ferguson*.

Top left: Steenbecque (Nord), where th
author was first hidden.
(Photo: Combier Imprimeur, Maçon).

Top right: The author passed this way
sixty-eight years ago.

Middle left: The author
with Yvonne Dillies, in
the hen coop,
Steenbecque, where he
hid, 8th-10th June 194

Middle right: No. 13 rue o
la Fraternité, Montauba
home of Charles and Pa
Cheramy.

Bottom: At the flat of
Gaston Nègre, Nîmes,
July-August 1942. First
left, standing, Mario
Prassinos; second left,
Gaston Nègre. 'Jacques'
(the author) seated on
left. Others in photo we
helpers of Gaston Nègre

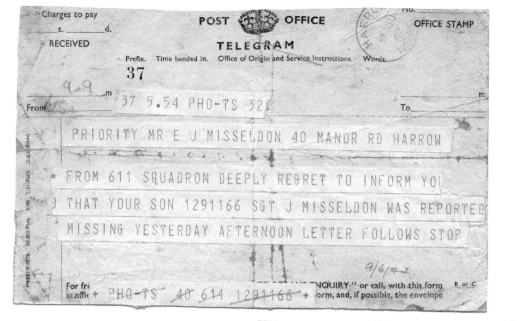

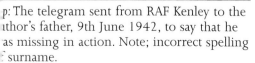

p: The telegram sent from RAF Kenley to the ithor's father, 9th June 1942, to say that he as missing in action. Note; incorrect spelling surname.

Above left: With Guy Walsh (left), North Africa. He was best man at the author's wedding in September 1945.

Above right: The author (left) in Jeep, North Africa.

Left: Mauricette and the author at their wedding, Oujda, North Africa, 6th September 1945.

Above: Wedding cake, French style, 6th September 1945.

Below: Leaving St. Louis d'Anjou church, Oujda, 6th September 1945.

Top and Bottom left: Spitfire TZ220, over the desert north-east of Cairo, 19th December 1947. Nothing but sand....

Below right: Benghazi harbour, 19th December 1947. (Photos via Flight Lieutenant W.J.J. Hudson RAF).

Left: With Pat Cheramy at RAF Odiham, where her portrait was hung, 1980.

Bottom left: Reunion at Steenbecque, 1988. Left to right: Yvonne Dillies; Mauricette; the author; Georges Lemettre.

Middle right: Steenbecque, June 1980. The author (centre) with Squadron Leader Holiday RAF and the mayor of Steenbecque.

Bottom right: Battle of Britain Day, Paris, 1990. Left to right: The author, David Ward, Reg Lewis. Mauricette (second from right) wearing sun glasses.

Above: Recent shot of the author refuelling, Digne, France.

Top right: The author in cockpit of P-51 Mustang, and *Middle*: Standing in front of Chance-Vought Corsair, Mandelieu airport, Cannes, France, September 2001. The author flew a number of these two types of aircraft whilst serving in North Africa and Italy.

Bottom: Arc de Triomphe, Paris, Battle of Britain Day, 1990. Second from left (holding wreath): Tom Wingham, fellow member of RAFES.

Painting by Duncan Robertson of John Misseldine's Spitfire on the day he was shot down.

reaction from the patrol but, fearing that the French family might make the attempt to follow our footsteps, we moved off rapidly across fields until we came to a farm. Approaching a cowshed we saw a farmhand who, after Albert had spoken to him, gave us a drink of fresh milk and a crust of bread.

Leaving the farm, we headed for the town of Loches, but must have taken a wrong turning for, when we entered what we thought was our destination, we discovered that it was called Mouzay. Walking into the village square we saw a café where Albert thought it would be a good idea to have a drink and at the same time get new directions for Loches. After serving us with a beer, the proprietor walked over to the corner and picked up the telephone. Albert and I watched him and noted that during his conversation, he was continually glancing in our direction. As I was still very conscious of my appearance, I nudged Albert, and indicated that we should leave. As we started to walk down the road we saw an individual in a uniform approaching, whom I thought was the village policeman, but Albert told me that he suspected he was a Milicien, who collaborated with the Germans. So we turned off into a side alley to avoid him and found our way to the edge of the village.

We covered a few more miles without incident until we arrived at a small stream, where we were able to wash. As it was getting dark but still very warm, we decided to sleep on some hay lying in a field close by. Returning to Mouzay the following morning we took the single-line train to Loches where we had been told that we could get a bus to Châteauroux and board a mainline train going south. However, after a few kilometres, when we discovered that the bus was going to a different destination, we got off and started to walk back to Loches, when we were lucky enough to be picked up by a Frenchman in a car who was going to Châteauroux.

Albert went to the ticket office in the booking hall, and came back to show me that he had first class tickets. I queried this, in view of my ill-fitting clothes, but he replied that, now we were in France Libre and, as things seemed to be going well, we might as well travel in comfort. We didn't have to wait long until the express train drew into the platform and, though it was fairly crowded, we found two seats together in one of the compartments. Amongst our fellow passengers, and sitting nearly opposite to me, was a man dressed in a navy-blue military uniform, who kept glancing at me and who eventually attempted to get into conversation with me. Albert had been aware of the interest that the man was showing, so he leaned across and spoke to him and, I presume, told him that I was deaf and dumb. In any event he made no further effort to speak to me, even though I was conscious that he continued glancing at my clothes. My distrust of him was confirmed when we arrived at Montauban and got off the train. He pushed past us and went over to the ticket collector at the exit and spoke to him, whilst pointing at us. As the train whistle sounded, announcing its imminent departure, he broke off his conversation and ran over to climb back on board.

We waited until all of the other passengers had passed through before we approached the barrier where the ticket collector, who appeared to be at least fifty, spoke to Albert at some length, during which time I heard Albert say "Aviateur Anglais". Much to my relief the railway employee turned to me and shook my hand saying "Bonne chance". Once clear of the station, I asked Albert what the ticket collector had said and, bit by bit, I was able to gather that the individual on the train had become suspicious of me travelling first class because of the way I was dressed, and had told the ticket collector to notify the police. However, after Albert had disclosed my identity, the railway employee told Albert that, as he had served in the 1914-18 war, he was only too willing to disregard the suspicions of the collaborateur and to let us pass.

We went into a café, and were able to borrow a Michelin map of the area, as I was still not sure of the address of the safe house. When we saw a road on the map running from Montauban, passing the villages of Nègrepelisse and Bruniquel, to Penne, the latter struck a chord in my memory, and I decided that it was worth visiting.

Crossing the square in front of the station we made for the bus terminal and saw on the timetable that there was a bus departing for Bruniquel at 5.00 pm that passed near to the village of Nègrepelisse. As we had more than an hour to wait for the transport, Albert suggested that we visit the hairdresser's shop that we could see across the square. Apart from a hair cut I also had a shave though, at nineteen years old, my facial hair did not grow fast. It seemed to be a good idea, even though I found that it was a painful experience due to my skin still being very tender from the burns. I did, however, feel more presentable and cleaner once the barber had finished.

We boarded the Bruniquel bus and, some thirty minutes later, were told by the driver that we were at the Nègrepelisse stop. We walked into the village, found the convent school in the principal street and, on approaching the main entrance, knocked on an impressive oak door fitted with a 'Judas' hatch. A man's face appeared at this aperture, and a voice asked, "Qu'est-ce-que vous voulez?" ("What do you want?"). I started to explain in English that I was an airman who needed help, but he didn't seem to understand. Albert intervened and, speaking to him in French, asked if we could see the person in charge. The hatch closed and we waited. After several minutes, I began to wonder if I had the right address, or whether it had been compromised? My anxiety increased when we saw two men in uniform hurrying down the street, so I beckoned to Albert and we crossed the road to hide behind a truck. The individuals stopped in front of the school door and were almost immediately let in, which seemed to confirm my suspicions that we were not welcome.

With a heavy heart we left the village where I had hoped to obtain assistance, and set off down a country lane heading back towards Montauban. We came across a disused railway line that seemed to be going in the right direction, and walked along the tracks, passing through a tunnel until eventually arriving at a point where the railway ran parallel to a road. As dusk was now approaching, we took to the road to look for a likely place to spend the night.

Soon a farmhouse came in view, and Albert knocked on the door. Moments later a person, whom we took to be the farmer, opened the door in company with his wife. While I stayed in the background Albert talked to the farmer and, though I understood little of the conversation, I again heard him say "Pilote Anglais". The farmer pointed down the road and we left them to walk a short way to a barn, where we climbed into the hay loft, and had just started to make ourselves comfortable when we heard a small voice from below saying, "Messieurs. Descendez s'il vous plait". Albert went down and found a young boy who said he was the son of the farmer and that his parents wanted us to go back to the house. When we got there the wife, putting her arms around me, said,"Mon pauvre enfant, et si jeune". ("My poor child, and so young").

I learned from Albert afterwards that, during his conversation with the farmer and his wife when we were eating a meal that she had insisted on cooking for us, he had told them that my aircraft had been shot down in flames and that I was only nineteen years old. When we had left to go to the barn, she had apparently told her husband that she would not be able to sleep that night unless he agreed that we could come back to the house to sleep. The following morning, after a typical French breakfast, the farmer gave us directions to get back to Montauban, where we arrived just before midday. I sat down on a bench in the main square with Albert feeling quite depressed after our failure to find the safe house.

Throughout the time I was in hiding, and then during our journey south, I had been buoyed up by the thought that, at the safe house, I would be able to get help to get out of France, and now the reaction was setting in. I knew that there was an alternative possibility, of making my way to the Pyrenees and hopefully finding a contrabandier (smuggler) who could be bribed to take me over the mountains into Spain. I knew that if I was successful in crossing over I would be arrested by the Spanish police but, as I had been told in the pre-flight briefing, I would be able contact the British Consul in San Sebastián who would arrange my release.

Across the square we noticed a queue of men approaching an abandoned shop, and Albert went off to investigate. He came back with the information that it was a soup kitchen run by the local Scouts for the benefit of the refugees from the Spanish Civil War. Albert suggested that we join the queue to get a meal and, as I felt a kinship with the refugees who were away from their own country and no better dressed than I was, I agreed. When I arrived in front of a Scout who was serving the food, I thought of the vow that I had had to make when I first joined the movement at school: "I promise on my honour to do my best for God and King and to *help other people at all times.*" I gave him the Scout salute and, as he handed me a plate, I said "Thank you", in English, and he smiled and replied "That's OK". After Albert and I had sat down, and everyone had been served, the Scout came across to our table and spoke to me. I asked him if he knew of any English people who might be living in the town, to which he replied that he did know of a Frenchman married to an English lady, who was helping him to learn English. He said that he would go and see them that afternoon and, if they were willing to meet me, he would tell her that I would be waiting on the southern side of the Pont Vieux (the old bridge), that straddled the River Tarn, at 6 pm.

After we had left the soup kitchen I explained the situation to Albert in our common means of communication, a mixture of German and my limited French. To pass the time away, we walked down to the river and along the bank for some distance, before returning to the bridge just before the meeting time. As the clock on a nearby church struck the hour I saw a Frenchman on a bicycle approaching and stop in front of us. He asked me in English if I was a Scout. Having replied that I was and had met a brother Scout earlier in the day, he introduced himself as Charles Cheramy, and said that he was married to Pat, an English lady, who would like to meet me. I introduced my companion, Albert. The three of us set off walking for about a mile, until we turned into the rue de la Fraternité and stopped at a small house, number 13, that Charles said was his home. Knowing that *fraternité* meant friendship, I thought that it was an appropriate name and a good omen for the future.

As we walked up the side path a lady in her early thirties came out, and said her name was Eleanor but that all her friends called her Pat. Going into the house we sat down in the living room and, when she asked me what I was doing in the area, I gave her a brief account of my journey with Albert. As the story unfolded, she cast several glances at him, particularly when I mentioned the event at Arras station and the incident on the train between Châteauroux and Montauban. When I had finished, and knowing that Albert did not understand English, she said that I could stay in her house but, as she had some reservations about my companion, she would prefer that he stayed in a local hotel that could be arranged. She told Albert, in French, of this arrangement, giving the excuse of limited accommodation in her house. Charles went off with him and, on his return, said that he had made suitable arrangements with the hotel for Albert to help out in the kitchen.

During the evening, we talked about England, the bombings, problems of rationing, the morale of the people and, inevitably, my family, particularly my parents, who would have had no news of me except that I was missing in action. As Pat remarked – had I been taken prisoner or killed, they would already have had notification via the Red Cross but, as this was obviously not the case, they must be worried. It was then that she suggested that she should send them a telegram to say that I was alive. Frankly, I was not only surprised at this proposal, but appalled at the possible consequences, and told her so. At about 11.00 pm we had a late supper, after which she showed me up to the attic, where she had made up a bed.

The following morning, as soon as I heard movement downstairs, I came down to find Pat feeding a young baby in a high chair. She told me that he was their son Michel. After a breakfast of bread and jam, she returned to the subject of getting a message to my parents. She explained that, as Vichy France was theoretically now a neutral country with a common border with Switzerland, she had on many occasions sent telegrams to England via the neighbouring country after completing the necessary formalities with the local police and Town Hall. Her proposal was that we should word a telegram couched in a way that would be plausible and not create any suspicion. Later that morning, after returning from shopping, she sat down at the table and, after several attempts, showed me a draft of the cable that she said could be sent. It read: "John arrived safely, all is well." She said that, as Michel was only nine months old, it would look as if it was an announcement of his birth. It seemed plausible, but I still hesitated.

After lunch Pat suggested that we take Michel in his pram and go for a walk in the park. There she asked me to look after him while

she went into town to do a little shopping. She was gone for nearly an hour but on her return, apart from a few groceries that she
was carrying, she was holding a form that she showed me and
explained that it was for sending telegrams. I had already noticed
that she had a strong character and, when referring to the enemy,
she always spoke of them in a disdainful voice as "The Boches". It
now became evident that she was determined to appease the
anguish of my parents. Back in the house she persisted in assuring
me that there was no risk, and so I relented, but added a few words
that would confirm to my parents that the telegram was genuine.
The wording of the text would read as follows: "JOHN ARRIVED
SAFELY ALL IS WELL CABLE ANN NEWS REPLY CHERAMY 13 RUE
DE LA FRATERNITE MONTAUBAN."

The following morning, 9th July, we again took Michel out in
the pram, and Pat went off to send the cable, after which we
returned home for lunch. I enquired how Albert was getting on,
and was told that, as he was busy in the hotel, we would not be seeing him until the weekend. I then spent the afternoon reading one
of her English books.

Several days later, Pat said that in the afternoon we would be visiting a couple of friends who, though they were French Jews, spoke
English very well. She said that they could be trusted, as they hated
the Germans for their attitude towards Jews in the East. She added
that, even in Unoccupied France, there was a danger looming from
certain Frenchmen who had succumbed to the German influence
and who were guilty of traitorous acts, including informing on
their neighbours. We walked some considerable distance until we
arrived at a very imposing mini-château called 'La Tourelle' and, as
we passed through the main gates, I could see that it possessed
extensive grounds. We were greeted by the owners, Monsieur and
Madame Clanc, and spent a very pleasant afternoon chatting over
cups of tea and cakes in a truly English fashion. On another outing
Pat took me to the wedding of a friend where, after the church
service was over, she took great delight in getting me to sign the
register as a witness to the ceremony.

I saw very little of Albert and wondered what he did all day, until
Pat told me that he was not staying at the hotel as a guest but as an

employee in the kitchen. This reminded her of an incident that happened in the autumn of 1940 when a British soldier, who had not been evacuated from Dunkirk, had managed to make his way south and had been helped by Pat. At that time, because of the trauma of the capitulation, the inhabitants of *France Libre* had become careful of any action that might get to the ears of the Germans. Nevertheless, Pat told me that she did what she could for the soldier and found him a job in the kitchen of the same hotel where Albert was now lodged. I asked Pat what became of the soldier, to which she worryingly replied that he just disappeared one day.

But she told me of an incident at the hotel, recounted by the soldier, when a small group of German officers stayed for lunch after inspecting the premises. They ordered steaks and, while the kitchen staff were preparing the meal, the dish containing the steaks fell on the floor. Before the chef could pick them up, one of the cooks proposed that they should be marinated. So, they all gathered round and relieved themselves on the meat and, for good measure, trod on them to 'tenderise the steaks', whereupon they were cooked and served. When the meal was finished, the chef was called into the dining room. On his return, doubled-up with laughter and having finally regained his breath, he explained that he had been congratulated on the preparation of the steaks and was asked: "What herbs did you use?"

Having been with Pat and Charles for about three weeks I had become increasingly restless, partly because of the risk that they were running by harbouring me but, more importantly, because I was determined somehow to make an attempt to get to Gibraltar and freedom. With the safe house no longer an option, I became convinced that I would have to try the alternate plan of escaping through Spain. The principal problem facing me, with my limited knowledge of French, was how to make contact with a Frenchman who was a smuggler and who could be trusted to guide me over the Pyrenees. In England, we had been told that it was risky, but that it would be possible to bribe one to act as a guide. As I still had most of the French money that I had been supplied with before leaving England, the question of paying him presented no problems.

One evening I discussed this idea with Charles and, looking at a map, we decided that the most likely town where a contact could be made was St Girons, some 140 kilometres south of Montauban. A few days later we resumed our talk after Charles had told me that, from discreet inquiries he had made, St Girons, close to the Pyrenees on the French side, sounded like a good bet. He added that, as he could obtain a second bicycle, he was prepared to come with me to find a contact, and that by leaving early in the morning we should be able to ride there in one day. If we left on the following Saturday he would be able to return to Montauban on the Sunday, in time to be at work on the following day. At this point I raised the delicate matter of Albert, asking Charles why the three of us couldn't go together. He replied that, as both Pat and he still had reservations about the Belgian and, because of the shortage of pilots, it was more important that I should get back to England with the minimum of risk. Though hating to abandon Albert, I accepted that it was probably prudent, and we decided that the two of us would make the journey the following Saturday.

Late in the evening of Thursday, 22nd July, two nights before our intended departure, the three of us were sitting in the living room when there was a knock at the front door. Pat told me to go into the kitchen where, because I had left the door slightly ajar, I heard her open the front door and converse with the visitor in English before inviting him in. Now that the person was in the house I could identify from the voice that he was a male talking in accented English, and was astounded as I listened to the conversation.

"My name is Mario Prassinos, and I believe you have an English friend called John."

To which Pat replied, "What makes you say that?"

"You sent a telegram to a Mr Misseldine in England some days ago mentioning his name."

"How do you know that?"

"I received a message from England and, to prove that I am a friend and to set your mind at rest, I will tell you that Ann, whom you mentioned in your cable, refers to John's American girlfriend."

At this point Pat called me into the room and introduced me to the visitor who, after shaking me by the hand, asked me my rank, name, and RAF enlistment number. It obviously satisfied him as to my identity and, to prove his own, he spoke of my schooling and other factors that could only have been known by someone who had the information from the UK. He then went on to explain that the telegram had been taken to the War Office by my father and had been passed on to the Ministry of Information Section MI9. They had decided to investigate the mysterious telegram and, as a result, had made contact with a radio operator belonging to the Pat O'Leary escape organization, of which he, Mario, was a member.

He asked me to recount in brief what had happened since I was shot down. This I did, including the fact that I had been accompanied by Albert, who wanted to get to England to join the Belgian forces. We discussed the situation, until Mario said that, because of the urgent need of trained pilots, his prime task was to ensure my safe return to England. He also had to be careful not to compromise the escape organisation, and therefore it was prudent that Albert should be left behind for the moment. He promised, however, that he had the means to investigate Albert's background and that, providing the results were satisfactory, he would arrange for him to be brought out at a later date.

He then said, "It's time for us to leave as we have to catch the night train."

"To where?" I replied.

"To a safe house in another town, some distance from here."

After going upstairs to collect my personal things that didn't even fill a small paper bag, I came down to thank Pat and Charles for their kindness and hospitality. I left with Mario, walked to the station with him, and boarded a train for Marseilles.

Chapter 9

THE LAST LAP
TO FREEDOM

While events had not turned out exactly as I had anticipated, my hopes of getting back to England now looked much better.

The train travelled through the night, stopping firstly at Toulouse station, and then through Narbonne, Béziers and Montpellier, until we finally arrived at Nîmes in the early hours of the morning. There, we walked through deserted streets until we arrived at what seemed to be a large grocery store. Mario knocked on the side door and, after a short time, it was opened by a woman, who embraced my companion. He then introduced me as Jack, and she came forward and in the true French fashion embraced me as well. Mario explained that she was the maid, employed in the household, who could be trusted implicitly. Her name was Thérèse. She led us up the stairs to a sumptuous flat over the shop, where I met the owner Gaston Nègre, a jovial character who obviously enjoyed the products of his wine and grocery business!

We all sat down at the dining-room table and drank real coffee, accompanied by fresh French bread and slices of ham that were brought in by Gaston's cook. Once we had finished the meal, I was shown to a bright and airy bedroom, given towels and soap and told that, after a bath, I should rest. I slept through the lunch hour, awaking about 5 o'clock to find that, during my sleep, Thérèse had taken my clothes, laundered and ironed them, before returning them to the bedroom. It was nice to get dressed and smell fresh and clean again. Gaston must have heard me moving, as he poked his head around the door and said that I should join them in the living room. There I found that he had already opened the bar and that, with Mario, they were drinking a milky liquid. He offered me a glass, pouring a moderate amount of a yellowish liquid from a bottle and then adding a quantity of water turning it a milky colour. Lifting my glass in a toast to my host, I tasted it and found that it had a liquorice flavour, making me wonder whether it was medicine or an alcoholic drink. By the time I had finished the glass and Gaston had refilled it again, I realised that it was the latter. Thus, I was introduced to *Pastis*.

Before dinner, Gaston took me on a tour of the flat that, apart from the living quarters, had seven or eight bedrooms. Mario said that on one occasion they had all been occupied at the same time by other escapees. The first dinner with them in the dining room was a pleasant event, but Mario explained that most days it would be necessary for me to have my meals in my bedroom as, in the course of Gaston's business as a wholesale grocer, he often had clients and important people visiting the flat.

Very occasionally I dined with Gaston and his companions of the escape organisation but, of all meals, the most memorable was an evening when he told me that he had some guests for dinner, and that I could join them on the condition that I did not speak. The meal passed well, but after the visitors had left he told me that amongst the diners were a local judge, the police chief and an important person with German connections. It was apparent that Gaston was engaged in the 'black market' and that his guests, probably, turned a blind eye to his activities as they benefited from gifts of food from his warehouses. Whilst I had felt uncomfortable under the glances of the visitors, it seemed that Gaston derived pleasure from the situation, and even went to the extent of agreeing that a photograph could be taken.

There was plenty of reading material in the flat, including a selection of English novels, so the time passed agreeably. I was the only 'guest' there at the time, and I thought it would have been nice to have had a companion. Gaston and his staff did all they could to make my stay comfortable and assured me that, with a bit of patience, I would soon be on my way on the next leg of my journey, a rendezvous near the Spanish border. He wouldn't give me any details, but his manner was so positive that I felt almost certain that all would go well. Even so, the days seemed long, particularly as I was not allowed out to stretch my legs.

Eventually, on 14th August, Mario arrived at the flat and told me that he had been confirming arrangements to get me out of France. I was overjoyed, but remembered the old adage 'Don't count your chickens before they are hatched'. After more than two months of avoiding capture, with its high and low points, particularly the disappointment at Nègrepelisse, I was still worried. It was true that there were, supposedly, no Germans in the area, but there was the Milice to worry about, and also the possibility of some locals being 'nosey' about Gaston's activities. However, Mario assured me that over the months he had helped a number of aircrew and many soldiers who, left behind at Dunkirk, had made their way south, many of them safely crossing the border into Spain.

So, early the next morning, after thanking Gaston and his staff for looking after me, I promised that when the war was over I would try and contact them. I walked with Mario to the main railway station in town, where we boarded a train for Toulouse and found an empty compartment. The train stopped at Montpellier and Béziers, where more passengers boarded and our carriage soon filled up. Though Mario spoke English, conversation between us was out of the question. As the train started to slow down approaching Narbonne station Mario rose from his seat, and I followed him down the corridor ready to alight when the train came to a halt. Stepping down onto the platform I noticed a train with only a few carriages waiting on the other side of the platform. Mario said "Parfait", and we climbed into one of the carriages. A few minutes later the ancient engine pulled the train out of the station and puffed its merry way at a sedate pace in a southerly direction, passing through a marshland area, to its first stop at Port-la-Nouvelle. Here I had my first glimpse of the Mediterranean that, on this hot, sunny day, looked as blue as advertisements portrayed it. The train continued on its way, following the coast for a while, until we crossed over a bridge spanning an inlet of the sea and arrived at Fort de Salses station, where we alighted.

As we left the station I noticed that the station clock showed that it was fifteen minutes after midday. We set off at a brisk pace passing through the villages of St Hippolyte, St Laurent-de-la-Salanque, Torreilles and Ste Marie without seeing a soul; no doubt the inhabitants were having a siesta after enjoying their lunch. After what seemed about a ten mile hike we approached the River Tet sometime in the afternoon, and I asked Mario if we could have a rest as my calves were sore, undoubtedly because of the lack of exercise whilst at Nîmes. We rested beside the river and, somewhat refreshed, set off again along the bank of the river until we reached the shores of the Mediterranean Sea. We walked along for a while until we reached the beach somewhere between the villages of Ste Marie-Plage and Canet-Plage. There he told me that he would have to leave me for a while, explaining that he had a rendezvous to confirm that all was in order for the next move.[23]

Before leaving he pointed to a group of bushes nearby that would be our rendezvous later that night. Lying there the time passed slowly, particularly after the sun had set and darkness had fallen around 9 o'clock. It was a moonless night and, as I lay there looking up at the starlit sky, I wondered which of the stars was my lucky one – for I was sure I had one. I knew that we were probably less than fifty kilometres from the Spanish border and, if it meant climbing over the Pyrenees, it would not be too arduous as, from where I was, the mountains at the eastern end of the Pyrenees did not look too high.

I must have dozed off, but woke up when I heard footsteps

---

[23] This account of John's time in France after leaving Nîmes is, however, at variance with his official 1942 report -Ed.

approaching. To my relief, I recognised Mario's voice calling my name. As he came closer I saw that he was accompanied by seven people – an RAF officer, a sergeant pilot, a woman and four men who were trying to get to England to serve once more with the Allied forces. Joining me beside the bushes it was then that Mario told me that, unless there were last minute problems, we were all going to be picked up by the navy.

Our party waited patiently until, in the early hours of the morning of 15th August 1942, Mario stood up and with a pocket torch, flashed a signal out to sea. Almost immediately I saw an answering flash and, in due course, heard the muffled sound of oars before making out the shape of a rowing boat that had grounded on the sandy beach. After we had climbed aboard, the sailors pushed the boat out and rowed us out to a ship that, as we approached, appeared to be a fishing trawler. Once alongside, we climbed on board and, even before the rowing boat had been completely hoisted, the ship was already under way. We headed in a south-easterly direction to get out of sight of land before daybreak. The captain allocated a cabin to the lady, while the officer, who by now had revealed himself as Pilot Officer Perdue, and myself, slept in bunks on the side of the main cabin. During the voyage, Pilot Officer Perdue told me that he had been working on a farm in Brittany for some months until he was picked up by a member of the Pat O'Leary line and had been brought to the south.[24]

The following morning, after a navy breakfast, including a strong cup of cocoa, the male passengers were asked to go on deck to help the crew. We were all given a can of grey paint and were allocated different parts of the superstructure that we were required to paint. I thought that this was odd, until a seaman explained that the ship, HMS *Tarana*, had left Gibraltar as a grey-painted Royal Navy Auxiliary vessel but that, as soon as they were out of sight of the Spanish coast, they had painted the superstructure brown to look like a fishing vessel. Now we had to reverse the process in order to

---

[24] Perdue was brought from a farm, near Ste Opportune-la-Mer, Normandy, by Louis Nouveau, a highly-trusted agent of the Pat O'Leary line, and shelterer of evaders and escapers at his home in Marseilles.

re-enter Gibraltar harbour. In the evening I was able to take a shower but I wasn't too happy as the hot sea water irritated my skin.

Three or four days later we arrived in Gibraltar harbour, and as soon as we had tied up at a quay in the south shore harbour an individual, accompanied by an MP, escorted our group to a barrack hut. I was allowed time to have a normal shower, and then taken to the medical officer, who gave me a thorough check-up. He told me that I had survived my ordeal well and that the scars from the burns would eventually disappear. To my relief, he said that the irritation that I was experiencing was no worse than scabies, due to poor diet and lack of a change of under clothes. The treatment was not so pleasant; a medical orderly painted the whole of my body with a purple-coloured liquid, which I believe was called Gentian Violet. He thankfully assured me that the problem would disappear very quickly!

Having dressed, I was then escorted to the intelligence officer, who introduced himself as Donald Darling. He explained that he worked for MI9, the War Office department whose function was dealing with the various escape organisations and, in consequence, the escapees. His interrogation was thorough, firstly questioning me to confirm my identity, then requiring details of my stay in Montauban and the sending of a telegram that had resulted in my being contacted by a member of the Pat O'Leary escape organisation. He then asked me my opinion of Pat and Charles, and whether I felt that the telegram could have been intercepted by the Germans. He was concerned that recently the Gestapo had managed, one way or another, to infiltrate and arrest a number of 'helpers'. I assured him that Pat Cheramy was very British, her husband Charles, anti-Vichy, and that the telegram wording was innocuous and similar to others that she had sent to relatives in the UK about her son.

I was then asked to give a full account of my perambulations, including the names and addresses of families and individuals who, I recalled, had given me assistance, together with any information that I might have gleaned concerning German activities in the north of France. Included in my story was, of course, the name of Albert Mestdagh, my companion all the way to Montauban, who had accompanied me with the stated ambition of getting to England and joining a Belgian parachute regiment. Despite Pat

Cheramy's doubts and precautions in not having him stay at her home, I asked Donald if Albert could be investigated and, if his identity was confirmed, be brought out by the same route at a future date.

When the interrogation was finished, Donald and I talked for some while about the bravery of the people who had helped me, and I told him that I wondered if we – the escapees – had the right to put other people at such a risk. He replied that it was the duty of members of the armed forces to try to return to their units, particularly pilots and aircrew, in view of the time and money spent on their training. In addition, he said that any attempt to avoid capture, even if unsuccessful, would have aggravated the German authorities, as they would have had to divert a considerable number of soldiers from their normal tasks in searching for a downed airman in the region where he came down. I could have added another reason for evading capture, namely that the idea of a prolonged stay in a prisoner-of-war camp was not appealing. Finally, he warned me that even when I got back to England, I was not to give any details, even to my family, of my escape and specifically not to mention the names of those who had helped me nor the escape line, and the fact that I was picked up by a ship off the French coast.

The next visit was to the stores to get a new uniform and the rest of an airman's kit. It seemed strange to be dressed properly again after weeks in civilian clothes. I was allocated a bed in the barracks, and was even glad to sleep on the biscuit mattresses, reminding me that, once again, I was back in the RAF. I was then directed to the paymaster, who explained that, as he did not have my records, he could only give me an advance, which would be deducted from any amounts due to me on my return to England. The sum that he handed over was one week's pay for a sergeant pilot, namely thirty-five shillings (£1.75).

I soon made friends with other members of the barrack who were stationed there, and who knew places on the 'Rock' where one could relax. A bar down the high street was a favourite place where they had a cabaret, consisting mainly of a group of Spanish dancers from across the border, which came to perform the Flamenco amongst many of their national dances. I was also surprised at the choice of food in the restaurants, and the selection of clothes and jewellery, until I realised that, with the neutral Spanish territory just across the border, the merchants were no doubt profiting from the shortages on the Rock. Most of all though, I appreciated being able to move about freely without looking over my shoulder, and to be able to speak English again.

On 28th August, I was told to report to Donald Darling again, who informed me that I would be leaving for the UK on the following day, and that I was to report to the SWO to obtain a movement order to board a troopship. I was disappointed to be going back by sea, as I was given to understand that Pilot Officer Perdue, who had been with me on the *Tarana*, had already left for the UK by air in a Sunderland flying-boat. It subsequently came to my knowledge that he had been on the same ship returning to Gourock, albeit in much better accommodation.

Saying goodbye to the friends that I had made in Gibraltar, I boarded a merchant navy ship converted to carry troops, was given a hammock to sleep in each night and taken to a large mess room, where I was allocated a spot to hang it. I was also told that I would have to take my turn as 'fire piquet' on a roster basis for eight hours each day or night. My first reaction was that that did not seem fair after the tribulations of the past three months, but it brought me down to earth and made me realise that I was not something special.

The ship left harbour on 29th August and, passing through the Straits of Gibraltar, made its way well out into the Atlantic, where it joined a convoy of ships heading in a north-westerly direction. The voyage was reasonably pleasant as the weather was kind and, most importantly, there were no scares of any enemy submarines being in the vicinity. Apart from piquet duties, sunning on the deck was a principal pastime during the day, with interminable games of cards being the main distraction in the evenings. Eventually we passed round the northern coast of Ireland, followed the coast into the North Channel and, rounding the Mull of Kintyre, steamed up the Firth of Clyde until we finally docked at Gourock on 8th September, three months exactly from the date on which I had been shot down.

I was told to remain in the mess room until the other troops had disembarked. When the last of them had left our temporary home, two MPs came in with orders to accompany me to London under guard until we reached our destination and my identity had been confirmed. I thought it was strange, but realised its advantage when we got to the station where the movement officer checked my name and told the three of us that we had a reserved compartment. He accompanied us to one of the carriages, and told the MPs that they should lock the door to the corridor. The train was due to leave at about 10 pm, crowded with navy, army and air force personnel, who shook angry fists at us when they saw the empty seats in our compartment and found that my guards would not let them in. They eventually left us alone and found spots to sleep on the floor in the corridor, whilst I slept in reasonable comfort on one of the seats, with an MP on the other and the third member making do by sleeping on the luggage rack.

The journey south took most of the night, with one halt for two hours caused by an enemy air raid which, fortunately, was not in our immediate vicinity. When the train eventually pulled in to Euston station, I descended and, with my escorts, reported to the movements office. When the situation had been explained to the officer in charge, transport was arranged to take us to the Ministry of Defence.

At MI9, I was interrogated at some length to elicit any additional information that I could remember to supplement the report that I had made to Donald Darling in Gibraltar. At the conclusion of the session, they suggested I might like to telephone my parents, telling me that I would be provided with a travel voucher to go on immediate leave for fourteen days, and another voucher enabling me to report to the Standing Committee of Adjustment at RAF Uxbridge on 14th September.

With so many men having been called up to serve in the armed forces my mother, like many other women, had taken an office job at Paddington railway station. Having looked up the phone number of the station, I spent many minutes explaining to the switchboard operator that I wanted to contact my mother, but didn't know in which department she was working. Eventually the girl was able to connect me and I recognised my mother's voice. She was overjoyed to hear my voice and we arranged to meet for lunch before going home together. My mother must have contacted my sister Barbara and Pop, for I found all of them waiting on the platform at Kenton station when we arrived.

Whilst relaxing at home, I had to parry the questions of the family, neighbours and friends concerning my adventure. Apart from Donald Darling's warnings, the debriefing officer in London also emphasised that I should not give any details of my evasion to anyone, as it could jeopardise the lives of the people who had helped me.

On the 14th I went to Uxbridge and, during an interview, was told that during my absence I had been promoted to flight sergeant. I was then directed to a special section, where the personal effects of airmen who had been shot down were stored. I was told that I was one of the lucky ones, as most of the items stored belonged to aircrew who were now prisoners of war. Their effects would be held until they were freed at the end of hostilities. There was another section for the personal belongings of airmen reported missing and believed killed, whose effects would be returned to their families after verification of the facts.

After checking their records, an airman eventually found my kit-bag, which had been packed by my fellow NCO pilots of 611 Squadron when I failed to return on 8th June. Apart from my RAF kit, it contained mementos, photographs and souvenirs which, customarily, would have been vetted by my friends to ensure that there was nothing included which could have caused pain to the missing person's family or girlfriend.

I was then directed to the SWO who told me that, at the end of my leave, I was to report to RAF Headquarters London for posting to a new unit. He added that before leaving the station, I should go to the paymaster's section where I could draw my pay. I hadn't thought about it, but a surprise awaited me – I was paid for the three months that I had been absent. Welcome news, as my twentieth birthday, on 17th September, was only a few days away and, with the windfall that I had received, I knew that I could celebrate in style, and then relax during my leave, even though I couldn't help wondering what my career in flying would be.

*   *   *   *

In 1948, and for many years after, I visited Pat Cheramy in a London flat, where I gradually learned of the sequence of events that followed my departure from 13, rue de la Fraternité, Montauban in July 1942. As to those who had helped me in the Pas-de-Calais region in June 1942, I had only been able to keep in touch with them by letter. Now, in the 1960s, after crossing the Channel from Dover to Calais, I was able to go and talk with them, in particular Yvonne, the daughter of Monsieur and Madame Dillies at Steenbecque, Albert, the son of Monsieur and Madame Caron-Dupont at Aire-sur-la-Lys, and the children of Madame Perel-Ferment at Haverskerque. On one occasion I diverted to Annecy so that I could visit Georges Lemettre and talk about those days in June 1942. They were all key figures in helping me during the first four days of hiding.

On the first of these visits, I was shown the field where I landed by parachute, the wood known as le fanque where I hid on the first night, and the chicken coop where I spent three nights in hiding, all of which I photographed. From Albert Caron-Dupont I learned that his sister, who had been a friend of my Belgian companion, Albert Mestdagh, had died but, as he had been fourteen years old in 1942, he had been old enough to remember many details. He was able to show me the place where his father's butcher's shop had been, even though it was now converted into a private residence. The children of Madame Perel-Ferment were able to give me some details of my short stay with them. Piecing together all this information it became clear that the area most touched by the events of that time was the village of Steenbecque. To ensure that I had the correct details, I asked them to put in writing their memories of that time. Translations of the pertinent contents of these letters have been included in the appendices.

On another occasion, in 1968, to confirm my memory of events, I routed my return from my home, in Grasse, southern France, to England via Nîmes, Narbonne, Canet-Plage, Montauban, and the village of Nègrepelisse. A lot had changed, with the grocery shop of Gaston Nègre at Nîmes now occupied by new residents; the sandy beach near Canet-Plage had succumbed to development for holiday makers; and, though the Cheramys' small house in Montauban had fallen into disrepair, I could still see the hayloft in which I had slept during July 1942. In Nègrepelisse, I found the school that I had visited and, above all, recognised the door where I had been unable to get an answer, before walking some fifteen kilometres back to Montauban.

When I was recently able to get a copy of the report of my debriefing in London, I noted that in my statement I had said that I went to Bruniquel and Penne. I do remember that the sign on the bus that I took with Albert was Bruniquel, but I certainly have no recollection of saying that I went to Penne. But the way in which I met the Cheramys was as I described. Details of my interrogation are vague, but, with a map and questions from the officer, I might have agreed that I went to Penne, especially as I had only just returned from a ten-week journey, with little knowledge of French and of the geography of France.

In the summer of 2000 my granddaughter, Vicky Honour, who is a journalist and author in her own right, drove a motor home down the route that I had followed, visiting the mayor of Steenbecque, and the wood with Yvonne, before continuing her pilgrimage to Haverskerque, Aire-sur-la-Lys, Montauban, and Nègrepelisse, where she was also able to identify the school as the Ecole St Thérèse, by then empty and derelict.

Chapter 10

RETURN TO DUTY

During my leave I visited Bentley Priory near Stanmore, the headquarters of 11 Group, controlling all fighter operations in the area of London and the south-east of England. I tried to get some information about my future but, though they were kind and helpful, they told me that that decision would be made in London, where I would be required to report at the end of my leave, on 6th October.

Arriving there on that date I was directed to the movements officer, who pulled my service record out of a filing cabinet. I asked him if it would be possible for me to return to 611 Squadron but, glancing at the file in front of him, he said that there was a notation that said: "This pilot can no longer take part in operations over Europe." He went on to explain: "There is a regulation in force that states that an aircrew member who had been shot down and escaped should not be permitted to fly over the same area again. It is for security reasons as, if you were allowed to rejoin your old squadron, which is still operating over France, and be unfortunate enough to be shot down again and taken prisoner, it might create problems. The Germans may already have some clue as to the name of the pilot who had been shot down on 8th June as your name was probably on a piece of flying equipment such as the Mae West that you buried. If so, it might give them a clue as to the individuals and organisation that had helped you to freedom."[25]

Under these circumstances, he suggested that perhaps I might like to transfer to a squadron flying Lysander aircraft, a high-wing monoplane whose main operations were communications and towing drogues in the UK for air-to-air firing practice by fighter planes. I laughed and said, "Having been shot at by Germans I don't fancy being a target of my own countrymen." I then asked if I could be posted to a squadron on Malta or the Middle East. He hesitated before saying that, in view of the time lapse since I last flew, he thought that it would be better for me to get some flying in, and posted me to 65 (Spitfire) Squadron, resting and reforming at Drem. He added that he would extend my leave to the last week in October, as 65 were at the moment on a special training exercise at Lympne, and would not be back at Drem until the end of October.

Though the extra time at home was pleasant, I was longing to get back in to the air again and waited impatiently for the confirmation of my posting, together with a travel warrant. On receipt of them I packed my gear and left home on 25th October 1942, for Drem, where I arrived late in the evening. A truck was waiting to take other airmen and myself to the airfield, where I reported to the orderly room of the squadron and was allocated a billet that I would be sharing with another pilot, who was due back from the exercise at Lympne airfield the following day.

On the morning of the 27th the adjutant took me in to meet my

---

[25] As it happens, I found out after the war that when Pat Cheramy was interrogated by the Germans, having had confirmation by radio of my safe return from England, she had seen no harm, under torture, in giving the names of the soldiers whom she had helped as well as the name of the RAF pilot, Misseldine, as the people she had sheltered. So the RAF were right in their policy of not letting me rejoin a squadron flying operations over France.

new CO, Squadron Leader (Commandant) Mouchotte who, I'd
been told, had also escaped from France in the early days of the
French capitulation, and was now the first Frenchman to command
an RAF squadron.

At the end of June 1940 Squadron Leader René Mouchotte DFC
'stole' a French air force Goéland aircraft from Oran, North Africa,
and flew it to Gibraltar. He sailed to England on 3rd July aboard a
French warship, which was acting as a convoy escort. Joining the
RAF, he went from an OTU in September 1940 to 245 Squadron,
and soon to 615 Squadron. In December 1941 he was posted as a
flight commander to 340 'Ile de France' ('Free French') Squadron,
before being given command of 65 Squadron with effect from 11
am, 31st August 1942. He wrote in his diary that it was "un grand
honneur que de me confier un tel poste" ("a great honour to be
entrusted with such a post"). His DFC was awarded at this time.
Commandant René Gaston Octave Jean Mouchotte was killed leading 341 'Alsace' Squadron into action on 27th August 1943.

As I entered the CO's office and saluted, he told me to stand at
ease, while perusing a folder on his desk that was evidently my
service record. He questioned me about my journey through
France, and said that he was glad that his countrymen had helped
me. Then, sitting back in his chair, he said: "I see that the last time
that you flew a Spitfire was on 8th June, so you haven't flown for
over four months." He went on to say, "Regulations state that if a
pilot has not flown for three months or more, he should be
checked out in a dual-control plane, but I think that's a waste of
time as nobody forgets how to fly. Get your flying gear and we'll
see how you get on. I'm sure that you won't have any problems
but, if you do, tant-pis, hard luck." Charming, I thought!

Having signed for a parachute, helmet and gloves I climbed into
Spitfire Mk V BL373 bearing the squadron code YT-X. It was like
coming back to an old friend as everything seemed familiar.
Nevertheless, I sat there for a while going through the pre-flight
checks and routines in my mind, before signalling to the mechanic that I was ready to start up. Calling the control tower for permission to take off, I taxied out and made a reasonable take-off and
flew away from the airfield, cruised around for a short while, and

then performed some aerobatics before returning to make a fair three-point landing.

I hadn't realised it, but the CO had been standing outside watching and, as I braked and shut off the engine, he came up to the aircraft and told me that I would join B Flight under the command of Pilot Officer Peter Hearne. He then told me to change planes and take YT-L (AB272) to practise three or four more take-offs and landings and then join Peter Hearne for some formation practice.[26]

To my surprise, having already flown twice that day, I was told that I would be required to take off at dusk and practise some night flying. I knew from my time with 611 Squadron, that the Spitfire was not the greatest of aircraft to fly at night, as vision is somewhat impaired by the long nose and the white-hot glow of the exhausts. It is not surprising, therefore, that the superb fighter aircraft that was the Spitfire, and which underwent many changes throughout the Second World War, was never employed on operations specifically as a night fighter. In 1931 the requirements of the original Air Ministry specification F.7/30, were in fact for a 'single-seater day and night fighter'. Four years later the specification, F.5/34 had changed to simply a 'single-seat fighter'. However a year after, in 1936, specification F.10/35 outlined requirements for a 'single-engine single-seater day and night fighter.'

As I was to discover, despite its wonderful daylight efficiency, the Spitfire was clearly not suitable for night flying. Nevertheless, such was the brilliance of its original design (production finally ended in 1949 after more than 22,000 Spitfires and Seafires – Spitfires 'with hooks' for the Royal Navy's aircraft carriers – had been built) that the Spitfire was unbeaten in the air, in its capacity as a short-range, high-performance fighter for the duration of

---

[26] Spitfire Vb AB272 survived the war, and was struck off charge on 19th June 1945. BL373, on the other hand, was converted to a Seafire Ib and joined the Fleet Air Arm, where it suffered damage on three occasions when flown into crash-barriers on aircraft carriers.

the war.

The following morning I took off with another aircraft of the squadron to fly a ground controlled interception (GCI), the other aircraft being the 'hare' while I was the 'hound' who had to intercept him. In the afternoon I took off again to practise air-to-air firing at a drogue towed by another Spitfire. Intensive flying was carried out by the squadron nearly every day, with more air-to-air firing, air-to-ground firing, height climbs to 31,000 feet, formation flying and dog-fight practice with other squadron members.

On 5th November we received news of the Allied landings in North Africa, and that gave me hope that I would be able to join a squadron over there. Three days later, I was told to report to the CO, who told me that he was very pleased with my flying ability and asked me if I thought about becoming an officer. I replied that I had been previously recommended when I was with 611 Squadron but that, at the interview at 13 Group headquarters in Newcastle, the group captain had deferred a decision for three months on the grounds that I was young and lacked experience. "Good," he said. "Then it should be a 'piece of cake' as your escape showed that you have initiative and persistence. I will arrange an interview with the AOC in Newcastle." Thus, on 12th November, I boarded a train for Newcastle and, as luck would have it, was shown into the same group captain's office for the interview. "I remember that you came for an interview last May," he said, "and I expected to see you again in August, after you had had some squadron experience. Why the delay?"

I explained that I had been shot down over France but, with help, had managed to return to the UK. After questioning me further, he said that the recommendation by Squadron Leader Mouchotte was sufficient for him to approve my being granted a commission as a pilot officer. Returning to Drem, my CO confirmed that he had received a signal from Newcastle and that, in consequence, I would be granted seven days leave to outfit myself as an officer. He added that on my return I was to report to the adjutant, who would explain my new responsibilities and introduce me to other commissioned officers in the officers' mess. I left Drem the following morning and reached home in the evening, where I was pleased to learn that my brother Geoff had also just been commissioned as a second lieutenant in the Royal Regiment of Artillery.[27]

Arriving back at Drem on the last day of November, I carried out several GCIs without any contact except that on 5th December, after being 'scrambled' and closing in on an intruder aircraft over the North Sea, I was recalled to base for fear that I might run short of petrol. The only other incident was a few days later when, orbiting with another Spitfire covering a convoy entering the Firth of Forth, a gunner on a merchant ship must have had an itchy finger for, though we were out of range, I could see tracer bullets being fired roughly in our direction.

On 10th December I was informed by the adjutant that he had received a signal from the Air Ministry posting me to an aircrew holding unit in Algiers. It brought to mind my interview with the movements officer in London, who had no doubt been aware of the planning of the North African liberation and had kept his word to post me to a new theatre of operations. I was granted seven days overseas posting leave, and left Drem on 10th December by train, but with a difference; as an officer I was now travelling first class, instead of being crowded into third class carriages.

Once again on leave, I enjoyed the time with my parents and my sister Barbara, knowing that it would be some time before I saw them again, but excited at the prospect of seeing another new country. On the 18th I said goodbye to them and took the train north to Glasgow and on to Gourock, where I boarded a troopship, and shared a cabin with another officer. We waited for three days until the last of the contingent had boarded before the ship left the dockside and started its journey down the Clyde. I had gone to sleep, undisturbed by the sound of the engines, but was woken up

---

[27] The announcement of Cadet Geoffrey Edward Misseldine's commission as second lieutenant (247628, seniority of 8th October 1942) appeared in the *London Gazette* on 6th November 1942. Then, on 22nd December 1942, the *London Gazette* announced that 1291166 Flight Sergeant John Ernest Misseldine had been commissioned pilot officer (134227, seniority 5th November 1942).

by an almighty bang and realised that the ship's engines had stopped. Soon after there was an announcement on the tannoy saying that we would be returning to our point of departure.

When daylight came and we went on deck, we could see the reason for our return to the dockside. The ship had suffered some damage caused by a collision with another ship in the blackness of the night. We were told that, as repairs would take a few days, we would be sent on leave and to await a telegram ordering us to return to Gourock. This meant that I was able to spend Christmas Day at home with the family, but the recall telegram arrived two days after and, once again, I headed north to Scotland. On 30th December the ship left harbour and joined a convoy of other ships sailing wide of the French and Spanish coastline to avoid U-boats operating out of their bases at St Nazaire and Brest. The days passed with boat drills, some light exercise, and plenty of hours playing cards or reading. We passed through the Straits of Gibraltar and headed for Algiers, where the aircrew members disembarked on 8th January 1943 before being transported to a temporary personnel holding centre based in a boarding college.

As the days went by waiting for a posting to a squadron, new friendships were made and the town of Algiers was explored, except for the Kasbah, the old Arab quarter that was strictly 'out of bounds'. Not so for the cafés. A group of us would frequently visit one that was not far from our billet, usually for coffee, but on one evening we decided to sample the contents of many, coloured bottles arranged on the shelf behind the bar. It was the first time that we had seen such an array of liqueurs and, having decided to taste a few, we found that, though they were sweet and seemingly innocuous, they soon made us change our minds.

At the beginning of February a dozen of us were informed that we would be taken by ship to Gibraltar, and amongst the group were Guy Walsh, Johnny Chandler, Roy Poole and myself (all pilot officers with previous experience on squadrons), who had become firm friends during our waiting period in Algiers. We were told that we were to collect some Spitfire Mk Vc aircraft and fly them to 351 Maintenance Unit (MU) at Maison Blanche airfield near the town of Algiers. We learned that the aircraft had come out by ship in crates and had been assembled by Italian prisoners of war, albeit under the supervision of RAF fitters for the engines, and riggers for the airframes. 'Fitter' and 'rigger' were trades dating back to the days of the 1914-1918 war and the Royal Flying Corps before it became the RAF. The thought that the aircraft had been assembled by ex-enemies made us pay close attention to the daily inspection that a pilot carried out before climbing into the cockpit. The runway at Gibraltar, at that time, was quite short with water at both ends of it. Once airborne, however, there was nowhere to make an emergency landing except 'in the drink', due to the fact that Spain was a neutral territory. The normal take-off direction was to the west over the naval base in the bay, then turn to port around the Rock avoiding the town of Algeciras. Once over the Straits the normal course was in an easterly direction avoiding Spanish Morocco which was also neutral territory.

Johnny, Roy and I had decided to fly together with Guy who had been nominated to lead the formation and, though we took off individually, by the time we had circumnavigated the Rock we had closed up on the leader. Flying under economical cruising settings with 30-gallon overload tanks under the belly of the aircraft, it took us nearly three hours to make the trip and land at Maison Blanche airfield.

Having handed the aircraft over to the MU, we reported to the movements officer, who arranged transport for us on a USAAC C-47 'Dakota' to return to Gibraltar via La Senia airfield at Oran with orders to convert onto Hurricanes. I enjoyed the experience of flying Hurricane IIc aircraft (HW856 and HW734) as well as the life in the town, which had an abundance of shops, tea rooms and a club where we could watch the female Flamenco dancers who, like many of the workers, came over the border from La Linea in Spain each day.

We continued ferrying Spitfires or Hurricanes from Gibraltar to Algiers until 14th April 1943, when Guy, Johnny, Roy, myself and some twenty other pilots were told that we were now to be formally known as 3 Aircraft Delivery Unit (ADU), with our home base at Râs el-Ma airfield near the town of Fes, some fifty miles south of

Oran.[28]

Though disappointed that we were not posted to a squadron, we were told that it was of equal importance to provide the support to fighter units and that, with our experience, we would have to deliver any type of single-engine aircraft to the forward positions of the squadrons covering the advancing Eighth Army. Which, having pushed Rommel out of the Western Desert, was now halted at the Mareth line, in southern Tunisia, where they were re-grouping together with the RAF squadrons, who were being reinforced before advancing again in conjunction with the US forces in the north, having battled their way from Algeria to Tunisia.

By now war material, including British and American fighters, was being shipped into Morocco, some of them flying in from aircraft carriers, while others were being assembled at airfields near Rabat and Casablanca in Morocco. This meant that we were collecting aircraft, including Mk IX Spitfires, from either of these airfields nearly every day for delivery to air stores parks near Algiers or, with much longer flights, via refuelling points at Algiers and Biskra on the edge of the Sahara, to airfields as far away as Tripoli in Libya. After overcoming the strong Axis resistance in southern Tunisia, the Eighth Army entered Tunis on 8th May, at the same time as the American army entered Bizerta. By 13th May the whole of Tunisia was in Allied hands.

It should be mentioned that a RAF aircraft delivery unit, 2 ADU, had been in existence for some time, with aircraft being assembled at Takoradi on the Gold Coast (Ghana) and then flown in formation with a twin-engine Beaufighter navigating them across Nigeria, Chad and the desert to Cairo.

With the increasing amount of aircraft to be delivered to front-

---

[28] No. 3 ADU was part of 216 Group (Transport Command), but was operationally controlled and administered by Middle East Command, itself a subordinate component of Mediterranean Air Command (Air Chief Marshal Sir Arthur A.W. Tedder GCB). Air Officer Commanding 216 Group was Air Commodore Whitney Willard Straight MC, DFC, who had himself been evacuated from France in July 1942, a month before the author, from the same place and also by HMS *Tarana*.

line squadrons and to air stores parks, additional pilots, including Canadians, Australians, New Zealanders and South Africans, were posted to what had now become 3 Ferry Control Unit (3 FCU). We were now commanded by a more senior officer (Wing Commander Mitchell of the Midlands brewery firm Mitchell & Butlers). Most of the newly-arrived aircrew came directly from operational training units, with some having twin-engine aircraft experience. This was good news for, as our unit now had a Lockheed Hudson, an Expeditor, and an Avro Anson, all twin-engined aircraft, it meant that instead of having to wait for a seat on an American transport plane to return to base, one of our 'twins' would follow us, enabling us to return to our Râs el-Ma base without delay.

In June 1943, as a diversion from operations, our unit received a challenge to play a rugby match against a French air force unit based at Sale, near Rabat. The challenge was accepted on the condition that they provided transport from Fes to Rabat and return. When the aircraft turned up, it was an old DC-2 passenger plane that had seen better days, and though normally in its civilian role it carried sixteen passengers in comfort, the aircraft had been stripped, and the French pilot, named Tissandier, assured us that he would be able to take the rugby team, reserves and twelve supporters. In fact some supporters cried off, and the number of passengers was reduced to twenty-five. Despite our misgivings the 'old girl' took to the air, albeit using most of the runway, and we landed safely at Rabat. The pitch was rudimentary, and the game quite physical, but though we lost by twenty-four points to six the worst part was that several of our team received grazes and cuts that, because of the state of the ground, turned septic over the following days. From then on we were banned from playing rugby. One bit of good news I did receive during the month, July, was my promotion to flying officer, meaning an increase in pay.[29]

In August, along with Johnny, Guy and some other pilots, we

---

[29] The promotion was gazetted on 23rd July 1943, with seniority back-dated to 5th May 1943.

were detached to the airfield at Sétif (over 400 miles east of Râs el-Ma) that had become an air stores park and MU. Apart from the usual tasks of delivering aircraft mainly to the advancing front line in Italy, we were now bringing back damaged aircraft for repairs. Once the damaged aircraft were checked out and were given a limited certificate of air-worthiness, I was nominated to air test them before they were flown back to the principal MU at Maison Blanche for a complete overhaul.

On 16th September I was required to fly a Spitfire Mk Vb to Pachino airfield on the southernmost tip of Sicily. I wasn't particularly pleased, as I had planned to celebrate my 21st birthday with my friends on the following day. Fortunately, after landing in Italy, I was able to organise a seat in an Anson aircraft that was flying to Sétif the following morning, and landed back at base in the afternoon. After the evening meal in the annexe of the aircrew mess the party got under way. Though none of us drank much alcohol when we were on flying duty, we were not scheduled to fly on the following day, so were able to 'let our hair down' and celebrate in style. Everything was jolly until late in the evening, when a tug-of-war was suggested, and we formed into two teams. My team were out-pulled by the heavier opponents on the first leg, but on the second leg they were unable to budge us. It seemed hard to believe, until I saw the anchor man on my team was smiling and giving the thumbs-up sign. He had tied the end of the rope round a radiator without the other team being aware, and they continued to pull, with the inevitable result that the radiator became detached from its mountings and water poured out onto the floor. We were able to turn off the control valves and limit the damage before, having more or less fixed the unit back in place, we staggered off to bed.

Later in the month I had a different aircraft to fly – an Auster AOP 6. Two of them were to be delivered to an army unit in Italy and, as luck would have it, my friend Johnny Chandler was to pilot the other one. The two aircraft were to be flown to Foggia airfield and handed over to an army observation post, where they would be flown by Royal Artillery officers for gunnery observation flights. The Austers were not designed to fly long distances and thus, for safety's sake, we would have to refuel approximately every 100

miles. Knowing this, we took great care in plotting our route, especially as we would have to cross a fair-sized strip of water between
Tunisia and Sicily, the so-called Sicilian Channel, part of the
Mediterranean. Fortunately, when the American and British armies
had advanced they had constructed numerous airstrips, and so we
were able to plan our route using those that were marked on our
navigational charts.

On 20th October, ground mechanics swung the propellers to
start our engines and we took off, heading for the airfield at
Constantine to refuel. It was then on to Bône to repeat the exercise,
finally crossing the border between Algeria and Tunisia to land at El
Aouina airfield near Tunis, where we stayed overnight. Next morning, we loaded some spare cans of petrol into the aircraft and set
course for Kelibia on the east coast of Cap Bon where, though there
was no airfield, we found a flat piece of ground near the town and
landed to top up our fuel tanks. With that accomplished, Johnny
climbed into his aircraft and I swung the prop for him and started
his engine. Leaving his engine idling, he climbed out of his aircraft
and started to walk over to swing my prop. As I watched him, I saw
that his aircraft had started to move, so I yelled to him, and he ran
after the slowly moving plane, climbed in, and applied the brakes
that he had forgotten to do. After having a good laugh and, having
started my engine, we took off for the small island of Pantelleria, in
the Sicilian Channel, a little over fifty miles, where there was a
small airstrip occupied by a small army detachment. We refuelled
there, and were able to get a soldier to swing the propellers before
we took off heading for an airstrip at Mazara del Vallo on Sicily, a
further seventy miles or so. Then it was on to Castelvetrano and
Ponte Olivo, refuelling at each strip, until we reached Catania airfield in the shadow of the Etna volcano (all 10,800 feet of it).

After a good night's sleep, we set off across the Strait of Messina
to Vibo Valentia in the toe of Italy. From there we headed for Foggia,
refuelling at Rocco Bernado and Metaponto before landing at
Foggia Main airfield, where there were many aircraft parked.
Checking in at flying control we were told that they were not
expecting delivery of an Auster aircraft, but suggested that they
were probably required by the Eighth Army unit at Foggia 1

airstrip. Landing there we were told that the unit that we were looking for was probably at Torremaggiore, to the north-west of Foggia. We felt like salesmen who couldn't sell their products, but took off again, even though light was fading. Spotting an army encampment near Torremaggiore we decided to land on a nearby football field. An officer approached the aircraft and, though very hospitable, told us that we were still at the wrong place. He said that we could leave the aircraft with him and that he would contact the unit who needed them and request them to send their own pilots to collect them. He then arranged transport for us to get to Foggia Main airfield, where the transport officer would be able to arrange a flight for us to return to Sétif. In fact it didn't turn out quite like that, as he gave me a movement order to fly to Catania where they needed a pilot to collect a Kittyhawk P-40 and fly it via El Aouina back to Sétif.

About this time we started receiving American fighter aircraft, and during the coming months I flew Curtiss Kittyhawk IVs (P-40N), including FX789; North American Mustang IIIs and IVs (P-51), including KH549; and Chance Vought Corsair IVs (FG-1D), including KD361. In all these types the method of learning to fly them was to sit in the cockpit with pilot's notes for a couple of hours, locating all the instruments and controls. The principle flying instruments were grouped in what was commonly known as 'the blind flying panel', consisting of: air speed indicator, altimeter, engine speed (rpm), climb and descent indicator, artificial horizon, gyro-compass and needle and ball. In addition, critical speeds for take-off, abort of take-off (V1), take-off speed (V2), rate of climb, cruise speed, maximum speed, etc, had to be memorized as well as the location of subsidiary instrumentation and controls. A short spell of taxiing to get the feel of the aircraft, and then the first flight on type was made.

Amongst other single-engine aircraft that I flew in was a Mk I Supermarine Walrus amphibious aircraft, W3080, which was quite amusing. I had flown to Casablanca to collect it, adopting the usual method of sitting in the cockpit to find out how things worked and, accompanied by Warrant Officer Palmer, I flew over Sale and then over the Atlantic avoiding neutral Spanish Morocco until we sighted the Rock of Gibraltar. It was then that things started to go wrong. We found that we couldn't contact air traffic control and so, because I had noted that the hydraulic pressure gauge for the brakes was showing zero, we wrote a note, attached it to a spare spanner and a handkerchief, and flew past the air traffic control tower, where we dropped it to advise them of our predicament. We circled the Rock and came in on our approach to the landing strip which runs parallel to the Spanish border, with approaches being over water in the westerly or easterly directions. The landing was made successfully but, because of the strong westerly wind blowing, the aircraft started to move backwards! Warrant Officer Palmer jumped out of the cockpit, ran over to the wing tip and swung the aircraft around whilst some airmen were running to assist. No damage was done.

On 4th November my spell on detachment at Sétif was over and I was able to get a flight via Algiers back to Oujda, on the Moroccan/Algiers border, where my unit, now renamed as 3 ADU, were based. The following day I took off to fly a Spitfire Mk VII to Algiers but, running into bad weather, diverted to La Senia airfield at Oran. Hardly had I landed when I was asked to take off to search for a missing plane flown by a sergeant pilot of our unit. After locating his crashed aircraft, he was recovered by the ground crew with nothing worse than a broken jaw.

One of the several advantages of the unit being re-located at the airfield, some ten kilometres (six miles) from Oujda, was the fact that it had been constructed by the United States Army and, therefore, was more luxurious than our previous base. On top of that, it was also only about twenty kilometres from the village of Saidia on the Mediterranean coast, where a rest camp had been created. Though Oujda was predominantly populated by Arabs in the Souk area, there were quite a large number of French families living in the French quarter who were very hospitable; our group were frequently invited to a *soirée* in one or other of their family homes or to dances at the French Club. Inevitably there was some pairing off with the daughters of our hosts and, to repay their hospitality, we were able to invite them to join us at the rest camp for an afternoon's swimming, sunbathing and impromptu dancing when we had a day off flying.

Flights were now getting longer as, apart from supplying new aircraft to various airfields in Italy, and flying damaged aircraft back to the maintenance and repair unit at Maison Blanche, Algiers, we were now starting to deliver Spitfire Mk IXs from Oujda to Cairo, for onward flights to the Far East. This entailed refuelling at Biskra, on the edge of the Sahara desert, then a flight over the desert to Castel Benito airfield, Tripoli. From there it was on to Marble Arch staging post in Tripolitania, then El Adem airfield near Tobruk, before landing at LG 224, Cairo West. As there were about nine or ten hours flying involved, together with refuelling and aircraft daily inspections, the trips usually took three days.

On 5th January 1944 I took off from Oujda early in the morning leading a flight of five Spitfires, equipped with 30-gallon overload tanks for such a flight to Cairo. Arriving at Biskra about noon, we found that the temperature there was around 45 degrees Centigrade (113 degrees Fahrenheit) in the sun. This meant that we were forced to stay overnight. Even with glycol added to the cooling system, the temperatures of our engines were near boiling point before we could even get to the take-off end of the runway. We spent a miserable night trying to sleep in that heat, even soaking the beds in water did not help. Needless to say we arose early so that we were able to take off in the coolest part of the day. I set course for Tripoli, flying over dry lakes, Shott El Hodna being one of the largest of them, until we landed at Castel Benito.

After refuelling and having had lunch, we took off heading for the staging post airfield at Marble Arch. It was a very useful navigational aid and, arriving there in the late afternoon, we checked in and were accommodated in the transit block. Surprisingly, we found that the airfield had a NAAFI canteen, where not only the RAF personnel on the base but also transient soldiers were able to purchase food and other items. This marble archway, *Arco dei Fileni de Mussolini*, built on the orders of Mussolini when the Italians were in control of Tripolitania (now Libya) at a point where its border touched Cyrenaica, was finished in 1937 to glorify the fascists. It definitely reminded one of Marble Arch in London. It was destroyed in 1973 by order of the ruler of Libya, Colonel Khadafi. I believe that the name Marble Arch was given to it by the Eighth Army.

The following morning I woke to find that a sandstorm was

blowing off the Sahara, and that there was no possibility of flying. We spent an uncomfortable day with the sand penetrating our clothes, and the food had a gritty taste. However, by late afternoon, the storm abated, allowing the mechanics to go out to the aircraft and carry out normal checks and, in particular, clean the filters in the oil and radiator intakes. I had planned to take off early the following morning, but two pilots of my flight were having difficulty in starting the engines of their aircraft and were standing-by whilst the mechanics had the panels off and were working on the problems. I waited a while then told the pilots of these aircraft to wait for the next convoy and join them. This left me free to take off with the other two aircraft and, hugging the coastline, I headed for Tobruk. But after we had been flying for about twenty minutes, the pilot flying the aircraft on my port side reported that his engine was getting hot and that he was losing power. I ordered him to return to Marble Arch, soon after the remaining pilot in my flight reported a similar problem and I gave him the same orders. My aircraft seemed to be without problems, so I decided to press on, choosing a direct course to my destination across the sand dunes toward Gambut III airfield near Tobruk. It wasn't one of my best decisions. When I was some thirty minutes from the airfield my engine started to play-up. However, by reducing the power and adjusting the mixture control, with the speed dropping to 140 mph, I found that the aircraft was still flyable. Nevertheless, as I approached the airfield, I asked for a priority landing, as I felt that it would be difficult to go round again if I had to abort the landing. The controller confirmed that I could land on Runway 210. On my final approach, I moved the undercarriage control lever to 'down' and, though I felt a bump that normally meant that the undercarriage was in the landing position, the warning system sounded and the green light did not come on to confirm that the wheels were down and locked.

Attempting to put power on to abort the landing, the engine didn't respond and I knew that I was in for an uncomfortable landing on the belly of the aircraft, but it didn't happen like that. As I touched down, the port wing started to drop and I thought at least I have one leg down. However, as my speed dropped further, the port wing came up, but the starboard wing dropped. Curious I thought, but nevertheless switched off the engine as the right wing dug into the runway and I saw bits breaking off the propeller. Coming to a halt I stepped out of the cockpit and looked at the weather cocks around the airfield; they indicated a strong, varying wind, and I realised that at the moment of touching down a gust of crosswind had initially caused the starboard wing to lift. The problem, though, had been that the locking pin in the starboard leg had not functioned, probably caused by an ingress of sand the previous day. Walking over to the control tower I reported the incident and watched as the ground crew towed my aircraft away for repairs. Luckily, a Beaufighter piloted by a member of our unit was preparing to take off, and I was able to get a lift to Cairo to await transport back to Oujda.

On 4th March 1944, I was posted to command the airfield at Râs el-Ma. It had been downgraded to a staging post, and was mainly used as a refuelling point. It was during my short stay there that I came face to face with death. The pilot of a Beaufighter had landed, refuelled and then taken off again but, as I watched him gain some height, he veered off to the left and disappeared behind the hills to the north of Fes. Soon after, I received a report that an aircraft had crashed. With the doctor, ambulance and crash crew we set off in the direction that had been indicated. Driving across barren countryside, we spotted smoke rising from behind one of the hills and headed in that direction. Arriving there we found that it was the Beaufighter that had so recently taken off and was still smouldering, with the charred corpse of the pilot trapped in the cockpit. The medical orderly took the identity discs and a ring from one of the fingers and the body was placed in the ambulance to be taken for burial.

I remained at Râs el-Ma for six weeks before being relieved by another officer but, apart from several test flights on aircraft that had become unserviceable and had been serviced by the mechanics, I was missing the joy of being in the air. However, to relieve the monotony of life for the ground personnel, during a flight test of one of the aircraft, a Spitfire Mk IX, I gave them a short display of aerobatics at various altitudes over the airfield, finishing with a full-power flight down the runway at 10 feet above the surface. This time there was no danger of being brought before the CO, unlike the episode in April 1942 when I was reprimanded for a less serious incident in a Tiger Moth.

Rejoining the unit at Oujda in May, I found that the number of aircrew in 3 Ferry Unit continued to grow with a predominance of single-engine pilots, mostly directly from OTUs. The work rate increased, and the number of incidents, accidents and the loss of some aircraft and pilots increased correspondingly. Included in the losses was one of my friends Flying Officer Ron Hartley, who was accompanying me in another Spitfire to a unit in the north of Corsica. After we had landed at Elmas near Cagliari in Sardinia to refuel, Ron took off in front of me, and I could see that he seemed to be having a problem in gaining height and was trying to return to the airfield. Unhappily, on the down-wind leg he had insufficient height to clear a grove of mature olive trees and crashed into these unbending trees. A sad loss.[30]

At the beginning of August 1944 I had a surprise when the wing commander called me into his office and told me that, on his recommendation, I had been Mentioned in Despatches again in the King's June Honours List.[31] When I asked him what for, he replied that he considered that I had leadership qualities, and had assessed me as being "Above average as a pilot and pilot-navigator".

At the same time our unit flew more and more Spitfires to Calvi, St Catherine and Calenzana airfields in Corsica, as reserves for the squadrons who were preparing to join in the liberation of southern France. With the amount of aircraft parked on these airfields it was not surprising that there were ground collisions. On 21st August, Guy and I suffered minor damage to the aircraft that we were taxiing, when another pilot misjudged the clearance distance of its wings and caused minor damage to both of our Spitfires. The following day another pilot managed to chew the tail of my aircraft

---

[30] Flying Officer Ronald Hartley (161791), aged twenty-four, was killed on 12th October 1944. He is buried in Cagliari (St Michele) Communal Cemetery.

[31] Published in the *London Gazette*, 8th June 1944. The author was also Mentioned in Despatches on 1st January 1943 for his evasion.

while I was still sitting in the cockpit!

In the middle of August I was sent on detachment to Elmas along with Johnny, Roy and a number of other pilots, with Guy in command. Our principal task was flying single-engine replacement aircraft to southern France, where the Allied armies and squadrons were advancing rapidly.

On the 22nd of the month I once again set foot on French soil, having delivered a Spitfire to an airstrip near Ramatuelle, which the bulldozers of the US Army engineers had carved out in an olive grove within a week after landing in the area.

Early in September 1944 an incident happened that was to change the course of my life. With Guy, Johnny, Roy and other friends we decided to have a break at the R&R (Rest and Recreation) camp at Saidia. Transport – a 3-ton RAF lorry – was organised, and those who had French girlfriends invited them to join us. After spending a lazy afternoon swimming and sunbathing, we returned to the patio for drinks and an impromptu dance session. I was quite taken by Guy's girlfriend, Mauricette, and, when I saw her walk away from him looking cross, I asked her to dance with me. Though my knowledge of the French language was limited and her knowledge of English wasn't much better, we seemed to get on well together. Later we went for a walk along the beach and I found out that she had a job as a typist working in the town hall. We spoke about Guy who, I told her, was one of my closest friends, and that I wouldn't want to break up her friendship with him. She replied that she wasn't over keen on him, which led me to ask if I could meet her whenever I was free from flying duties.

The following week the same group of us arranged to go to Saidia and, though I expected to spend the afternoon with Mauricette, she seemed to prefer to chat with my other friends. I couldn't understand it, as the previous week we seemed to get on so well. Later in the evening I found an opportunity to ask her if I had done something to upset her, to which she replied that she quite liked me, but that she didn't want to go out with me as she had been told that I was married. I then realised why, on several occasions, my 'friends' were having a good laugh. It took me nearly two weeks to convince Mauricette that I was single, after which we started dating regularly.

In mid-September I spoke to Guy about returning to Oujda, so that it would allow me to see more of Mauricette and, though he wasn't in agreement, I managed to get a flight on a South African Dakota that was flying via Algiers to Oujda. Apart from ferrying aircraft to Corsica, I was also back on the Cairo run, adding Mustangs, Corsairs, a Vengeance and a Hellcat to the growing number of different types of aircraft that I flew.

I was able to see Mauricette quite frequently and, as our friendship developed, I was invited to her home. I'll never forget that first visit. Arriving on the doorstep expecting to see her open the door, it was her mother who did so. She invited me in and managed to make me understand that her daughter would be home from work a little later. As I sat there waiting, conversation was lacking, until a fox terrier came into the room and conversation perked up.

I managed, "Joli chien", to which she replied "Oui. Chien de Mauricette. "

Moments later: "Nom de chien? "

"Bobby. "

Inspired by the conversation, I asked "Quel age? " No words, but four fingers held up.

Fortunately at this moment Mauricette arrived and, after greeting her mother, she suggested that we go for a walk and return later to meet her father. The introductions were made despite the language problem, and I found him likeable even though, over the next few weeks whenever I went to their house, he insisted that I should attempt to speak French when in his house and that, when he was able to understand what I was trying to say, he would correct me. At first I found this method tiring but, with the aid of an English/French dictionary, I made good progress and became more confident in speaking the language. On the other hand, whenever we were by ourselves or with our friends, Mauricette and I spoke mostly in English, as she had more of a gift of learning English faster than I did the French language.

Things were getting serious between us and, now that I had been promoted to flight lieutenant and the end of the war seemed not too far away, I decided to ask her if she would marry me.[32] She accepted, on the understanding that I got permission from her father. It took me several weeks to find the right moment before I plucked up enough courage to do so, and was happy find that her parents had no objections. I didn't appreciate it at that time, but it must have been a hard decision for them to agree and to give their blessing, as she was their only child and they would have realised that, eventually, we would be making our life in England.

Having been given their approval, the next step was to obtain permission to marry from my CO who, if he agreed would forward it to 216 Group, Transport Command, at Headquarters Middle East Command in Cairo for their confirmation. I knew that it would take some time as, during wartime, the military command tended to discourage marriage with 'foreigners'. The fact that North Africa had been part of Vichy France until liberated, would mean that they would, no doubt, make enquiries not only about Mauricette but also her family. Having set the paper trail in motion, we decided to have an engagement party early in the New Year of 1945, and make plans for the wedding ceremony in June.

December 1944 was a quiet month of flying for me. Apart from doing some air-testing of aircraft, I had one delivery flight of a Hurricane to Algiers and a short flight in another Hurricane to get some dental treatment at the American base at Oran. I did have an interesting experience flying a Walrus, an amphibious bi-plane air-craft with the engine and 'pusher' propeller behind the cockpit. Apart from that I did manage to organize a flight to collect a Corsair IV from Gibraltar that enabled me to do some shopping and, especially, buy an engagement ring in a jewellers shop, owned by an Indian in the town.

I had been invited to a Christmas lunch by my fiancée's parents, where I would meet other members of their family, which would, in part, also be a celebration of our engagement. Among the relatives was her uncle Maurice who, when I was given the honour of opening the first bottle of champagne, told me to shake the bottle

---

[32] This promotion was gazetted on 24th November 1944, with seniority of 5th November 1944.

before opening it. Never having opened a bottle of champagne before, and not realising that he was a practical joker, the result was that, as the cork popped, the champagne spurted out and the ceiling and walls were showered with the contents. I was embarrassed, but they all laughed, as they realised that the joke had backfired on them.

On 11th January 1945 I invited Mauricette's parents and my RAF friends to an engagement party lunch at the Hotel Terminus in Oujda, where we told our guests that we had decided to get married at the beginning of June. With this date in mind, when I was required to deliver a Corsair in the middle of the month to the airfield at Cairo West, before arranging a return flight back to base I had time to do some shopping, bargaining for the gold wedding rings plus a length of white satin material for Mauricette to make her wedding gown.

However, at the end of February I was disappointed to learn that I was posted to 76 Staging Post at El Aouina airfield, Tunis, as OC Flying and second-in-command to Squadron Leader Fry, the commanding officer. I suspected that this was probably a move by Mediterranean/Middle East Command to allow me to reflect on the question of marriage.[33]

The base was shared with the US Air Force who had frequent communication flights to different airfields and, after making friends with the American movements officer, I was able to get a couple of days leave at the end of March and a seat as a passenger on a Dakota going to Oujda. This enabled me to celebrate Mauricette's 22nd birthday on the 26th of the month and continue with our plans for the wedding.

The only flying that I did during March was a short flight in a Hellcat, but the situation improved in April as a Harvard (North American AT-6) had been left at the airfield for servicing, and I was able to get some local flying in it before delivering it to Oujda and then returning to Tunis. Soon after my return, there was a 'flap on' concerning a missing aircraft over the Mediterranean Sea but,

---

[33] Headquarters would have been well aware, of course, that 75 Staging Post was located at Oujda.

though I took part in the search flying a Hurricane, no trace of an aircraft was found.

By now it was apparent that the war in Europe was in its final stages and, when the Germans capitulated on 8th May, apart from the relief that I felt at the ending of hostilities in our part of the globe, there was always the possibility that I might be transferred to the Far East. However, as the days went by with no signs of my being moved elsewhere and, having at last received permission to marry, I found a flat in Tunis. Though we had originally planned to marry in June, because of the delay in getting authorization, it was no longer possible, and so we set a new date – 6th September.

On 7th August I was over in the American sector of the airfield to see my opposite number, when I heard a discussion about the damage that an American bomb had done on the town of Hiroshima in Japan the day before. I heard the figure of 80,000 deaths mentioned, and I thought it was a typical American exaggeration. But a second bomb was dropped on the 9th over Nagasaki, with reports of a very high death toll, and I was told we had entered the atomic age. However, horrifying as the death toll was, it brought about an unconditional surrender by the Japanese on 14th August 1945. At first there was an adverse reaction over the use of this terrible weapon, but it was justified by the High Command on the grounds that, had they not done so, to subjugate Japan would have meant a prolongation of the war in the Far East with conventional weapons on the ground, sea and air. It was estimated that this would probably have cost the lives of many more Allied personnel than those who had lost theirs in these two bombed towns. The awful decision that the High Command had to make can always be criticized by those who have never been in such a situation.

With the Second World War now over, everyone started to think about going home and being demobilized, but my thoughts were more immediate. I could continue with the arrangements necessary for our wedding in September and, after, I could look forward to returning with my wife to the flat I had rented in Tunis, until the time came for me to return to 'civvy street'. These plans seemed to be thwarted when some unkind soul in movement control in Cairo decided that I should be moved at the end of August to take command of 16 Staging Post at Marble Arch in the desert. The good news, however, was that, though the posting would not be cancelled, Wing Commander Mitchell, now stationed at Blida airfield near Algiers, was able to convince Cairo that I should be permitted to have two weeks leave at the beginning of September in order to get married and have a short honeymoon before taking command of the staging post. The bad news was that being an isolated airfield there was no possibility of my wife accompanying me.

The wedding arrangements progressed, the banns had been called at the church of St Louis d'Anjou in Oujda, the town hall booked for the civil ceremony that precedes the church service, and the British Embassy in Rabat notified so that they could send a member of their staff to witness the marriage and provide a British certificate of marriage. I also made a reservation at Saidia for the first week of the honeymoon and a week at the officers' club in the Hotel Aletti in Algiers for the following week.

I arrived in Oujda on 4th September, where I had booked a room at the Terminus hotel. My best man, Guy, and other friends arrived the following afternoon, having managed to organize 'training' flights from Blida to Oujda. Their intention was to have the customary 'bachelor night', and for this purpose they had come well supplied with bottles of alcohol bought from the NAAFI in Algiers. As the daytime temperature was over 100 degrees Fahrenheit, to keep these bottles cool they commandeered my bath and filled it with cold water. That being done, they went in search of somewhere to sleep the night. Using their charm and initiative, they ended up at the local hospital, where they managed to coerce the sister in charge to make available a dozen beds in a ward that was not in use. Try as they might to get me sozzled that evening, I managed to remain sober enough to kick them out just after midnight and climb into the bath, albeit surrounded by the bottles, in order to cool off and regain some semblance of sobriety.

6th September turned out to be even hotter than previous days. I passed the morning with my friends until, dressed in my new lightweight khaki uniform, we set out for the town hall just after lunch. This day was even hotter than the previous ones so that, by the time that we arrived there, the creases in my trousers were prac-tically non-existent. Mauricette's family and friends were already seated and we had not long to wait before my bride-to-be arrived with her father for the brief civil ceremony.

Once it was over I was driven with Guy to the church, whilst Mauricette and her father waited for a short while so as to arrive after the congregation had taken their seats and Guy and I had sat down in the front pew on the right-hand side. As the music of the Wedding March sounded I looked round and saw my bride looking fabulous in her wedding gown and train, arriving on the arm of her father. The religious ceremony started and, to be honest, I don't remember much of the detail as it was in French and Latin, as was customary in the Catholic Church in those days. But it seemed very similar to that of the Church of England where, as a choir boy, I had sung with other choristers at various weddings. After Guy had handed the two wedding rings to the vicar and they had been blessed, and he had recited the responsibilities of a husband and wife, I placed the smaller ring on the left finger of my wife, fol-lowed by her doing the same thing on my left finger. Once the service was over, we walked down the aisle out into the fresh air and a surprise. A dozen of my fellow officers were holding an arch-way of sabres, which they must have somehow coerced on loan from a French army unit. It really made our day.

After the usual round of wedding photographs we all made our way to the home of my wife's parents where a reception was being held. With plenty of food, champagne, wine and the spirit left over from the 'stag night', the party soon developed into a lively affair to say the least, with the English contingent mixing well with my new family. Sometime, around 10 pm, Mauricette disappeared to change into a suitable outfit to leave on honeymoon with me. Having previously completed RAF Form 658, application for mechanical transport, we were driven, after the usual high jinks of attaching tin cans to the back of the car, by an RAF driver in a small Hillman car to Saidia, where we spent the first seven days of mar-ried life.

At the end of the week the same small Hillman returned to take us back to Oujda where, after spending the night at her parent's home, we boarded a train bound for Algiers, to continue our honeymoon at the Hotel Aletti. We spent some time exploring the French quarter of the town, during which we found a nice restaurant where we celebrated my 23rd birthday. Sadly, the time flew by, and it was time for me to leave to take up my responsibilities at the RAF staging post at Marble Arch. Before leaving Algiers, with a heavy heart, I took my wife to the railway station, where she boarded the train to Sidi-bel-Abbes to attend a cousin's wedding before returning to her home in Oujda.

I then organized my flights, via Blida to Tunis, where I picked up the rest of my gear before getting a flight via Tripoli to my new station on 23rd September. My brief was to organize the gradual closure of the staging post, but it was not long before I found out that I was required to make unpleasant decisions, firstly relating to a minor incident. The adjutant reported to me that the NAAFI manager had a complaint that some of the airmen had bent a quantity of eating forks into different shapes – it was not difficult, as they were made of fairly pliable metal. Under the advice of the adjutant I ordered a parade for the following morning to establish who the culprits were but, as was to be expected, nobody owned-up and, after I had warned them that if it happened again I would take action, the parade was dismissed. It wasn't the end of the affair however as, the following day, the manager complained that his spoons had now been tied into knots. Once again I ordered a parade, this time at 7 o'clock in the morning and, with nobody owning-up again, I had to decide what to do, and opted to tell them that they would all have to do an hour's drill with the SWO. Whilst it had the effect of stopping the vandalism, I couldn't help hearing some unsavoury comments about me and, over the days that followed, I felt sad that I had opened a chasm in my relationship with the men.

During my time with the squadrons, most pilots were friendly with their ground crews, fitters, riggers, armourers and radio technicians etc, as our lives depended on their efficiency but, when on parade, discipline was paramount. My lack of experience of commanding a fairly large group of airmen, and the enforced separation from my wife, probably contributed to the way that I treated the affair. However, a couple of weeks later a problem arose that, unwittingly, enabled me to re-establish a rapport with the airmen.

I was called to the control tower early in the afternoon after the controller had received a message from the pilot of a twin-engine Anson aircraft who reported that, even though he was only about thirty miles from the airfield he was going to have to make a forced landing as the engines were spluttering and the petrol gauges were showing zero. As he would be flying close to the Tripoli main road, I suggested that the safest course of action would be to make a 'wheels up' landing in the sand beside the road. I then contacted the flight sergeant in charge of engineering and told him to take a crew, load up the necessary equipment in the 3-ton truck and, together with the ambulance, follow my 30-cwt Bedford truck until we found the crashed aircraft.

We had travelled along the road to Tripoli for about thirty minutes before we spotted the downed aircraft on its belly, quite close to the road. The pilot had chosen the spot well, and had made an excellent landing with the engines stopped and the wheels retracted to minimize the damage. The flight sergeant and his crew examined the aircraft and decided that it was possible to raise it up by laying lifting bags under the wings and inflating them with a portable pump that they had brought along. This took some time and it was well into the afternoon before the aircraft was raised high enough for the undercarriage to be lowered and locked. As there was rarely any traffic on this section of the highway, I decided that we would tow the aircraft back to the airfield along the road. The crew manhandled the Anson onto the road, where the tail-wheel support of the aircraft was attached to the back of the heavy lorry. The convoy set off with me in the lead so that, in the event of meeting any on-coming vehicles, they would have time to pull off the road and let us pass. The fire engine and ambulance covered the rear.

All went well until, about a mile from the airfield with the light fading fast, we came across a snag. Close beside the road there were sign boards, indicating the proximity of the NAAFI, transit accommodation and other facilities, which were fixed to 4x4 wooden posts. The convoy came to a stop, as it was obvious that the wings would foul these structures and it would have taken some time to dismantle the obstructions. Knowing that the area would be abandoned shortly, I took the decision to drive my vehicle off the road and knock down the offending signs, by pushing them over with the bumper of my 30-cwt vehicle, to clear the way, much to the glee of the watching airmen. My relations with the men improved and, as I had word that an ENSA (Entertainment National Service Association) show was performing in Tripoli, I was able to arrange for them to visit our station. That also helped greatly.

By the end of November 1945, I was receiving daily signals for the despatch of items that were 'on charge', i.e. recoverable. We had some difficulty in finding one item – a petrol tank trailer (known as a bowser) until an airman remembered that he had seen a burnt out trailer beside the road not far from the outskirts of the airfield. Bit by bit items were sent to destinations indicated on the signals, as well as the posting of the personnel, most of whom were scheduled to return to the UK for demobilizing. On 29th November I flew with Flying Officer Davis to Castel Benito airfield, in the Anson that had been serviced, in order to finalise arrangements for the closure.

On my return to Marble Arch on 1st December the closure was soon completed, and I left with a convoy of the last vehicles to drive to Benghazi on 4th December. There I was able to get a flight in a Dakota to Kilo 40, an airfield on the outskirts of Cairo.

Having obtained a movement order to return to 3 Ferry Unit, I got a flight via Algiers to Oujda, where I was given new orders. I was to be posted to Blida to perform the same function as at Marble Arch, namely to close it down. However, it was not all bad news, as I was able to be reunited with my wife at her parents' home and, whilst there, discovered that she had relatives in the town of Blida. Because of this I opted to travel to my destination by train with my wife, knowing that we would be able to spend some time together in accommodation provided by a member of her family.

Blida was an air stores park, where dozens of Spitfires, Hurricanes and other aircraft were being kept. The airfield was some twenty or thirty kilometres from the main airfield of Maison Blanche near Algiers and, in consequence, little air traffic came into

Blida. Therefore, apart from the fitters and riggers, voluntarily and for the love of working on some of the aircraft to keep them in flying condition, the wind-down of the airfield proceeded in an orderly fashion. After supervising the routine of the airfield during daylight hours, leaving Flying Officer Smith in charge, it allowed me to spend the evenings and nights with Mauricette.

As a change from the daily routine an English lady arrived, announcing that she was a psychologist who was acting as a careers advisor, and was present in order to meet with any airmen seeking advice about his career after demobilization. I remember an incident involving one of the cooks who had a flair for preparing meals, from basic rations subsidised by purchase of local produce, worthy of a good-class hotel. He was interviewed by her and she suggested that on his return to Britain she could arrange for him to be trained as a chef.

When he refused, she asked him why.

He replied: "I prefer to return to my old job."

"What was that?"

"Sweeping roads. I get on with my job in the fresh air without anyone complaining or standing over me telling me what to do. What more can I ask?"

Little by little, the stores 'on charge' were disposed of, either to the airfield at Maison Blanche, or to the port of Algiers, whilst, one by one the personnel received movement orders – posted to other stations in Africa, the Middle East, or to Algiers to await repatriation to the UK by ship. Finally, on 21st February 1946, the job was finished and, with a heavy heart, I took a last walk around the Spitfires and Hurricanes, knowing that they would soon be turned into scrap metal. Little did I realise that one day they would become an aviation collector's item, and that sixty years on a Spitfire would change hands for over £1,000,000.

I had already received my movement order to travel to 70 Staging Post, now at Rabat-Sale, to await demobilization instructions. As my wife would be travelling with me, instead of waiting for a place on an aircraft, we left by train. This allowed us to break our journey at Oujda and to spend a few days with her parents before leaving to embark on our new life. Though it was sad for her parents, my father-in-law assured us that he had always wanted to see England, and that once we had settled down they would visit us.

Arriving at Rabat-Sale, my wife and I were given two rooms in the transit quarters, a bedroom and another room that we could use as a private lounge and, though we had no cooking facilities, it didn't matter as we were able to dine in the officers' mess. A stray puppy took a liking to us and made itself quite at home, the only drawback being that, from time to time, he piddled in our quarters and so was christened 'Bowser' (after the petrol tank trailers that were used to re-fuel aircraft and which often left a leaky trail when the filling hose was disconnected).

We stayed there for nearly two months waiting to be repatriated but, fortunately, as Mauricette had spent some time at a college in Rabat and had distant relatives living in the region, we were able to visit them. My movement order to return to England, that also included my wife, eventually came through and we were able to get two places (you could hardly call them seats!) on an RAF Dakota aircraft that was flying to Gibraltar. There, whilst waiting for a place on a plane bound for the UK, we stayed at the Rock Hotel, which at that time was reserved for officers in transit. Our stay there was not unduly long as the movements officer was able to find two places on another Dakota that was due to fly via the military airfield at Istres near Marseilles to refuel, before taking off for Blackbushe airfield, in Surrey.

Crossing the English coast we eventually arrived over the outskirts of London, where my wife could not help but comment on the mass of similar houses that she could see out of the window; not surprising, as, in the French quarters of main towns in Morocco at that time, most of the houses were of individual design. My own thoughts centred on the fact that more than three years had passed since I had last seen the English countryside, and I wondered what changes I could expect.

On disembarking at Blackbushe airfield, I found that transport had been arranged for the passengers to take them to London. Fortunately, I had time before the bus was due to depart, to telephone my parents and tell them that we had arrived in the UK and were on our way to London. I added that we intended to leave the bus at Hyde Park station, where I would give them another call giving them an estimated time of arrival at Kenton station. There waiting for us were my mother, father and sister Barbara, together with Muriel, my brother's wife.

Because of the wartime restrictions it had been impossible for them to be present at the ceremony, and their only knowledge of Mauricette came from the photographs of our wedding and my letters. This was, therefore, the first time that they had seen her in the flesh. As the name Mauricette was not commonly known in the UK I introduced her as Toni, my pet name for her deriving from her other Christian name, Antoinette. They immediately took to her, especially my father, who said to me, "What a lovely girl you have chosen".

Chapter 11

A RUDE AWAKENING

Having been away from England for over three years and generally having lived in decent quarters with adequate food, the problems of accommodation and rationing on our return were not things that I had thought about deeply. It therefore came as a great shock to both Mauricette and me that rationing was still in force and accommodation was difficult to find. Back at 40, Manor Road with my parents, we found that they had resolved the first problem by ceding their own bedroom to the 'newly weds', whilst the second bedroom was now occupied by my brother Geoff, his wife Muriel and their eighteen-month-old son, David. Barbara retained her small bedroom, whilst my parents had installed a convertible bed in the dining room.

Once settled in I travelled to Wilmslow to complete the necessary formalities of demobilisation. I was required to hand in certain equipment, including my fur-lined flying jacket. Later, I had cause to regret that during the long, cold days of winter, but I retained my officer's uniform as, having been placed on the reserve list, I was liable for recall if a situation warranted it. My pay book was handed to me, and I was happy to see that, since my marriage and the abandonment of bachelor life, with flying pay, overseas and marriage allowances, I had a reasonable amount of savings.

Ration cards were obtained for my family, and I returned home to find that, with good will, the three families settled down into a comfortable routine. It was obvious that something had to be done about the overcrowding problem. My brother Geoff had already been demobilised, and had found a job as a representative for a food manufacturing firm that had allowed him to start the process of buying one of the houses being built in Clonard Way, Hatch End.[34] And so I decided to make an application to the town hall for a place to live. As a result, a housing inspector came round and decided that, according to 'the book', we were a half a person over-crowded. I suppose that the fact that my wife was some four months pregnant accounted for this assessment!

Meanwhile, the three families lived together for most of the year, during which time our son, Ronald Edward, was born in a nursing home in Sheepcote Road, Harrow, coincidentally on my father's birthday, 14th October. We named him Ronald after his French grandfather René, and Edward after his English grandfather. This augmentation of the number of people at 40, Manor Road led to me being offered a prefabricated bungalow at 1, Scott Crescent, Rayners Lane, not too far from my parents' home and, early in November 1946, we were able to move into the bungalow. We found that it was well designed, with a fully-equipped kitchen and built-in cupboards, a reasonably large living room and two bed-rooms. Once we had completed furnishing it, we were able to set-tle down to a real married life.

During this period I had returned to the firm that I had worked for as a clerk prior to enlisting. They gave me a position as assistant manager in the Finchley Road branch of the company, but the problem was that, during my absence in the forces, the work had been carried out by two ladies who knew the routine well. They showed their resentment of the fact that I was in a position above them by not co-operating. Fortunately the manager saw the prob-lem and, as I now had a home in Rayners Lane, he was able to arrange a transfer to an office in that area.

This was fortunate for, on the 2nd of October of that year, 1947, I received a telephone call from a neighbour who said that she

---

[34] Having been in the Territorial Army before war was declared, Geoff joined the Royal Artillery, and eventually took part in the battles for Normandy and beyond.

thought that my wife was going into labour. I got one of our coal delivery lorry drivers to take me home, and a neighbour took us by car to a nursing home in Harrow. I believed it was a false alarm for, by the doctor's calculations, our second child was not due until November. As my mother was not far away, I left Mauricette in good hands and went round to see her. At my mother's I telephoned the nursing home to see if everything was all right and, to my astonishment, was told that I now had a daughter. She had been born prematurely, less than an hour after I had left her in their care. We named her Jacqueline, knowing full well that she would be called 'Jackie' in memory of my wartime nickname, Jack, and its French equivalent, Jacques.

The other problem with my employment was that my salary at the time of only £5.50 per week was not enough to bring up my family as I wanted. This led me to apply for, and obtain, a job as a sales representative with the Rowntree chocolate manufacturer with a much better salary, and a bonus. Furthermore, as I was required to visit shops in Hertfordshire and Bedfordshire, they provided me with a small Morris Minor car. This made life easier for the four of us, as I was able to use it, with the sanction of the company on a mileage repayment basis, for visiting the family and friends.

My father-in-law, who retired at the age of fifty-five from the CFM (Chemin de Fer du Maroc), made annual visits to us in England with my mother-in-law. However, in 1955, I had a proposition from him to move to France, so that he could see more of his only daughter and our children. He was planning to have a house built at Grasse in the Alpes Maritimes region of France, with money from a share of an inheritance that my mother-in-law was expecting from the sale of her father's farm at Sidi-bel-Abbes. The proposal was that they would be able to finance a small business with its own accommodation near to them. As it was July, and the children were on holiday, I grabbed the opportunity to take the family and explore the possibilities.

In a hired car, we had a look at a number of possibilities, including a small hotel, and the prospects looked good. As a result, my wife and I returned to England. I resigned from my job, put most of our furniture in store, advised the landlord of our departure, and returned to Grasse. Continuing our search, it became apparent that my father-in-law had been over-optimistic about the financial aspect, and the amount of the inheritance, when it was confirmed, was barely sufficient to pay for the new house. They would, there-fore, be unable to assist in the purchase of a small business. On top of this, our daughter Jackie became ill, and the doctor considered that the climate didn't suit her. So we were back to square one, and had to return to England to pick up the pieces.

I was lucky enough to find a two-bedroom flat to rent immedi-ately, and soon found a job to 'keep the wolf from the door' while searching for something more permanent. Somehow we managed over the next two years, until I saw an advertisement in the *Daily Telegraph* seeking a person, with a good knowledge of French, to set up a London sales office for a French manufacturer of electric mini-switches, a range of small motors and timing devices, designed to be incorporated into domestic appliances. I applied and was select-ed to go for an interview at the factory in Valence, situated in the Drôme region of France. I was engaged, and spent three weeks at the factory to familiarise myself with the products and their possi-ble uses.

In 1959, I was joined by a Frenchman, Phil Moutet, who had been sent from the factory as a technical salesman. He was single and a 'workaholic' so between us, working sometimes fourteen or fifteen hours a day, the embryo company progressed and became a limited company based in Brentford, Middlesex. Both of us were appointed as directors, Phil covering sales and marketing, while I controlled purchasing and employment, and another Englishman was engaged as company secretary and controller of accounts. Two senior French employees from Valence were also appointed. As the sales increased we came to the point where a factory was needed, and we acquired suitable premises in Hemel Hempstead where parts, mainly imported from the parent company, enabled us to respond to customer requirements more easily.

With the progress of the company and a much improved salary, in 1964 I was able to obtain a loan from a building society and buy a three-bedroom house in Hanworth. At last, it gave each of the children their own large bedroom, not that our son Ronald used it for very long, as he was a great enthusiast of aviation and joined the RAF for a five-year period, where he trained as an electronics engineer. When daughter Jacqueline left school, she trained to be a secretary and, because she spoke French fluently, was engaged as the secretary of one of my director colleagues.

I needed to visit the main factory at Valence frequently and, at first, travelled by train but, as business progressed, I bought a better car and made the long journey to Valence by road, the first of these visits being in July 1960, ostensibly to ensure that, amongst other matters, all the parts that I had ordered for England would be delivered before the main factory in Valence closed for the annual holiday in August. I profited from this visit by taking my family with me so that, after the meetings were over, I was able to continue on to Grasse with them and stay with Mauricette's parents in their new house.

In 1972, my career changed direction when I had the opportunity to get back into an aeronautical atmosphere. I joined the Fairey group of companies, and was transferred to the Britten Norman division where, because of my knowledge of French, I was appointed as sales manager covering France and all the ex-French territories in Africa. In one of these countries I sold three 'Defenders', a military version of the 'Islander', for use in a local dispute over frontiers. Unfortunately, competition in this range of aircraft was very severe and, with lack of sales and over-production within a short time, Britten Norman went into administration. Happily, Short Brothers, based in Belfast, took on the sales team, with Hugh Wilson as sales manager and two other aircraft salesmen including myself. Again, I covered the same French-speaking territories, but the Short 330 was not suitable for that market, and I left the company in 1979 to join two of my nephews, David and Stuart. They had a company specialising in converting local shops into mini-supermarkets, and I joined them as a controller of accounts. I stayed with them for a few years and then decided to take early retirement.

Part of the reason for this was to spend more time on the affairs of the Royal Air Force Escaping Society (RAFES), in particular to raise money for its charity fund. I joined the panel of guest speakers and attended many functions, rotary dinners, and WVS meetings amongst others, and 'sang for my supper', i.e. received the contents of a hat that was passed around, or a donation. In addition, I was co-opted onto the committee to help plan an international marathon run to commemorate the many escape lines. The route chosen was that of one of the most notable of them, the Comet Line. My brief was to produce a booklet for the event, to be sold down the route from Brussels in Belgium to St Jean-de-Luz in south-west France, near the Spanish border. The event took place between 14th and 22nd May 1982.

As I have already mentioned, when working at the end of the 1970s covering the ex-French colonial countries in Africa, I was frequently in touch with the commercial department of the British Embassy in Paris, where I also met the air attaché, an air commodore. At a later date, during a reception at the embassy to commemorate the help given by French people to members of the Royal Air Force Escaping Society, I again met the air commodore and, during the course of conversation, mentioned that I was going back to Steenbecque on the thirty-eighth anniversary of the day I was shot down. I was returning to meet the mayor and to thank the people who had helped me, as well as those who had been taken hostage. The air attaché thought it was a wonderful idea, and promised to advise the consul at Lille and to send a serving RAF officer to be present at the event. He added that he would contribute a case of champagne for the occasion.

On Sunday, 8th June 1980, my wife and I duly met the British Consul of Lille, Mr F.M.A. Cargill; Squadron Leader D. Holliday, who had been sent as the representative of the embassy by the military attaché in Paris; Mr Sydney Holroyd, chairman of the Royal Air Force Escaping Society at that time, and his wife; and also Yvonne and Georges. I took them to lunch at a country restaurant, before we set off to visit Steenbecque to meet the mayor and surviving hostages.

Approaching the village I was surprised to see that the square was so full of people as to make it difficult for us to approach the Mairie. When we finally made it to the entrance we were stopped by the Garde Champêtre (village policeman), who blocked the entrance and told us that we could not enter as the mayor was expecting an important visitor. I said: "My name is Jack Misseldine, and I have an appointment with him at 3 o'clock." He stepped back, smiled an apology, and allowed our party to go in. We were taken to the parlour to be greeted by the mayor who, after making a speech of welcome, handed a beautiful bunch of flowers to my wife, and a glass of champagne to each of us. He then went on to explain the afternoon's programme and that it would start with a wreath-laying ceremony.

Descending the stairs and out into the square, the village band struck up, and the majorettes led the way in a parade to the war memorial for the wreath-laying ceremony. Happily, I had anticipated laying a wreath from the RAFES, as also had Squadron Leader Holliday. In company with the dignitaries of the village with their tributes, the ceremony took place with the *Marseillaise* and a creditable version of *God Save the Queen* played by the band. When this was over, with the majorettes and village band leading the way, and the mayor and our group just behind, we were followed by practically everybody in the village to the village hall for refreshments and speeches. I thought, "My goodness! A case of champagne won't go far". I needn't have worried as the mayor told us that we all were the guests of the village, and that plenty of wine and refreshments had been provided to celebrate such a memorable occasion. I was at loss for words at the generosity of the mayor and villagers, to whom I felt I owed so much.

During the festivities in the afternoon, I was asked to make a speech, and was glad to do so, expressing my regrets, particularly to the hostages, for their suffering nearly forty years previously, and also for the inconvenience that the villagers had suffered because of my presence in 1942. I met some of the hostages, including Georges Boncours, Madame Decool, Madame Houdière, Auguste Rensy, Madame Buret Hooghe, Madamoiselle Hameau, Marcel Vermeulen and Michel Glowa. Glowa claimed that he had hidden my cast-off equipment and parachute under a pile of manure, where he was sure that the enemy wouldn't soil their hands. He was wrong. The parachute material was unearthed by the villagers, to make underwear I believe! Several of the villagers also affirmed that, at the same time as I was shot down, an enemy aircraft was also seen to fall not too far away, and the German pilot landed by parachute a few kilometres from Steenbecque.

Towards the end of the evening, an old man approached the top table, where we were sitting with the mayor, and asked if he could speak to me. He told me that on the day that I was shot down some pieces of my aircraft dropped in the field where he was working, and he had picked up a souvenir. He then opened a bag and withdrew a Spitfire tail wheel that he had found amongst the debris. As he was sure that it came from my aircraft, he insisted that I should have it as a souvenir. I accepted it with thanks, and some years later sent it to the president of the ex-members of 611 Squadron Society who, I believe, handed it to the Liverpool War Museum, where it was displayed with other 611 memorabilia.[35]

On 15th September 1992 I met a group of my RAFES friends and their wives in Paris to participate in the fiftieth anniversary of the Battle of Britain. The British Embassy and our RAFES representative in Paris had liaised with the French authorities, who gave permission and arranged that our group would be allowed to march up part of the Champs Elysée, led by the French military band, then to take part in the ceremony at the tomb of the Unknown Soldier lying beneath the Arc de Triomphe. It was a moving experience rounded off by a garden party at the British Embassy.

My journey to safety, however, could not have been accomplished without help from the several people whom I met along the way.

Eleanor 'Pat' Cheramy

During my visits to Pat Cheramy in London from 1947 onwards, I learned of her involvement with the Pat O'Leary line and of her horrifying experiences in German prisoner of war camps.[36]

---

[35] Liverpool War Museum was chosen because 611 Squadron, formed in London during February 1936, had moved to Speke airfield, near Liverpool, in April of the same year. The squadron was then adopted by the city, and the squadron crest bears evidence of this – a trident and the red rose of Lancashire.

[36] 'Pat' Cheramy, baptised Eleanor Maud on 29th April 1906, was the fourth of five children of Edward and Mary Ann Hawkins (née Stroud) of Aldbourne, Wiltshire. [Thanks to Trish Rushen and especially to John Dymond for their help with this information.]

She told me that, after I had departed with Mario Prassinos, he returned and asked her and Charles if they would allow their home to be used as a safe house for escapees. They agreed but, because their own house was very small – just a living room and one bedroom downstairs, and the hay loft upstairs – Mario asked them if it would be possible for them to rent a larger property, financed from England. Pat's thoughts turned to their Jewish friends, the Clancs, who, because of the increasing danger of deportation by the Vichy French government, had decided to leave France.

Thus it was that Pat and Charles, their son Michel, and Tom Groome, moved in to la Tourelle. Thomas Gilmour Groome, an Australian but with a French mother, had been sent by MI9 from London as a wireless operator to help the Pat O'Leary line in their contact with England. All went well for a while but, as a result of the American and British forces landing in North Africa on 10th November 1942, German soldiers moved into Vichy France. This enhanced the dangers for the escape organisations in Unoccupied France as, up to this date, apart from plain-clothes Gestapo officers, there were no visible signs of enemy soldiers. Now, a garrison of German soldiers and radio-detector vans were stationed in Montauban.

Though Pat, Charles and Tom Groome thought that they had taken all possible precautions, on 11th January, 1943 German soldiers burst into the grounds of la Tourelle, and rushed to the tower where the wireless was located. They surprised Tom Groome in the process of transmitting a message, and the officer in charge ordered him to end the transmission or be shot. Groome seemingly did so, but he omitted a vital key that warned the operator in London, who was receiving the message in Room 900 at MI9's headquarters in London, that he had been compromised. Pat, Charles and Tom, were arrested. However the Germans did allow young Michel to be collected by his paternal grandmother, whilst the prisoners were taken to Gestapo headquarters at Toulouse and brutally questioned by the Gestapo.

Tom Groome jumped from a second-floor window, but suffered only a badly sprained ankle. He was re-arrested and sent to Fresnes prison, Mauthausen and Dachau concentration camps. He survived, and was admitted an MBE after the war.

Pat was also sent to the infamous prison at Fresnes in Paris, where she suffered intensive interrogation and torture in the Gestapo's attempts to extract information about the escape organisation. After weeks at this prison, Pat was sent first to Ravensbrück and then to Mauthausen concentration camps, to live in indescribable conditions until her liberation by US forces in 1945. They found her in a pitiable condition, weighing little more than 56 pounds (26 kilograms). And during a medical examination the doctors discovered that her head had been fractured from inhumane treatment by the camp guards. The American medical team arranged for her to be flown immediately to a clinic in Switzerland, where an eminent surgeon operated and released the pressure on her brain, before inserting a steel plate. It did, however, leave her with a lack of motor control in one arm and while, though over the subsequent years this problem improved with treatment, her damaged brain brought other problems. For her bravery she was awarded the French Croix de Guerre, the British Empire Medal, and the American Medal of Freedom, and many others.

On one of the frequent occasions that I met her, she was invited to attend a ceremony at RAF Station, Odiham as Guest of Honour. Because of her health problems, the CO had intended to send a helicopter to pick her up from a place near her home in Brighton. Unfortunately, the weather forecast was for a lot of cumulus cloud around and, as a result, the flight was likely to be turbulent. In view of her health, therefore, it was thought prudent to collect her in a staff car. After a full-dress lunch in the officers' dining room, there was the short ceremony of hanging a portrait of this brave lady in the entrance to the officers' mess.

RAF Odiham was a fitting place for this honour, as many clandestine operations were planned there, and agents often flown to France from the airfield in Lysanders, which frequently brought back those whose safety had been compromised and, on a few occasions, an escapee.

Pat was interviewed in 1973, and her story told in The Weekly News editions of May and June that year. However, in 1977 an event occurred that upset her and made conversation with her difficult.

BBC 2 made a counterpoint production to the drama series *The Secret Army* and '*Allo 'Allo!* and entitled it *Behind the Scenes*. Six episodes were scheduled, relating stories of airmen who had escaped, usually with the initial help of ordinary citizens. Several members of the Royal Air Forces Escaping Society, including the president, Sir Lewis 'Bob' Hodges, the chairman at that time, Bill Randle, and Pat as one of the people who had sheltered escapers and had suffered from her involvement, were invited to contribute.

Filmed in various locations, each of us gave a short version of our experiences, and the series was put together. However, when the episodes were shown on TV, starting in December of that year, Pat found that the producer had cut out most of the footage of her interview, and had concentrated on the stories of the aircrews. She was not at all pleased, and I took the brunt of her wrath when I next saw her. Her argument was that the RAF aircrews who had been helped had had an easy time, whilst she and other helpers took all the risks. She was right, up to a certain point.

Escapers, helpers and members of the escape lines were unhappy with the portrayal of the characters in the two drama series *The Secret Army* (ITV, 1977-79) and '*Allo 'Allo!*, a BBC series (eighty-five episodes) that is remembered by such phrases as "Good moaning" – "It is I Leclerc" – "You stupid old woman" – "The Gestapo? I 'ate zem" and "Listen very carefully. I shall say zis only once", amongst many others. I believe that *Behind the Scenes* was made in an effort to record the reality of that period. To my regret Eleanor (Pat) Cheramy died a lonely person, as she and her husband had parted ways in the 1950s. Apart from her son and a number of members of the RAFES, including myself, there was no official presence at her burial in a Brighton cemetery in 1987.

Albert Mestdagh

Albert Mestdagh, the Belgian who accompanied me on my trip to Montauban, must have been checked-out following my request at the interview with Donald Darling, the MI9 interrogator in Gibraltar. He was brought out at a later date and, referring to a 2004 publication, *Detachment W*, by Derek Richardson, I suspect that he may have been brought out with a group of people who were evacuated from Canet-Plage on Operation *Titania* on 21st September 1942. Unfortunately, I was never able to meet him again. After the war, when visiting the Carons, I learned that he had arrived in England at the end of 1942. Albert Caron also believed that he had joined a Belgian parachute brigade, but had been killed during the ill-fated Arnhem operation.

Happily, I can record that Albert did indeed survive the war. Thanks to some recent research by Belgian historian Peter Verstraeten I now know a little more about him. Born in Namur, Belgium, on 1st December 1915, and given the names Albert Fernand Ghislain, he enlisted in the 2nd Regiment of the Belgian Army on 25th February 1937. When the war came he was taken prisoner by the Germans on 29th May 1940, but was freed a few weeks later, on 2nd July.

On 21st May 1942 he decided to leave Occupied Belgium, and it was not long afterwards that our paths met in France. Looking at the dates, I must have met him for the first time about 15th June, at the Caron-Duponts. He left with me on 30th June, arriving at Montauban about 3rd July. I never knew that while I was on my way to Spain so, too, was Albert. He crossed the Pyrenees on the night of 1/2nd August, and was immediately interned by the Spanish. Released on 20th September, he went to Gibraltar, and was sent to Britain by boat on 1st October. After a voyage of ten days he landed in England.

He quickly joined the Belgian Independent Parachute Company, attached to the British SAS, and went on all the necessary courses at the Allied Special Training Centre, Inverlochy Castle, Fort William, in Scotland. By the time he had finished 11 Special Training Course, it was 18th December 1943, and his report described him simply as a "good soldier". He was promoted to Soldier 1st Class on 26th June 1944, and a month later was parachuted with his company into an area to the north-west of Le Mans, France, on Operation Shakespeare. Their task was to cause maximum confusion to the enemy as they retreated west of Paris, but by the time the Belgians had arrived the Germans were well on their way home. Instead, Albert and company found themselves assisting Major Airey Neave retrieve the 150 or so allied evaders who had been gathered in a forest near Châteaudun.

The Belgians returned to England, and Albert was once again dropped with his company (Captain Courtoy and forty troops, in two parties) into the Belgian Ardennes during the first week of September 1944, on Operation Bergbang. Their task this time was to cut enemy communications east of the River Meuse, but the operation proved to be not successful due to a 'blind' drop too far from the specified area. Despite this, Albert and his fellow troops fought their way through Holland and on into Germany. When it was all over, Albert was awarded the Croix de Guerre 1940 avec Palme, the citation for which read:

> "Parachuté le 29.7.44 dans la region du MANS (France) il contribua activement au succès d'une opération combiné avec le SAS. Britannique, qui avait pour but, de traverser les lignes ennemies et de délivrer 300 aviateurs cachés dans un bois.
>
> Il fut parachuté une seconde fois le 9.9.44 dans les Ardennes Belges. Il participa à l'action contre l'offensive von Rundstedt et aux campagnes de Hollande et d'Allemagne.
>
> Dans toutes ces opérations, il fit preuve de cran et de courage."

Gaston Nègre

A number of years later when visiting Nîmes, I found the grocery store and flat of Gaston Nègre where I had stayed, hoping that he would still be there, but I discovered that the business had been sold. The new owner was, however, in a postition to to tell me that Gaston had been arrested by the Gestapo and had spent many months in a concentration camp.

Talking to some of his old neighbours, I was able to establish that they thought that he had moved to Marseilles and now owned a bar. I drove down to the area and, after buying many a drink in the small pubs near the old port, I found him drinking his inevitable Pastis, surrounded by his old cronies. He was a shadow of his former self, and I am not sure that he really recognised me, which is quite understandable when one realises the number of evaders he had housed and, the treatment that he had suffered in German hands. However, with pride, he did point to a wall of the bar where he had hung the medals that had been bestowed upon him by the governments of Great Britain, the USA and, of course, the French. I learned on a later visit that he died in the early 1980s.

Mario Lambros Achilles Prassinos

Mario, who played such a vital part in the final days of my escape, got back to England in December 1942. He returned to France as a lieutenant in the British Army for Special Operations Executive, but was also arrested and tortured before being sent to a prison camp. Sadly, he died at the age of forty-seven of typhus in the camp at Schwerin on 4th March 1945. The British awarded him the OBE posthumously.[37]

The Pat O'Leary Line

Much has been written about this escape line and, although I never met him personally, Dr Albert-Marie Guérisse, was the driving force of the escape organisation known as the 'Pat O'Leary Line'. He too suffered betrayal, imprisonment and torture, but survived and was released at the end of the war in April 1945. Even after hostilities finished, he continued 'in action'. For his deeds he was decorated with the George Cross and DSO by the British, the Legion d'Honneur and Croix de Guerre by the French, the Croix de Guerre by the Belgians, and the Medal of Freedom by the Americans.

---

[37] Mario, born in Egypt to Achilles and Hélène Prassinos, was married to Marguerite.

CHAPTER 12

FLIGHTS DOWN
MEMORY LANE

In 1996 my wife and I flew to the United States for a family reunion and we were able to book our return flight on Concorde. Once having cleared the runway, in no time we reached 50,000 feet where we accelerated to Mach 2. Sitting in the warmth and comfort of the pressurised cabin, I looked down at some clouds well below that we were flying over, which gave the only visual indication that we were flying fast.

I couldn't help making comparisons with the altitude performance of my first love, the Spitfire. The first time that I made a height climb with a Spitfire Mk Vc, I think that it took me some twenty minutes to attain 30,000 feet wearing an oxygen mask, and I found that it was very cold, despite wearing the traditional rollneck pullover and a fur-lined Irvin jacket, silk gloves and gauntlets.

In retirement I would also be free to travel more frequently to Grasse, in the south of France, where my wife's elderly mother was ailing. This led to a decision to rent an apartment near her, whilst we arranged to sell our house in England. Unhappily, my wife's mother died in 1989, but we stuck to our decision to move permanently to Grasse. Instead of continuing to rent a flat, however, we moved in to what was now Mauricette's property, where we have enjoyed living in harmony ever since.

As I said in the introduction, my desire to become a pilot stemmed from a short flight in a biplane when I was sixteen years old. That flight gave me the itch to fly, and led me to become an RAF pilot. As age started to take its toll any thoughts of piloting an aircraft again were seemingly a pipe dream but, at the age of seventy-seven, a chance came my way.

In 1999, I happened to meet Hugh Wilson, whom I had first met in my days with Britten Norman. During our conversation, he mentioned the fact that he owned a vintage biplane, and suggested that the next time I was in England we should have a flight together. This idea germinated and, eventually, as he was arranging a business trip to Toulouse, we planned a route to fly over some of the places I had passed through in 1942. He suggested that he could meet me at Heathrow and, after spending a night at his place, we could then fly his biplane from White Waltham airfield and over to France. Afterwards we could continue on and land at a small airfield at Fayence, near Grasse. I was thrilled by the idea of flying in a light aircraft again and, perhaps, to be able to do some of the flying myself.

On 14th August 1999, I arrived in London and was met by Hugh, who drove us over to White Waltham airfield to see his biplane, a Bücker Jungmann, which had two open cockpits.[38] Before getting into the front cockpit, Hugh insisted that I should watch the mechanic, who would swing the propeller by hand in order start the engine as, he said, I would have to do it several times on our trip. The following morning we set off flying south to Southsea, and then followed the coastline to Lydd, where I was surprised to see my journalist granddaughter, Vicky Honour. Aware of the intended flight she had driven to the airport, principally to meet her 'flying grandfather', but also to write an article for the local paper.

After being her guests at lunch, we took off to fly over the Channel heading for a point off Le Touquet airport where, as required by air safety regulations, we called the control tower

---

[38] The Bü 131 Jungmann was a primary basic training aircraft for the Luftwaffe before the Second World War.

advising them that we were en route for Blois. Minutes later we lost contact with them. Soon after, I felt a tap on my shoulder, and Hugh passed a note to me asking if I had inadvertently knocked out the connection from the battery to the VHF radio that was located behind the joystick. I looked down and found that the leads were disconnected, probably by my feet but, in the cramped space, I was unable to bend down to reconnect them. We could have landed at a local airfield but, after passing a series of notes to each other, we decided that we would possibly have problems if there were no customs facilities and that it would be better to continue on to Blois, where custom facilities were available, and would be in accordance with the flight plan.

One of Hugh's notes suggested that we should share the flying, to which suggestion I was only too happy to agree. As the forward cockpit only had two basic instruments, altimeter and air speed indicator, I flew 'by the seat of my pants'. Navigating from a Michelin map brought back memories of my early days of learning to fly, and we landed at Blois three hours after take-off. Hugh immediately phoned Le Touquet who, having lost contact with us by radio over two hours before, were beginning to be concerned. After reconnecting the radio, the following morning we headed for Toulouse but, when we were approaching the town of Sarlat, we could see heavy rain clouds ahead and, as we were flying under visual flying rules, we had to avoid inclement weather.

The map showed that there was an airstrip at Selves nearby and, though it looked deserted except for some aircraft wrecks, we were surprised on landing to see a 'character' appear from a wooden building. Admiring Hugh's aeroplane he offered us lunch – stale bread and a portion of over-ripe Camembert cheese – before filling it up with petrol. When it was time to leave, I was having some difficulty in getting the engine started by swinging the propeller, but the man pushed me out of the way, saying that it would give him great satisfaction to do this once again.

We flew on to Toulouse, where we fell foul of the air traffic controller at the busy airport and home of Airbus production. We were ordered to circle over a specific point until he came back on air with instructions that we were to land at Muret airfield. The following day we flew eastwards, passing over the ancient fortress town of Carcassonne, then Narbonne, Pezenas, Nîmes, and north of Marseilles to our destination at Fayence, where I was met by my wife and daughter who had been concerned that, at my age, I should have undertaken such an adventure.

A few years ago, I believe in September 2001, I attended a fly-in of vintage aircraft at Mandelieu airport, near Cannes. Whilst enjoying the pleasure of seeing 'cousins' of a number of aircraft that I had once flown, I got into conversation with the pilot of a Mustang who, having learnt that I had flown this type of aircraft during the Second World War, kindly allowed me to sit in the cockpit and to be photographed in it. The pilot of a Corsair was also happy to take a photograph of myself in front of his aircraft.

All seemed well until 2006, when I was diagnosed as having suspected cancer, and received treatment of the prostate. The situation deteriorated in 2007 and the bladder became infected. By September 2007 my health was in a very poor state and the specialist told me that there was only one answer, a major operation to remove both organs and to construct an alternative system (total cystectomy). I signed the necessary waiver, and the operation took place on my eighty-fifth birthday. A biopsy confirmed that it was cancer. After five days of intensive care, two weeks later I was discharged from the clinic, but home nursing was necessary until January 2008. The following March I had to see the surgeon for a check up, and he seemed amazed that I had made a full recovery. I am still in good health as the photograph with my wife, Jacqueline my daughter, and grand-daughter Vicky gives evidence.

Whilst I am still a member of the Royal Air Force Association (RAFA), travel to meetings has become difficult but, nevertheless, I still 'fly the flag'. This came about due to my friendship with a retired *Gendarme*, Joseph Macari, who, during his career, had been part of the 'Garde Royale' at the Elysée Palace in Paris, where on one occasion he stood guard outside the bedroom occupied by H.M. Queen Elizabeth. He still is a standard bearer at various ceremonies, amongst which is an annual event commemorating the liberation of two local villages, Opio and Rouret, a few kilometres east of Grasse, by the British, Canadian and American forces on 24th

August 1944. Each year they have a service of remembrance at their local war memorial, where the flags of the liberators are hoisted. Through this contact I was asked to raise the Union Jack on behalf of the British. I accepted this honour that, for me, has now become an annual event.

One day, thinking about my life, Frank Sinatra's song *My Way* came to mind, particularly the line "I made mistakes, not just a few". With a very optimistic outlook on life I have survived though, and now look forward to my next goal – celebrating sixty-five years of marriage with Mauricette on 6th September 2010.

APPENDIX I

Letter of 9th June 1942 from Squadron Leader D. H. Watkins

Officers' Mess,
R.A.F. Kenley
Nr. Whyteleafe, Surrey
9th June, 1942.

"Dear Mr. Misseldine
I am sorry that I had to give you such bad news last night about your son.

We went over France at 1 o'clock yesterday and we attacked about twenty enemy aircraft who came up to try and stop us – we saw Sergeant Misseldine diving down to attack, and later what seems almost certain to be his aeroplane with its tail dropped off due, apparently, to a collision. 'Paddy' Finucane saw the pilot bale out and land apparently quite safely in France.

While there is always the possibility of mistakes of identity in the heat of these battles – from all information, including the fact that we only had two casualties, it is most reasonable to assume that he is a prisoner of war.

Jack was a very popular member of the squadron and a boy in whom I had great confidence and hope – I had recommended him for a commission and was looking forward to seeing him taking a leading part in battles to come.

Unfortunately it was not to be and we can only wait for an opportunity to do ourselves what he would have done.

It takes anything from three weeks to six weeks or sometimes longer to hear from the Red Cross who will probably write to you direct.

All his personal effects have been listed and locked up and these will go to the Standing Committee of Adjustment at Air Ministry who will forward them to you in due course.

I enclose the wings off Jack's tunic as I think you will probably like to have them as a memento.

If there is anything further that I can do to help you, do please write or ring me up or come and see me; and in the meantime, we all wish to thank you for giving us such a grand comrade and member of the squadron.

Yours sincerely
[signed] Douglas H Watkins, S/Ldr
CO 611 Squadron."

.

APPENDIX II

Despatches

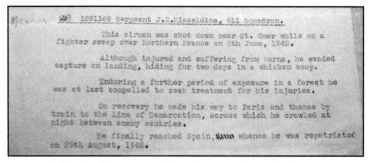

Copy of the draft citation for John Misseldine's first Mention
in Despatches [The National Archives, AIR 2/5684]

1st Jan 43: Notice of Mention in
Despatches, New Year's
Honours, 1943.

8th Jun 44: Notice of Mention
in Despatches, King's Birthday
Honours, 1944.

APPENDIX III

Letters from Jack's Helpers – translated from French

Georges Lemettre

"On Monday, 8th June 1942, I was eating my midday meal in our house in Steenbecque, when I heard the sound of machine guns firing in aerial combat. I hurried outside and looked up into the blue sky, relieved by a scattering of white clouds drifting lazily by, and saw an aircraft that I recognised as a Spitfire falling in flames. I then noticed an airman suspended under a parachute floating down towards a field on the outskirts of our village. I ran to my bicycle, mounted it and peddled quickly to the area where I guessed he would land. On arriving I discovered that there were many people from my village and the adjacent village of Morbecque, who were standing around watching the airman burying his parachute and flying equipment. The fact that he was doing this convinced me that he was not a German pilot and, as I approached, this was confirmed by the fact that he was dressed in a RAF uniform even though it was scorched. I could see that he had burns on his face and wrists, and realised that he needed help. I approached him and, in my limited English, asked him if he wished to surrender to the 'Boches' to get medical treatment, or did he want to try to escape? He replied "Escape". I then told him that my name was Georges, and he replied that his name was Jack.

Though I knew that the few Germans located in the village were known to be somewhat easy-going, I hoped that they would still be occupied with their lunch; nevertheless I realised that I had to act quickly. The first thing that I did was to tell the crowd to disperse and, above all, not to talk about the incident. As they moved away, I turned to Jack and pointed to a small wood, known as le fanque, some 500 metres away, and started to walk in that direction with him. Nearing the wood I told him to hide there and left him with a promise that I would try to return later that night.

Fortunately the Germans had not yet arrived on the scene, but the problem for me was what to do next. Undoubtedly a thorough search for the airman would start at any moment and, as I passed through the village, I was discouraged by the sight of many of the villagers who had been at the field, standing in groups obviously discussing the event. I realised that it was imperative to find a new hiding place for the airman for, when the Germans started to interrogate the residents, as surely they would, it was quite likely that someone might let slip the fact that they had seen the pilot disappear into the wood.

Turning the problem over in my mind as I arrived home, I knew that I needed to confide in someone in whom I could trust and, after thinking it over, decided that the most likely person was Monsieur Henri Dillies, who was known to be very patriotic and lived on the outskirts of Steenbecque. During the afternoon I went to see him and, after giving him the facts, he agreed that, if the airman had not been captured and I was able to guide him to a property that he owned across the road from his house, he would be waiting there. He added that the house was surrounded by a high wall and had a brick-built hen house where the airman could hide temporarily in reasonable comfort. Thanking Monsieur Dillies, I told him that I would go to the wood that night and bring the airman to the outside of the wall around midnight and give a signal. Monsieur Dillies confirmed that he would be waiting in the garden and that he would give a signal if it was safe for the two of us to climb over.

About 11 pm that evening I set out for the wood, taking care that I was not being observed, and entered into it. I didn't know exactly where he might have hidden himself, but as I progressed I whistled a tune softly and called "Jack" in a low voice. I then saw the pilot emerge from a pile of leaves, stand up and grip my hand firmly in a gesture that seemed to say "Thank you for coming back".

After leaving Jacques in the hen house and saying goodnight to the Dillies, I returned home to a sleepless night, knowing that it was dangerous to leave the pilot where he was. I knew that I had to try to find a way to move him urgently. Sometime during the night I remembered the name of Madame Perel-Ferment, who lived in modest circumstances in a fairly isolated spot several kilometres away. Her patriotism was well-known, not only for several acts of heroism she had displayed during the 1914-18 war, but also for the help she had given to soldiers after the collapse of France early in June 1940.

The next day I cycled to Haverskerque and met Madame Perel, who agreed that she would help but that, first, she would visit a person she knew who lived in a town not far away and who would be better able to hide the airman. Returning to the Dillies, I visited Jacques, and was concerned over his evident fever. It made me wonder if he would be fit to travel in the near future, and I wondered if I ought to tell the airman to give himself up and have his burns treated. I knew that this would condemn him to an unknown number of years in a prisoner of war camp, and decided that I must leave the decision to him as long as there was an improvement in his health overnight.

On the following day I met Yvonne, and she told me that our airman seemed a lot better, so I rode over to Madame Perel to ask her if it was possible for her to accept Jacques this same night. She said that she could, and moreover that, as she could speak some English, she would come over to meet me later in the evening, then collect the airman from his hiding place and leave immediately. True to her word she arrived after dark and spoke to Jack in English and, though I accompanied her for part of the journey, she continued on with Jack making for her cottage in Haverskerque.

Jack had left just in time for, apart from the German soldiers who were visiting all the houses in the village, they had enlisted the aid of the village policeman. In fact it was he who called on me and said that I was to accompany him to the town hall. There, I was interrogated by the Germans who said that, from information they had received, they believed I was the person who had helped the pilot to evade capture and ordered me to give the names of any other people involved. I feigned astonishment, and said that the only reason I had been near to the pilot, was to practise a few words of my limited English.

As I expected, this explanation did not go down well with them and, as they became more and more angry, they threatened me with all sorts of punishment. Eventually, reaching the end of their patience, they took me to their headquarters in the château dominating the village of Cassel, where I was imprisoned in the dungeon. Several days later, believing that the time in solitary confinement with the minimum of food, would weaken me, I was taken back to the town hall in Steenbecque for further interrogation and accusations. They were no more successful in their efforts to make me admit that I had helped the British pilot than they had been on previous occasions. Losing patience they then carried out their threat of 11th June, and took eleven other hostages, mostly from Steenbecque with a few from Morbecque, and transported us to the main prison of Loos in the town of Lille, where we were locked up four to a cell.

Several days later I was taken to a room where a French lawyer, hired by my parents, was waiting and, after discussing my case, he told me that I was to be brought before an examining magistrate who was suspected of being too close to the occupying powers, and in whom I had little confidence. At the hearing he was not satisfied with some of my replies, and reminded me that, as the accusations brought against me by the Germans included collaboration with the enemy, a guilty verdict would result in capital punishment. After continuing to question me for a long time he informed me that his findings would be passed on to the Germans.

Many weeks later, towards the end of October, I was brought before a German court-martial. There I was confronted with witnesses, who had come forward at the time of the assembly in front of the town hall on 13th June, and made certain statements. My lawyer defended brilliantly, emphasising my assertion that my only crime, if it was a crime, was that I had spoken to the pilot in English. Furthermore, none of the testimonies of the so-called witnesses had proved anything to the contrary and, so being, the accusations were without foundation.

I knew that, apart from the Dillies family, nobody had any knowledge of what happened between 8th and 11th June, and I had felt reasonably certain that, even if the Dillies family had been questioned, they would have denied any involvement for their own safety. But I still had a feeling that the Germans might make an example of me.

Fortunately, all Germans were not Nazis, and the officers of the court behaved correctly as, for want of proof, they gave me the benefit of doubt and dismissed the accusations. It will always remain a mystery to me as to why they had not pursued the matter further, making me wonder whether some unknown person with influence had intervened on my behalf to obtain my acquittal.

Six weeks later, early in December 1942, along with the other eleven hostages, I was released to return home and prepare to celebrate Christmas as a free man."

Note: Georges's bravery was eventually acknowledged by the French government, albeit sixty years after the event, with the medal of the Chevalier de la Legion d'Honneur.

Yvonne Dillies

"On the morning of 8th June I returned home at about 1 o'clock from shopping in the nearby town of Hazebrouck and, as I arrived, I was told by René, an employee of my father, that an airman had landed by parachute in the field of Jules Boddaert behind the bakery of Marcel Chrétien. Being curious, I set off on my bicycle to the area, passing several people en route who told me that the airman was a British pilot who had already left the scene after talking to Georges Lemettre, a neighbour and long-time friend of mine. I returned home disappointed that I had not seen the event.

As I sat down to lunch with my father, René confirmed that the aircraft was British and had come down in flames some distance away and the young pilot, who had escaped by parachute, had suffered some burns. My father said that he had heard that Georges seemed to have taken charge and, as he was a level-headed person who would remain calm and resourceful, there was a chance that the airman could avoid capture.

The afternoon was warm and we closed our shutters, but we could still see German soldiers beginning to search the village and making their way to the surrounding countryside. I was talking with my father when suddenly there was a knock on the door, and Georges walked in. He was pale and preoccupied but, finally, in an embarrassed fashion, came to the point by asking my father if it would be possible for him to hide the airman overnight. He couldn't risk taking the pilot to his own house, due to the fact that there had been many villagers who had seen him talking to and accompanying the airman part of the way towards the wood and, also, that the Germans frequently dropped in to the café next door to his home.

My father replied that as he had a German officer billeted in the house it would be impossible to have the pilot stay there. Looking at Georges's crestfallen face he continued by saying that the only thing that he could suggest was that, as he had a spacious hen house in his property across the road, he would allow the airman to hide there, temporarily. Calling my mother into the room, he explained to the two of us that there was a risk involved and that he would not make the decision without our consent. We agreed and my father told Georges to check that the pilot was still in the same hiding place, and, if so, bring him to the back wall of the property later that night. If the coast was clear, my father said that he would be waiting, and give him a signal to climb into the garden.

Around midnight I went with my father across the road and down to the bottom of the garden. At first there was no sign of anybody on the other side of the wall but, after waiting about fifteen minutes, we heard someone whistling a tune. Recognising it as the pre-arranged signal, my father gave a reply, and soon after George's face appeared, followed by his companion. As I looked at the airman I could see, even in the limited light of the moon, that his clothing was scorched and his face, particularly his lips, eyebrows and eyelids, were burnt, as well as the lower part of his arms. He must have had some difficulty in walking from the wood, as I noted that he was wearing a pair of shoes that appeared too small. Georges introduced him as Jack.

The next morning I crossed the road with a basket of corn and some water to feed the hens, but mainly to take some food to our 'guest'. I tried to get him to eat the food that I had concealed under the corn, consisting of a slice of bread that I had brought, together with a fresh egg that I had collected from one of the hens. It seemed, however, that as his lips were burnt and appeared to be very painful, he didn't want to eat. He also had some difficulty seeing, since his eyelids had swollen and were almost completely closed. There appeared little that I could do for him, even though it seemed to me that he was running a temperature. My father came with me in the evening and was not happy about the state of Jack's health, so much so that he posed the question: "What if he becomes seriously ill?"

None of us slept well that night but Jack, whom I discovered was only nineteen years old, was in much better spirits as his fever had abated. Additionally, Georges had called in during the morning to say that he had found a more secure place for our airman and told us that he would return around midnight with a lady, who would take him to her house several kilometres away. Prudently, Georges would not say who she was or where they would be going. I was more than relieved that Jack would be on the move, not only for the sake of my parents and me, but also for the pilot. I prayed that with the help of Georges, and the contact he had made, Jack would avoid falling into German hands and hopefully find a way to get back to his own country and family.

The following morning when I went into the village to do some shopping and meet my friends, I found that many of the villagers were standing around talking in front of the town hall, reading a notice that had been placed there by the Germans."

ORDER MADE BY THE KREISKOMMANDANT OF CASSEL – 11TH JUNE 1942

BY ORDER OF THE AUTHORITY GIVEN BY SUPERIOR MILITARY AUTHORITY

I ORDER THAT:–
TOMORROW 12TH JUNE AT 9 AM ALL INHABITANTS OF THIS COMMUNITY SHALL ASSEMBLE IN FRONT OF THE CHURCH. THE MAYOR WILL SPEAK TO THE ASSEMBLY AND ADVISE THOSE PRESENT TO SUPPLY ALL INFORMATION THAT THEY HAVE CONCERNING THE PARACHUTIST WHO LANDED LAST MONDAY (8th JUNE) IN THE AREA OF THE COMMUNITY. ABOVE ALL EACH PERSON MUST GIVE THE NAMES OF ANYONE THEY SAW IN

THE VICINITY OF THE PLACE WHERE THE PARACHUTIST
LANDED.

IF BY 5 PM TONIGHT NO INFORMATION IS GIVEN, OR,
IF THE INHABITANTS PRETEND TO KNOW NOTHING,
SEVERE SANCTIONS WILL BE TAKEN AGAINST THE
WHOLE COMMUNITY. EACH PERSON WHO CAN GIVE
ANY INFORMATION WHATSOEVER MUST GO TO THE
STEENBECQUE TOWN HALL AND MAKE HIS STATEMENT
WHICH WILL BE TAKEN DOWN IN WRITING.

Note: Mr and Mrs Dillies and their daughter were thoroughly interrogated by the Germans on 12th June, in particular Yvonne, who
had been pointed out as someone who was at the scene where the
pilot had landed. Her interrogators gave her a hard time, but she
was able to prove that she had been shopping in Haverskerque and,
therefore, could not have been at the scene at the time the parachutist landed. The fact that there was a German officer billeted
with them, who vouched for her, was no doubt helpful in clearing
Yvonne and her parents from any suspicion. That is ironic, when
you consider that I was a 'guest' in their nearby chicken coop for
the three days prior to this questioning.

Madame Perel-Ferment (*passed on by her children after her death*)
"On Monday, 8th June, at about 2 o'clock in the afternoon, when I
was in the garden hanging out the washing, I saw Georges Lemettre
arrive. He asked me if I had seen the aerial combat that had taken
place at lunch time and, when I answered, he told me that one of
the aeroplanes that had been shot down was that of a British pilot
who had landed by parachute close by Steenbecque and that he had
ridden over there on his bicycle. Seeing that a large crowd had collected around the pilot in a field, he had made his way through the
throng and, approaching the airman, he had asked him if he wanted to escape and had helped him to hide in a little wood. Georges
hesitated and then said that he knew that I had helped some soldiers to escape previously and asked me if I could do the same for
the young airman who said his name was Jack. He continued by

telling me that he had seen Mr Dillies, who had agreed to hide Jack temporarily, and that he intended to collect him from the forest that night and take him to an unoccupied property of Mr Dillies.

I said that I would try and help, as I knew a young girl, Marcelle Caron who, in 1940, was able to obtain false papers for two soldiers that I helped. Georges' last words were "It's urgent".

The following day I walked the ten kilometres to Aire-sur-la-Lys and saw Marcelle, who agreed she would be able to help. Two days later, on Wednesday, 10th June, she came to my house bringing some cigarettes and pastries that she said were for Jack. Taking these, I decided to go and see Georges at his home. Arriving at the estaminent of George's parents, I found his father alone in a terrified condition, as the Germans had already visited his place and searched every room along with all the dwellings nearby. Georges himself arrived soon after, and said that Jack must be moved as soon as possible, as even the house of Mr Dillies had been searched. Happily they had not thought to look in the hen coop.

In view of the urgency of the situation, I decided to take a risk and told Georges that I would return later that night, and would take him with me through the forest of Nieppe to my home and hide him until Marcelle came back with news. Early the following morning my husband, who was worried about his presence in the house, insisted that Jack should hide in the fringe of the adjacent wood. Happily, Marcelle arrived during the morning of the 11th with a spare bicycle, and I went to the edge of the wood and brought Jack back to the house. Marcelle left on one of the bikes, with Jack following at a safe distance behind."

Albert Caron (written after the death of his parents and of his sister Marcelle)
"Marcelle brought you to my parents' house about midday on the 11th June, passing the Feldgendarme on guard at the entrance to Aire-sur-la-Lys without any problems. You stayed with us, sharing my bed, for nearly three weeks, during which time Doctor Lambrecht visited every day to attend to your burns, and the necessary medicines were supplied by the chemist Mr. Kerleveo. Mr. Vallen supplied you with a false identity card. You also met Albert Mestdagh, and the two of you left our house at the end of the month."

Note: The Caron-Dupont family survived the war without too many problems, even though I learned from Albert that, on a number of occasions, Marcelle acted as a courier between Occupied France and Vichy France without ever being arrested. Unhappily, she died in the late 1950s before I was able to obtain her memories of the occasion and thank her for her help.

INDEX